The Globalization

The Globalization of Internationalization is a timely text which gives voice to emerging perspectives as an increasing range of countries engage in the process of internationalization. The pressure to internationalize cannot be ignored by institutions anywhere in today's world, yet the dominant paradigms in the conception of internationalization traditionally come from the English-speaking world and Western Europe. This book sets out to offer alternative viewpoints. Different dimensions and interpretations of internationalization in countries and regions whose perspectives have received little attention to date provide food for thought, and help to broaden understanding of its application in alternative contexts.

Combining diverse perspectives from around the world, this new volume in the *Internationalization in Higher Education* series seeks answers to key questions such as:

- What are the main characteristics of internationalization viewed from different cultural and regional backgrounds and how do they differ from traditional models such as in Western Europe, North America and Australasia?
- What issues in different global contexts have an impact on internationalization processes?
- What are the key challenges and obstacles encountered in developing innovative and non-traditional models of internationalization?

With contributions from world-renowned international authors, and perspectives from countries and contexts seen only rarely in the literature, *The Globalization of Internationalization* offers distinctive overviews and insights while exploring a range of thematic and regional issues arising from these considerations. This will be essential reading both as an academic resource and a practical manual for university leaders, academics, higher education policy advisers and non-governmental organizations which fund higher education.

Hans de Wit is Director of the Center for International Higher Education (CIHE) at Boston College, USA, and Professor in International Higher Education at the Department of Higher Education and Leadership of the Lynch School of Education, Boston College.

Jocelyne Gacel-Ávila is General Coordinator of the UNESCO Regional Observatory on Internationalization and Networks for Tertiary Education in Latin America and the Caribbean, Vice Dean of the research division for Social Sciences and Humanities, tenured researcher and professor of the PhD programme on Higher Education at the University of Guadalajara.

Elspeth Jones is Emerita Professor of the Internationalisation of Higher Education at Leeds Beckett University and Honorary Visiting Fellow at the Centre for Higher Education Internationalisation, Università Cattolica del Sacro Cuore, (CHEI) Milan, Italy.

Nico Jooste is Senior Director of the Office for International Education at Nelson Mandela Metropolitan University, Port Elizabeth, South Africa and President of the International Education Association of South Africa (IEASA).

Internationalization in Higher Education

Series Editor: Elspeth Jones

This series addresses key themes in the development of internationalization within Higher Education. Up to the minute and international in both appeal and scope, books in the series focus on delivering contributions from a wide range of contexts and provide both theoretical perspectives and practical examples. Written by some of the leading experts in the field, alongside others earlier in their career, books in this series reflect contemporary and emerging concerns, focusing on critical issues for the field as it develops.

Titles in the series:

Internationalization in Higher Education

Series Editor: Elspeth Jones

This series addresses key themes in the development of internationalization within Higher Education. Up to the minute and international in both appeal and scope, books in the series focus on delivering contributions from a wide range of contexts and provide both theoretical perspectives and practical examples. Written by some of the leading experts in the field, alongside others earlier in their careers, books in this series reflect contemporary thinking on emerging concerns, focusing on critical issues for the field as it develops.

Titles in the series:

Tools for Teaching in an Educationally Mobile World
Jude Carroll

Developing the Global Student
Higher Education in an Era of Globalization
David Killick

Governing Cross-Border Higher Education
Christopher Ziguras and Grant McBurnie

Comprehensive Internationalization
Institutional Pathways to Success
John K. Hudzik

Internationalizing the Curriculum
Betty Leask

The Globalization of Internationalization
Emerging Voices and Perspectives
Hans de Wit, Jocelyne Gacel-Ávila, Elspeth Jones and Nico Jooste (Eds)

The Globalization of Internationalization

Emerging Voices and Perspectives

Edited by

Hans de Wit, Jocelyne Gacel-Ávila, Elspeth Jones and Nico Jooste

Routledge
Taylor & Francis Group

LONDON AND NEW YORK

First published 2017
by Routledge
2 Park Square, Milton Park, Abingdon, Oxon OX14 4RN

and by Routledge
711 Third Avenue, New York, NY 10017

Routledge is an imprint of the Taylor & Francis Group, an informa business

© 2017 selection and editorial matter, H. de Wit, J. Gacel-Ávila, E. Jones & N. Jooste; individual chapters, the contributors

British Library Cataloguing in Publication Data
A catalogue record for this book is available from the British Library

Library of Congress Cataloguing in Publication Data
Names: Wit, Hans de, 1950– editor. | Gacel-Ávila, Jocelyne, editor. |
Jones, Elspeth, 1956– editor. | Jooste, Nico, editor.
Title: The globalization of internationalization: emerging voices and
perspectives / edited by Hans de Wit, Jocelyne Gacel-Ávila,
Elspeth Jones & Nico Jooste.
Description: Milton Park, Abingdon, Oxon; New York, NY: Routledge, 2016. |
Includes bibliographical references and index.
Identifiers: LCCN 2016030445 (print) | LCCN 2016049103 (ebook) |
ISBN 9781138100640 (hbk: paper) | ISBN 9781138100664 (pbk: paper) |
ISBN 9781315657547 (ebk)
Subjects: LCSH: International education–Developing countries. |
Education and globalization–Developing countries. |
Education, Higher–Developing countries.
Classification: LCC LC1090 .G594 2016 (print) | LCC LC1090 (ebook) |
DDC 370.11609172/4–dc23
LC record available at https://lccn.loc.gov/2016030445

ISBN: 978-1-138-10064-0 (hbk)
ISBN: 978-1-138-10066-4 (pbk)
ISBN: 978-1-315-65754-7 (ebk)

Typeset in Galliard
by Out of House Publishing

Contents

About the Editors

Hans de Wit is Director of the Center for International Higher Education (CIHE) at Boston College, USA, and Professor in International Higher Education at the Department of Higher Education and Leadership of the Lynch School of Education Boston College. He is former Director of the Centre for Higher Education Internationalisation (CHEI) at the Università Cattolica Sacro Cuore in Milan Italy, and Professor of Internationalization of Higher Education at the Amsterdam University of Applied Sciences. He is a Research Associate at the Unit for Higher Education Internationalisation in the Developing World at the Nelson Mandela Metropolitan University (NMMU), Port Elizabeth, South Africa, and at the International Business School of the Amsterdam University of Applied Sciences, the Netherlands.

Hans is Founding Editor of the *Journal of Studies in International Education* (Association for Studies in International Education/SAGE publishers), member of the Editorial board of the journal *Policy Reviews in Higher Education* (SRHE) and of *International Journal of Educational Technology in Higher Education* (Springer/Universitat Oberta de Catalunya), Associate Editor of *International Higher Education* and co-editor of the book series *Global Perspectives in Higher Education* (Sense Publishers). He publishes a monthly blog in *University World News* on internationalization of higher education, and contributes to *The World View* at Inside Higher Ed on a regular basis. He has (co-)written several other books and articles on international education and is actively involved in assessment and consultancy in international education, for organizations like the European Commission, UNESCO, World Bank, IMHE/OECD, IAU and the European Parliament.

Jocelyne Gacel-Ávila has a PhD in International Education and Master of Arts in Foreign Languages and Civilizations (University of Paris). She is General Coordinator of the UNESCO Regional Observatory on Internationalization and Networks for Tertiary Education in Latin America and the Caribbean, Vice Dean of the research division for Social Sciences and Humanities, tenured researcher and professor of the PhD programme on Higher Education at the University of Guadalajara where she was in charge of the internationalization process for 25 years and Member of the National Research System of Mexico (Level 2).

She is considered a leading expert and researcher on the internationalization process in Latin American and the Caribbean, collaborator of the World Bank and member of the OECD expert team on the contribution of higher education in regional development, President of the Mexican Association for International Education (AMPEI) (1996–2000/2014–2016), NAFSA Senior Fellow in Internationalization (2011–2014), Vice-President of the Board of OECD Higher Education Programme (2010–2012), Vice-President of the Board of the Consortium for North American Higher Education Collaboration (CONAHEC) (2005–2007), Member of the expert team of the International Association of Universities for the Global Survey on Internationalization, Consultant of the Inter-American Organization for Higher Education, and founding director of the magazine *Global Education* (AMPEI).

Jocelyne was winner of the 2010 CONAHEC Award of Distinction for outstanding contribution to academic collaboration in North America and 2006 AMPEI Award for the enhancement of the internationalization of the Mexican higher education sector.

Elspeth Jones is Emerita Professor of the Internationalisation of Higher Education, Leeds Beckett University, UK, and Honorary Visiting Fellow, Centre for Higher Education Internationalisation (CHEI) Università Cattolica del Sacro Cuore, Milan, Italy. With a background in languages and applied linguistics, she worked in Singapore and Japan before becoming International Dean at Leeds Metropolitan University, where she was responsible for its ambitious internationalization agenda. She has over 35 years' experience in international education and her specialisms include personal, professional and employability outcomes from international mobility, strategic leadership, internationalization of the curriculum at home and abroad, global citizenship and intercultural competence development. She has published widely, including several edited and co-edited books, such as *Internationalising Higher Education*, *Internationalisation and the Student Voice* and *Global and Local Internationalisation*. She is series editor for the Routledge book series, *Internationalization in Higher Education*.

Elspeth has undertaken consultancy, research, training and presentations for universities around the world and organizations such as the British Council, International Education Association of Australia, the International Association of Universities, Idiomas sem Fronteras, the Association of Southeast Asian Institutes of Higher Learning, European Commission and the European Parliament. She is a member of the Scientific Committee of CHEI, Milan and the Editorial Board of the *Journal of Studies in International Education*. She is Chair of the European Association for International Education's Expert Community on Internationalisation at Home and is Visiting Professor at several European universities. In 2014 Elspeth received the EAIE's Tony Adams Award for Excellence in Research.

Nico Jooste is Senior Director of the Office for International Education at Nelson Mandela Metropolitan University, Port Elizabeth, South Africa, and

President of the International Education Association of South Africa (IEASA). With a PhD in history from the University of the Free State, Nico began his career in higher education as a Lecturer in History at Fort Hare University in 1982, leading to his becoming Acting University Registrar until 1996. He then worked in private higher education while also being Executive Director of the Eastern Cape Higher Education Association before becoming responsible for the Office for International Education at the then University of Port Elizabeth in 2000. During this time international student numbers grew from 130 in 2000 to 2,500 in 2014.

Nico is considered a leading expert in the field of higher education internationalization in South Africa and is recognized internationally. In 2014 he organized the first Global Dialogue on Higher Education Internationalisation, attracting leaders of HEI organizations from across the world to Port Elizabeth, and establishing the Nelson Mandela Bay Global Dialogue Declaration on the Future of Internationalisation of Higher Education, aimed at emphasizing the importance of decision-making and practices in internationalization being imbued with ethical considerations and inclusivity. In 2014 Nico established the Unit for Higher Education Internationalisation in the Developing World, a first in Africa. The Unit published its first book, *Higher Education: Partnerships for the Future*, in 2015. Nico is also editor of the *Study South Africa* publication.

About the Authors

Kamal Abouchedid has a PhD in Education from the University of Manchester, UK. He is a full-time faculty member with the rank of Professor in the Faculty of Humanities at Notre Dame University–Louaize (NDU), Lebanon, and currently Dean of the Faculty of Humanities. His research interests lie in the scope of quality assurance in higher education and citizenship education. In addition, Dr Abouchedid has published a number of research articles in refereed journals, contributed chapters to books and provided consultancy to UNESCO, UNDP and other regional and local organizations.

Adil Ashirbekov is a junior researcher at the Research Institute of Nazarbayev University Graduate School of Education. He has been part of the international research team on the project 'Advancing Models of Best Practice in Internationalization of Higher Education in Kazakhstan'. Before joining the Graduate School of Education, Adil did his master's degree in international relations and also worked at the international office of Gumilyov Eurasian National University. Based on his professional experience and academic background, Adil has co-authored articles focused on issues of internationalization in higher education.

Fanta Aw is President and Chair of the Board of Directors of NAFSA: Association of International Educators, the largest international education association with over 10,000 members. Dr Aw is Assistant Vice President of campus life and Hurst Senior Professorial Lecturer in the School of International Service at American University in Washington, DC. She advises senior leadership on matters related to campus internationalization, diversity, inclusion and equity. With 25 years' experience in the field of international education and higher education, she is a frequent international presenter and speaker. As a sociologist, her areas of specialization include transnational migration, international education, social stratification and intercultural communication. Dr Aw is originally from Mali, West Africa.

Maria Bou Zeid is Assistant Professor and Chair of the Media Studies Department at Notre Dame University–Louaize (NDU), Lebanon. She holds a Doctorate in Media Studies from Université Paris II, France and a DES in Journalism from the Lebanese University in collaboration with the French Press Institute–IFP and the Center for the Formation and Perfecting of Journalists–CFPJ, Paris, France. Her expertise is in the role of media in safety and awareness, and the impact of media campaigns on the public health sector in Lebanon. She also has extensive television experience in the field of production and research and is engaged in research on higher education in the Arab world.

Magdalena Bustos-Aguirre is an Associate Professor at the University of Guadalajara. During the past 15 years she has held top managerial positions at internationalization offices of two Mexican universities. She is currently a CONACYT doctoral fellow working on the dissertation 'Elements that contribute to student mobility among Mexican higher education students'. She has participated in several international and national committees and associations related to internationalization and international cooperation and has been a presenter and panelist at many of their conferences and meetings. She served on the Board of Directors of AMPEI, the Mexican association of international cooperation, from 2003 to 2006.

César Cáceres Seguel is a researcher at the Center for Social Inclusion and Innovation, Universidad de Viña del Mar, Chile. His research focuses on urban transformation linked with the tourism industry, social inequalities in residential areas, metropolitan development and urban governance. His career began as consultant in rural development and land planning. He became Professor of Spatial Planning at the Universidad Católica de Temuco and assessor for the Metropolitan Plan of Temuco, Chile. In 2008 he joined the Fundación para la Superación de la Pobreza (Foundation for the Overcoming of Poverty) as adviser for neighbourhood plans in low-income areas of Santiago de Chile and Valparaíso. His PhD topic was 'Social Inequalities in Periurban-Residential Spaces of Santiago de Chile'.

Tapas R. Dash is a Professor and Senior Vice-President of Academic Affairs at Build Bright University (BBU), Cambodia and an active PhD supervisor. He is founding Editor-in-Chief of the *International Journal of Business and Development Research* published by BBU. He is also on the editorial and review board of other international journals such as the *International Journal of Business and Emerging Markets*. He has participated in a number of international conferences and seminars in the United States, France, India, Singapore, Malaysia, Thailand and Cambodia. He specializes in economics of education and rural economics. Dr Dash has the privilege of commissioning research and consultancy projects funded by several national and international agencies including the Royal Government of Cambodia.

Eva Egron-Polak became Secretary General of the International Association of Universities (IAU) in 2002, having held senior positions at Universities Canada, including Vice President. With an academic background in political science and international political economy, her career has been devoted to international higher education and development cooperation. At IAU, an international NGO bringing together more than 630 HE institutions and organizations worldwide, Eva contributes to reflection and debate on diverse HE policy topics and frequently takes part in expert panels reviewing HE systems or universities. She serves on numerous advisory boards including at UNESCO and the European Commission and represents IAU in many international forums. She is Council Member of the Magna Charta Observatory and holds an honorary doctorate from Mykolas Romeris University.

Jose Celso Freire Jr graduated in Electrical Engineering from the Federal University of Rio de Janeiro (UFRJ). He has a master's degree in Computer Science from University of São Paulo (USP) and a PhD in Software Engineering from Université de Grenoble I (Joseph Fourier University), France. He is an Associate Professor at São Paulo State University (UNESP) in Brazil. He is the Associate Provost for International Affairs at São Paulo State University and was formerly Head of the Department of Electrical Engineering. He is also the President of FAUBAI – Brazilian Association for International Education and as such has participated as a panelist in several international events like Going Global, EAIE, AIEA, CAIE and NAFSA.

Oforiwaa Gifty Gyamera is a Lecturer at the School of Public Service and Governance at the Ghana Institute of Management and Public Administration (GIMPA). She holds a PhD in Education from the University of Roehampton in the UK. Among others, she teaches policy studies and African studies. Her research interests include internationalization of higher education, international and comparative education, gender, postcolonial studies and curriculum development. She is particularly interested in challenging marginalization of minorities and discourses and practices perpetuating colonial ideologies and philosophies, particularly in relation to higher education and gender. Her PhD focused on internationalization in the public universities in Ghana. Since her PhD she has done extensive research in higher education.

Cornelius Hagenmeier is an international education administrator and legal academic rooted in the German and South African jurisdictions. His academic focus includes internationalization of higher education and human rights. He obtained his qualification as a judge in Germany before settling in South Africa in 2002. He holds a South African LLB degree (UNISA) and LLM degree (UCT) and is a non-practising attorney of the High Court of South Africa. He has worked at the University of Venda since 2007 in the Department of Public Law and since 2011 as the first Director of International Relations. He is also a member of the

Management Council of the International Education Association of South Africa (IEASA), and Treasurer since 2015.

Savo Heleta works as the Manager of Internationalisation at Home and Research at Nelson Mandela Metropolitan University's Office for International Education (OIE). He is also a researcher in OIE's Research Unit for Higher Education Internationalisation in the Developing World. His current research focuses on higher education internationalization, higher education in fragile and post-war settings, conflict analysis and post-war reconstruction and development in general.

Zakir Jumakulov is a junior researcher at the Research Institute in Nazarbayev University Graduate School of Education. He conducts research for the project 'Advancing Best Practices of Internationalization of Higher Education in Kazakhstan'. In addition, he is a coordinator of the Eurasian Higher Education Leaders Forum, which is held annually at Nazarbayev University. He obtained his bachelor degree from L. N. Gumilyov Eurasian National University, and his master's in Public Policy at the University of Michigan with the Bolashak Scholarship of Kazakhstan.

Sulushash Kerimkulova is Associate Professor in the Graduate School of Education, Nazarbayev University, Kazakhstan. She has studied in Russia, Scotland and the United States, where she obtained her PhD. She has won 11 grants (including a Fulbright grant) and has 37 years' teaching experience and 22 years' administrative and managerial experience in higher educational institutions, including Nazarbayev University. She is the author of more than 50 scholarly and methodological papers and manuals dealing with issues related to higher education, educational reform, language education and ICT.

Manja Klemenčič is Lecturer in Sociology of Higher Education at the Department of Sociology in the Faculty of Arts and Sciences, Harvard University. She researches, teaches, advises and consults in the field of international and comparative higher education, with particular interests in student experience and student agency in higher education, teaching and learning, institutional research and internationalization. Klemenčič is Editor-in-Chief of the *European Journal of Higher Education* (Taylor & Francis), thematic editor of the *International Encyclopaedia of Higher Education Systems and Institutions* (Springer), co-editor of the book series *Understanding Student Experiences in Higher Education* (Bloomsbury) and serves on the governing boards of the Consortium of Higher Education Researchers (CHER) and the Global Forum on Improving University Teaching (IUT).

Aisi Li is an Assistant Professor of Nazarbayev University Graduate School of Education. She holds a bachelor's degree in Business Management from Sichuan University, China. She then studied an MSc in Comparative and International Education, followed by DPhil in Educational Studies at the University of Oxford.

Her research takes a comparative and international perspective on educational policy borrowing, internationalization of higher education, and education in digital society.

Francisco Marmolejo is the Global Lead of the Tertiary Education Solutions Group at the World Bank. Previously, he served as founding Executive Director of the Consortium for North American Higher Education Collaboration (CONAHEC), a network of more than 160 tertiary education institutions primarily from Canada, the United States and Mexico, based at the University of Arizona, where he also worked as Assistant Vice President for Western Hemispheric Programs, Affiliated Researcher at the Center for the Study of Higher Education and Affiliate Faculty at the Center for Latin American Studies. Previously, he was an American Council on Education Fellow at the University of Massachusetts and Academic Vice President at the University of the Americas in Mexico.

Cynthia Miller-Idriss is Associate Professor of Education and Sociology and Director of the International Training and Education Program at American University, USA. Her research follows two trajectories: nationalist and extremist expressions of youth culture in Germany and the production of knowledge about the world within US universities. She is the author of *Blood and Culture: Youth, Right-Wing Extremism, and National Belonging in Contemporary Germany* (2009) and is co-editor (with Seteney Shami) of *Middle East Studies for the New Millennium: Infrastructures of Knowledge* (in press). She has forthcoming books on the production of knowledge about the world within the US university and on the commercialization of far right youth culture in Germany.

Lynne Parmenter is a Professor at Nazarbayev University Graduate School of Education. Before moving to Kazakhstan in 2013, she taught at Fukushima University and Waseda University in Japan, and at Manchester Metropolitan University in the UK. Her main research interests and publications are in global citizenship education and intercultural education, at all levels from early childhood to higher education. She is currently working on a three-year research project on internationalization of higher education in Kazakhstan.

Anh Pham is a university lecturer with over 15 years' experience in tertiary education, especially in internationalization of higher education in Vietnam. Her recent doctoral research at RMIT University, Australia, focused on the contribution of transnational higher education to workforce development in Ho Chi Minh City. She has worked for RMIT, Deakin University, HCMC University of Technology and Education (Vietnam), Heriot-Watt University and Sunderland University (UK), and in a voluntary capacity with organizations in Vietnam and Australia including Don Bosco Vocational and Settlement Project and UNESCO Cultural Exchange Programs in Vietnam. She has presented a number of papers at international conferences and has begun publishing her research work as book chapters and journal articles.

Carolina Pinto Baleisan has a PhD in Sociology from Université Paris-Est, France and is a researcher at the Social Innovation Regional Center, in Viña del Mar University, Chile. Her main research areas are social mobility and higher education, international migration and life path studies. She has done postdoctoral research at the Universidad de Chile and conducted qualitative fieldwork in Chile, France and the United States. In addition to her academic career, she was Programme Officer at the Ministry of the Interior (2005–2007) and Consultant in CEPAL, United Nations (2004). Her most recent publications relate to social mobility and individual life paths of Latin American professionals who studied abroad and returned to work and live in their own countries.

Carlos Ramírez Sánchez is Vice President International Relations of the Universidad Viña del Mar, Chile and Director of the Regional Center for Inclusion & Social Innovation. He is Professor of Education and Teaching Methodology and holds master's degrees in Education and in International Relations. Formerly he was a teacher of history and geography as well as Director of International Relations at the Universidad de Valparaíso and Universidad Autónoma de Chile. He is President of the Association of the Center of Voluntary Workers of the Valparaíso Region. He has participated in the 'Alfa Projects' of the European Union and Cooperation Networks with European Universities. He is an Expert Member for Consejo de Alta Dirección Pública for the Chilean government.

David Rampersad is a member of senior management of the University of the West Indies (UWI). As Executive Director responsible for the implementation of the outreach priority of the UWI Strategic Plan 2012–2017, his responsibilities include ensuring that a greater focus by the UWI on addressing needs in capacity building, training as well as research, development and knowledge transfer, results in maximum benefit to the Caribbean. As the UWI extends its global presence, his mandate also includes the development and strategic management of relations with international stakeholders including funding agencies. He served in the Foreign Service and the Central Bank of Trinidad and Tobago and has worked with government ministers, senior public officials, national and regional public agencies, as well as multilateral funding agencies.

Fazal Rizvi is a Professor of Global Studies in Education at the University of Melbourne Australia, as well as an Emeritus Professor at the University of Illinois at Urbana-Champaign in the United States. He has written extensively on issues of identity and culture in transnational contexts, globalization and education policy and Australia–Asia relations. A collection of his essays is published in *Encountering Education in the Global: Selected Writings of Fazal Rizvi* (Routledge, 2014). Professor Rizvi is a Fellow of the Australian Academy of the Social Sciences and a past Editor of the journal *Discourse: Studies in Cultural Politics of Education*, and past President of the Australian Association of Research in Education.

Jasvir Kaur Nachatar Singh received an Endeavour Postgraduate Scholarship Award in 2011 from the Australian government to undertake PhD study at

La Trobe University, graduating in 2015. Her PhD thesis is titled 'What Is Academic Success for International Postgraduate Students? A Qualitative Study of Student and Staff Perspectives at a Malaysian University'. She has published journal papers and presented at numerous higher education conferences in Malaysia, Hong Kong, New Zealand, Thailand and Australia. She is a member of the International Education Association of Australia. She has also recently been invited to join the National Higher Education Research Institute in Malaysia and the Management Education and Learning Research Interest Group at Monash University, Australia.

Jason Sparks is an Associate Professor and Vice-Dean of Nazarbayev University Graduate School of Education. His current research focuses on internationalization of higher education in Kazakhstan and the role of international large-scale assessments in Kazakhstan's national education policy-making and reform.

Bernhard Streitwieser, PhD Columbia University, is an Assistant Professor of International Education at the George Washington University Graduate School of Education and Human Development. His research looks at global educational mobility, issues of inequality and notions of the scholar-practitioner in comparative and international education. From 2010 to 2013 he was a Visiting Professor and Lecturer at Berlin's Humboldt Universität on Fulbright and DAAD grants; from 2002 to 2010 Associate Director and Senior Researcher at Northwestern University's Teaching Center and a Lecturer in Comparative Education; and from 2006 to 2008 Associate Director of the Study Abroad Office. In 2014 he published *Internationalisation of Higher Education and Global Mobility*, and in 2016 *International Higher Education's Scholar-Practitioners: Bridging Research and Practice.*

Carlos Alberto Vigil Taquechel is Associate Researcher of the Regional Observatory on Internationalisation and Networks in Tertiary Education in Latin America (OBIRET) and consultant on internationalisation, international cooperation for development and project management. His professional activity has focused on strategic association in higher education, science and technology between Latin America and the European Union. He has more than 20 years' experience coordinating and evaluating cooperation programmes and projects. He was in charge of the International Project Office of the Ministry of Higher Education in Cuba and was process coordinator of the EU Programme of High Level Scholarships for Latin America (Alβan). Through his blog, he has been a great advocate for the internationalization of Latin American universities.

Olga Ustyuzhantseva is Senior Research Fellow at the Center for Policy Analysis and Studies of Technologies, Tomsk State University, Russia and CEO of the Russian–Indian Center for cooperation in education, science and technology. Her PhD is in the science, technology and innovation development of India. She has several years of practical experience in educational cooperation between Russian and Indian institutes of higher education and participates in the Russian–Indian intergovernmental working group on science and education. This combination of academic knowledge and practical experience makes her a unique expert in Russian and Indian science, technology and education systems, especially regarding internationalization challenges for both countries. Her current research interests include changes in innovation systems arising from growing innovation activity in society.

Rui Yang is Professor and Associate Dean (Cross-border/International Engagement) at the Faculty of Education, University of Hong Kong. With an academic career of over 25 years in China, Australia and Hong Kong, he has an impressive track record on research at the interface of Chinese and Western traditions in education. Bridging the theoretical thrust of comparative education and the applied nature of international education, his research interests include education policy sociology, comparative and cross-cultural studies in education, international higher education, educational development in Chinese societies, and international politics in educational research. He has an extensive list of publications, research projects, invited keynote lectures in international and regional conferences, leadership in professional associations and membership in editorial boards of scholarly journals.

Christopher Ziguras studies varied aspects of the globalization of education, particularly the ways in which governments and institutions manage and regulate cross-border provision. His latest book is *Governing Cross-Border Higher Education* (Routledge, 2015). He is Deputy Dean, International in the social sciences at RMIT University, where he oversees a variety of international projects, ranging from intensive courses in Myanmar to an International Summer School in Melbourne. Chris received the RMIT University Vice-Chancellor's Distinguished Teaching Award in 2011, was Tony Adams Visiting Senior Scholar at the Centre for Higher Education Internationalisation at Università Cattolica Del Sacro Cuore in Milan in 2013, and in October 2015 he was elected President of the International Education Association of Australia.

Foreword

Fanta Aw

The Globalization of Internationalization is a very timely book and a much-needed contribution to the field. Globalization and internationalization are not new phenomena. In this contemporary era, however, the scope, reach and breadth of each, together with their intersections, have garnered greater attention at institutional, national and regional levels. Within higher education in key regions of the world (Europe, North America, Middle East, Asia-Pacific and more recently South America), the pressure to internationalize in response to globalization cannot be ignored either by institutions or states. Concepts such as 'comprehensive internationalization', 'internationalization at home', 'global learning' and the 'race for global talent' are ever-present among the lexicon of terms characterizing discourses, attitudes, policies and practices.

As nation-states compete for global talent, prestige, recognition, share of mobile students and scholars, along with knowledge transfer, internationalization is increasingly perceived as a means to achieve these multiple objectives. However, ongoing debates about the benefits and risks of internationalization and its unintended consequences abound: for example, identification of and responses to structural inequities, imbalances in student flows and the absence of multiple perspectives and voices. The fact remains that there is a lacuna of research that provides a comprehensive picture of the state of internationalization globally. The International Association of Universities (IAU) Global Survey is a primary source of data on internationalization in higher education. The most recent IAU Global Survey results (Egron-Polak & Hudson, 2014a) provide important insights into the state of internationalization of higher education globally. According to the IAU findings, student mobility and international research collaboration remain the dual priority activities of institutions aiming to internationalize, while the commodification of higher education constitutes a most pressing societal risk, alongside unequal access to international opportunities. Moreover, Europe remains a strong focus for most regions engaged in internationalization efforts.

Discourses and research related to internationalization reveal persistent challenges. These may be characterized along three broad spectrums: knowledge, access and relevance. It is essential that scholars and practitioners interrogate some of the fundamental paradigms that have driven internationalization to date and their outcomes. If we are vested in internationalization work that reflects more equitable policies and practices and translates into relevant and sustainable models, we must have the courage and duty of care to ask and seek answers to important questions relating to the broad domains of knowledge, access and relevance:

- What is the relationship between culture, context, time and place in internationalization efforts, and why do they matter?
- Whose and what knowledge is privileged in international education and what are the implications?
- How do we ensure that internationalization advances collaborative research?
- How do we integrate community-based learning and research in the work of internationalization to ensure that outcomes are relevant and of benefit to communities, societies and nation-states?
- How do we leverage diaspora communities in our collective efforts to advance internationalization, particularly capacity building in teaching and research?

Below, I will offer some reflections on the key questions posed above in the hope of stimulating dialogue and setting the context for the significance of this book and its potential contribution to expanding perspectives and shifting paradigms.

As a scholar practitioner originally from the South, and who has worked in the field of international education in the United States for over 25 years, I have witnessed a major phenomenon characterizing internationalization practices. Ideas are flowing from the North to the South, whether it is people from the South coming to the North for advice, or so-called 'experts' from the North enlisted by institutions and/or nations to implement Western forms of internationalization. We simply need to look to countries and/or regions of the world that are promoting internationalization in the higher education sphere to see Western models being touted as 'modern' and successful approaches to internationalization. The unidirectional flow reflects power relations and the dominance of Western cultures. Internationalization practices are not value-neutral and cannot be devoid of cultural dimensions. The work must be contextualized. How scholars and practitioners conceptualize and implement internationalization activities must take into account the specificities of the environment it is emanating from and aims to benefit. Most regions choose to engage Europe as a principal partner. However, rarely are such partnerships reciprocal and/or balanced. It is important for internationalization efforts to remain contextualized and rooted in culture, place, time and manner.

Internationalization involves knowledge exchange and transfer. However, the current practice is to privilege a form of knowledge originating from the North and flowing to the South. It is important that knowledge flows be multidirectional. Knowledge generation and dissemination need to be decolonized. Forms of knowledge such as Indigenous Knowledge need to be valued and considered legitimate. This book attempts to lead by example in its focus on internationalization initiatives occurring in regions that are rarely examined and by showcasing the work of scholars there.

Another important priority for institutions and nation-states engaged in internationalization is the realm of research. More and more, technological advances encourage researchers to work and network with colleagues across borders to further common research agendas. Although international research collaborations are on the rise, evidence suggests that much of the collaboration remains at a regional level or within geopolitical borders. This may be shaped by funding structures for research. Interregional collaborative research is uneven among regions. It is imperative that we identify and incentivize collaborative research activities that are more inclusive and cross-regional. Collaborative research has the potential to not only expand shared knowledge, but also, more importantly, contribute to solving critical issues of our times that are not the domain of a single nation or region.

Institutions can further the mission of teaching and research by integrating community-based learning and teaching. Participatory community-based research can, and does, reinforce the importance of engaging community-member organizations as purveyors of expertise and knowledge, and as key partners in identifying appropriate solutions. Institutions should be encouraged to partner with communities as main sources of vital knowledge and with the agency to help determine viable solutions to critical issues.

Diaspora communities ought to be intentionally engaged in internationalization efforts because they straddle multiple societies and have vital social networks connecting them to home and host cultures. Members of the diaspora possess cultural and political capital and can serve as important gateways for helping to build capacity in research and teaching.

The work of internationalization is complex, multifaceted and fraught with power relations. The need to examine carefully the role of culture, access, knowledge and relevance in internationalization practices, policies and initiatives cannot be understated. *The Globalization of Internationalization* expands our awareness and understanding of these issues by presenting perspectives and voices from nations and regions rarely explored.

Introduction

Hans de Wit, Jocelyne Gacel-Ávila, Elspeth Jones & Nico Jooste

The chapters in this book address new voices and perspectives on internationalization of higher education, in particular from regions, countries and institutions that normally do not have a strong presence in the discourse or the literature on this important theme. As editors we set out to offer answers to the following statement, written by two of us in 2012:

> Internationalization has become a mainstream notion in higher education around the world and has evolved thematically and regionally from the concept as it was developed in the 1990s. As the international dimensions of higher education have developed their own momentum and become a global topic of interest, the 'globalization of internationalization' requires a more nuanced approach to its interpretation and delivery. We continue to talk as though we share the same understanding, but in fact there are many different interpretations of 'internationalization'. It is timely to consider whether this variety of interpretation is a barrier or a benefit and to question whether we are learning sufficiently from other global contexts.
>
> (Jones & de Wit, 2012, p. 35)

Through this book we seek to give voice to some of those emerging perspectives as an increasing range of countries engage in the process of internationalization. Dominant paradigms in the conception of internationalization have traditionally come from the English-speaking world and Western Europe. The different dimensions and interpretations of internationalization in countries and regions whose perspectives have received little attention to date provide food for thought and help to broaden our understanding of its application in alternative contexts.

Eva Egron-Polak and Francisco Marmolejo, in their contribution, argue that the emerging voices of those countries once seen as peripheral will be key to the future shape and global relevance of higher education. Fanta Aw in her foreword addresses this issue even more forcefully. She states that:

the current practice is to privilege a form of knowledge originating from the North and flowing to the South. It is important that knowledge flows be multidirectional. Knowledge generation and dissemination need to be decolonized. Forms of knowledge such as indigenous knowledge need to be valued and considered legitimate.

In that context, key questions we wanted to answer are:

- What are the main characteristics of the current state of internationalization and how is this different from traditional models such as in Western Europe, North America and Australasia?
- What are the new and innovative ways of internationalizing higher education viewed from different cultural and regional backgrounds?
- What are the key challenges and obstacles encountered in developing innovative and non-traditional models of internationalization?

Fanta Aw argues that:

If we are vested in internationalization work that reflects more equitable policies and practices and translates into relevant and sustainable models, we must have the courage and duty of care to ask and seek answers to important questions relating to the broad domains of knowledge, access and relevance.

For that reason, she adds some additional relevant questions to this list:

- What is the relationship between culture, context, time and place in internationalization efforts, and why do they matter?
- Whose and what knowledge is privileged in international education and what are the implications?
- How do we ensure that internationalization advances collaborative research?
- How do we integrate community-based learning and research in the work of internationalization to ensure that outcomes are relevant and of benefit to communities, societies and nation-states?
- How do we leverage diaspora communities in our collective efforts to advance internationalization – particularly capacity building in teaching and research?

The chapters in this book try to answer these questions. They take a range of approaches, from the thought-provoking introductory chapter by Eva Egron-Polak and Francisco Marmolejo, to Fazal Rizvi's provocative discussion on the importance of internationalization in school education, and implications of this for the higher education sector. Other chapters take regional, national, institutional or thematic approaches. Case studies come from Africa, Asia, the Caribbean, Middle East, Latin America, Russia and Eastern Europe and from a range of contexts. Together they give a rich overview of obstacles, challenges and opportunities for new and innovative approaches to internationalization in emerging and developing regions. The book does not provide a final answer to the questions raised above, but together and on their own merit they show a range of pathways towards internationalization, which we hope will be of value to others in alternative contexts.

Part I

The Global Context

Chapter 1

Higher Education Internationalization
Adjusting to New Landscapes

Eva Egron-Polak & Francisco Marmolejo

Introduction

The title of this volume, *The Globalization of Internationalization*, marks or at least signals a certain shift in the conceptual discussion about internationalization of higher education (HE) that has been going on for close to 30 years. Various scholars and practitioners alike have elaborated and debated definitions of this process, tracked its evolution over time and studied its various approaches and dimensions. Common themes in many articles and books over the past three decades have explored whether or how internationalization of higher education differs in fundamental ways from globalization. Frequently the two terms have been used as if they were the same phenomenon and thus interchangeable. At the same time, the view that internationalization is the response of the HE sector to globalization is also not uncommon. Each of these contending views has its supporters, and each sheds new light on the analysis of the processes that are changing HE in important ways. For analytical purposes and for greater understanding and thus predictability of developments, knowing how similar or distinct the processes of globalization and internationalization are, and how they impact on HE, is crucial.

This volume's title invites us to examine the two concepts in a slightly different way. The focus is on globalization OF internationalization. The first section of this chapter will attend to that, while the second takes a closer look at emerging voices in the new HE landscape around the world. Here, too, it is necessary to reflect on who or what ought to be covered by 'emerging voices'. Are we to concentrate on higher education in emerging nations in the economic sense? This is clearly an option that must be explored. Which nations do we find in this category? What characterizes them as nations and what characterizes their HE systems and institutions more specifically? What are the specificities of their 'voices' in terms of the globalization of HE internationalization? Do they have a single voice or are they highly diverse, and if so, what distinguishing features colour their positioning in this process? What are the messages they share with the rest of the world? As well, it is necessary to consider what challenges are faced by HE institutions in emerging nations and the extent to which these may be unique or different from the rest of the world. Similarly, what are, if any, the opportunities that are unique to these (or some) emerging nations and their HE institutions in the context of internationalization?

Finally, in the last section of this chapter, another 'unifying' set of forces or context-setting realities that may impact on HE internationalization will be examined and their potential as alternatives to the globalization framework will be considered. Can the new Sustainable Development Goals (SDGs), adopted by the United Nations in September 2015, and which are structuring the new global agenda, offer this alternative? In comparison with the previous global agenda known as Millennium Development Goals, the SDGs include HE. Moreover, and also for the first time, they address all nations, not simply the developing world. By doing so, this ambitious agenda is truly global and sketches a new policy framework and potentially a unified conceptual landscape, including for HE. It also places emphasis on internationalization of HE, since it sees international mobility as an important path to fulfilling the education goal.

Shifting the Focus from Globalization and Internationalization of HE to Globalization of HE Internationalization

Among the numerous articles and analyses of similarities and differences between globalization and internationalization and their respective roles in transforming HE in the modern era (Knight, 2008a; Scott, 1998), a comprehensive study by the OECD focusing on globalization stands out (OECD, 2009). In particular, this in-depth examination of the distinctive features of globalization of HE, as opposed to internationalization of HE, can still serve as the starting point here. In that volume, Marginson and van der Wende (2009) treat globalization first in the generic sense – applicable to and transforming many sectors, not specifically HE. They opt for one of the simplest descriptions of globalization (though globalization has no simple or single definition) as the 'widening, deepening and speeding up of interconnectedness' (Held, 1999, cited in OECD, 2009, p. 18). Arguing that this concept can be viewed as a neutral process of convergence, they nevertheless also agree that globalization entails the formation of worldwide markets operating in real time in common financial systems (Marginson & van der Wende, 2009).

Taking a very different view, while recognizing that productivity and competitiveness are, by and large, a function of knowledge generation and information processing, Castells has argued that globalization has the capacity to

link up everything that is valuable according to dominant values and interests, while disconnecting everything that is not valuable, or becomes devalued. It is this simultaneous capacity to include and exclude people, territories and activities that characterises the new global economy.

(Castells, 1999, p. 5)

Thus, far from being neutral, when pervasive economic globalization rests on knowledge, the impact of this exclusionary and inclusionary process can be of major proportions on the institutions and systems that generate and disseminate knowledge, namely on higher education.

Internationalization, on the other hand, tends to be defined and used to describe more traditional relations between nations (or institutions within these nations). Crossing borders and moving or linking up with actors outside a national system are thus the defining features in this case. In addition, an important distinction between the two processes is the end-state that emerges. In globalization, there is a progressive integration or convergence, leading to the creation of a new common, global system (Beerkens, 2004, cited in OECD, 2009). This distinction is critical and will be used here to illustrate the extent to which current trends in internationalization of HE reflect how globalization is indeed exerting so strong an influence on the process that we now must speak of globalization OF higher education internationalization. Furthermore, it is clear that this influence brings both positive and negative results depending on the context of the HE institution or even system in question.

A second clear distinction between the two processes has to do with primary drivers. In globalization, the creation (or perception) of a single worldwide market (for students or faculty members in HE, for example) also demonstrates the extent to which the central drivers of globalization are economic, no matter what sector is being transformed. In this sense, the neutrality of the process must be questioned at all times. Globalization in its current form, unlike internationalization, is a relatively recent phenomenon in human history. It only dates back to the late 20th century and its global spread to the post-Cold War era and the era of decolonization. Starting at this time, international relations among nations, including collaboration in higher education, stopped serving primarily as an ideological glue helping to build or consolidate links between nations and peoples within the orbit of the Western democratic/capitalist or Eastern communist alliance, respectively, or as a means of structuring and maintaining the power relations within the colonial context. In both of these aspects, the political and diplomatic purposes dictated the relationships and patterns of cooperation between nations. Linkages created among academics and universities clearly served these purposes as well, and mapped the mobility patterns of students and scholars to a large extent. By no means were these relations neutral or value-free either, but their geopolitical purposes were never denied.

As noted by de Wit and Hunter (2015), this shift away from political drivers became especially visible from the second half of the 1990s, since when the principal driving force for internationalization has become economic, with international student recruitment, preparing graduates for the global labour market, attracting global talent for the knowledge economy, etc. becoming primary pillars of the internationalization of higher education (de Wit et al., 2015).

Thus the shift from political to economic rationales and the spread of a single economic model are central to globalization and have had a deep impact on higher education and all policies related to its transformation and development, including the policies for internationalization. This reversal in the primary rationale of the purposes of HE, coupled with the perception that internationalization is a response to this globalizing process, are among the root causes for internationalization being viewed at times critically and not always only in a positive light. There is no doubt that internationalization brings many benefits – it remains critical to the improvement of quality in HE, builds understanding among peoples and nations, offers new opportunities for research collaboration to improve lives etc., but it is also perceived as bringing with it commodification and commercialization and increased competition among institutions (Egron-Polak & Hudson, 2010, 2014a).

A second, important way in which globalization, understood as bringing about a new and integrated global system, has coloured HE internationalization strategies and processes can be seen in the extent of policy mimicry among both national policy-makers and institutional leaders worldwide. Despite the recognition that diversity of contexts, at all levels, dictates the actual capacity to pursue certain policies and strategies, policy imitation worldwide is very high. As leaders of most nations seek to succeed in and adjust to the global Knowledge Economy (whether or not this is a realistic or even real option), they look to the performance of their HE institutions and strive to ascertain and improve their contribution to national (and increasingly regional, as in the case of Europe) competitiveness. Though many countries have different starting points, the same trends are apparent everywhere; there is increasing global convergence in aspirations, if not yet in actions (De Wit et al., 2015). In this sense, the concept of competitiveness being adopted by governments is not always strictly in economic terms, but also in reputation, prestige and pride.

The path chosen to reach this goal is quite similar no matter which national policy or institutional mission is examined. The key milestones include a system, and at least one institution within the system, becoming globally competitive; attractive on the international scene; focused on research excellence as measured by indexed journals; enjoying prestige and reputation, which are measured by world institutional rankings; and having a solid track record of graduate employability in an increasingly globalized local as well as international context. In a nutshell, it could be argued that many policy-makers equate international stature with the capacity to have the equivalent of the so-called 'world-class university' and, consequently, many policy actions and resources at national and institutional levels are aimed at achieving such aspirations.

Though not completely absent, other considerations – such as equity in terms of access and success, social cohesion, affordability, sustainable development and related policies – are present in HE policies at national and institutional levels, especially in the rhetorical and aspirational sense. Too often, in reality and out of declared necessity, they remain secondary to the pursuit of economic competitiveness through more internationalized, and globally better integrated, HE institutions or systems.

The rapid and ubiquitous spread worldwide of HE policy or quasi-policy instruments – such as qualifications frameworks; academic credits as valid measures of learning achievement (e.g. ECTS); shared understanding of learning outcomes as critical output descriptors in HE (despite some failed projects with global reach, such as the OECD-sponsored AHELO[1]); the implementation of regional quality assurance processes; the increased popularity of international rankings and benchmarking; and the establishing of multinational universities – are among the numerous ways in which a new global landscape is being fashioned. The signposts to guide HE development and to help international navigation of the system are similar everywhere. Even more so, the now accepted notion of a global race for talent, global competition for market share of international students and the positive view associated with HE being a top export service in several countries also demonstrate (a) the way in which policy-makers align and copy strategies with and from others, (b) the extent to which the global dimension has become the acceptable unit of analysis in HE development and, perhaps most importantly, (c) how much HE policy is driven by economic considerations.

Hearing New Voices Assess the Impact of Globalization of HE Internationalization

Yet, just as with globalization in general, when globalization fashions internationalization policies, there are strong concerns that this process results in winners and losers. This does not stem from a negative view of the idea of competition; rather it is due to the fact that the starting blocks, and the terrain on which the competition takes place, are vastly different. Indeed, as internationalization has become a central lever in HE policy, and as it is increasingly driven by globalizing forces and drivers, the approaches adopted and impacts they bring locally and globally are increasingly, and rightly, subjected to scrutiny and regularly questioned. This is both a natural and a healthy development in a continuously changing context and offers the only path towards adjustments and improvement, both of which are necessary.

Of course, the discussion on the importance and shifting nature of the globalization of international HE requires consideration of differing perspectives and 'voices' from a wide array of stakeholders. Understandably, views on the importance, affordability and impact of HE internationalization vary among contexts, institutions and individuals. Still, the implicit predominant view in more advanced economies is that active participation in the Knowledge Economy is a way for them to preserve and improve the welfare of their citizens (and, for that matter, to retain a more advanced status than others), while emerging and low-income economies predominantly tend to see active involvement in the global economy as a key opportunity to reduce the gap with more advanced economies (as well as translating into significant improvement of life conditions and opportunities for their citizens, and a more advantageous place in the global geo-economic-political landscape). Such discourse is also often reflected in HE policies, including those focusing on internationalization. All of this, as expected, results in tensions and contradictory views about the goals and means of globalized international higher education.

In other words, it should be noted that the rationale used by proponents of greater internationalization of HE is interpreted differently by the institutions and individuals that act as the 'globalizers' than it is by those perceiving themselves as the 'globalized'. Each may see globalization of international HE through different lenses. Failing to understand and acknowledge these distinct perceptions, related motives, reference frameworks and goals can result in significant misunderstandings, and indeed a rejection of the internationalization process by some stakeholders.

A good example of such misperception is the case of migratory policies linked to international education and employment, established and promoted with significant enthusiasm in several high-income countries, to attract well-qualified international students to their HE institutions and retain them after graduation in order to fully take advantage of their potential as key players in the Knowledge Economy. Proponents of such policies usually argue that this is a legitimate and humane pathway to enable highly qualified individuals to achieve their full potential and productivity (a pathway that would not otherwise be possible given very limited opportunities in their countries of origin). Even elaborate theories of 'brain gain', 'brain exchange', 'brain circulation' and even 'reverse brain drain' have been developed to explain and somewhat justify actions on this matter. However, governments and HE institutions in the 'receiving' countries devote limited attention to analysing the impact, both positive and negative, that the aforementioned policies will have on the 'sending' countries.

The development of partnerships between HE institutions in different countries presents another visible case of differing perspectives on the process of globalization in international HE. It is common for institutions in more developed countries to impose their own scope, standards and protocols to formalize partnerships, leaving 'lower-status' institutions with limited room for manoeuvring. A 'take it or leave it' attitude can be prevalent in these uneven inter-institutional relationships.

On a larger scale, such asymmetries in relationships are reflected in the development of regional frameworks for international education. Two decades ago, the negotiations conducted to facilitate cross-border mobility of professionals between Canada, the United States and Mexico, as part of enacting the North American Free Trade Agreement, failed mostly due to the position of professional bodies and accrediting agencies in the United States, which argued that existing US criteria for quality should take precedence.

Similarly, other manifestations of the globalization of HE internationalization are interpreted differently and must be taken into consideration if we are to understand their full complexity and their multiple effects. In today's world, such multidimensional analysis is highly relevant. This makes it necessary to go beyond the traditional domestic view of internationalization, usually confined to the institutional or in some cases the national scope, to a more comprehensive analysis that reviews regional and global trends inside and outside the HE sector more explicitly. Such an expanded conceptual framework makes more explicit recognition of the globalization of internationalization in HE, and forces consideration of players or 'voices' and their perspectives that, under a narrower framework for analysis, receive only limited or no attention.

Yet, these perspectives of 'emerging voices' in international HE must, on the contrary, receive serious attention. The reasons for this abound. But, where are those 'emerging voices'? It is not as simple as just identifying and segmenting trends and perspectives and assuming that the 'emerging voices' are those from low- and middle-income countries and their HE systems. On the contrary, even in high-income countries there are 'emerging voices' being marginalized from a globalized higher education. At the same time, within low-income and emerging economies, a small share of the HE sector is often already actively engaged in international education at similar or even more advanced levels of intensity than institutions in rich countries.

But, why analyse the internationalization of HE through globalization lenses? Does it make sense to review what it is happening not only within but also beyond HE? What is the benefit of listening to the 'emerging voices' in the field of internationalization?

From Periphery to Centre Stage: Emerging Voices in HE Internationalization

As a case in point, a simple review of the current provision of HE is sufficient. Here, it should be noted that, globally, low- and middle-income economies are the ones experiencing most of the growth and transformation in higher education. It would be naive not to recognize that as developed economies continue greying, their HE institutions will be affected in different ways, including by a shrinking of their size (and some may argue of their influence). In fact, the larger and most dynamic share of global HE enrolment is now situated mostly in emerging economies followed by the low-income countries. Consequently, the way that HE evolves in low-income and emerging economies will greatly influence its overall future shape on a global scale and of its internationalization. Simply considering the magnitude of the HE sector, it is important to remember that from 2000 to 2013, the share of global HE enrolment in the United States, Canada and Western Europe shrank from 27% to just 20% (World Bank, 2015). In contrast, in the same period, the share in the BRICS countries alone (Brazil, Russia, India, China and South Africa) grew from 26 to 40% (British Council, 2015).

A few facts help to demonstrate the magnitude and complexity of the challenge associated with the shift in pressures for HE provision:

a   Youth with limited opportunities: Half the population in countries in the Middle East and North Africa region (MENA) is under the age of 20, but

32.3% of youth between 15 and 24 years of age are neither working nor in school (De Hoyos et al., 2015);

b   Interregional demographic shifts: From 2015 to 2050, the total population in most of Europe will decrease by 5% while most of Africa will grow by more than 40% (World Bank, 2015). In fact, by 2030, 42% of youth globally will live in Africa;

c   The vicious circle of poverty: Currently more than 70% of youth in Africa live on less than US$2 per day (Ping, 2016); globally more than 360 million youth between 15 and 24 years of age are neither working nor in school, mostly in the MENA region (32.3% of the total cohort), South Asia (30.3%) and Africa (23.9%) (De Hoyos et al., 2015).

Does any of the aforementioned information affect the internationalization of HE? The answer is obvious. The landscape of higher education around the world is being and will be transformed, and so will the internationalization of higher education. In a way, those that once were on the periphery have gradually been gaining prominence and their 'emerging voices' can no longer be ignored or minimized.

Nevertheless, as indicated before, this so-called periphery is not only situated in low- and middle-income countries. It is also present in developed economies, especially in countries with significantly stratified HE systems. The case of US study abroad data presents easily observable patterns of disparity. For instance, when studying abroad, more than 60% of all US students are enrolled in doctoral/research-oriented institutions, even though the national enrolment in those institutions is only 25%. In contrast, only 2% of US students studying abroad come from community colleges offering two-year degree programmes, even though such institutions enrol more than half of the total HE population (IIE, 2014). Although efforts have been made to address this acute asymmetry, evidently the 'voice' from community colleges is still unheard. Similar conclusions can be drawn from data on the socioeconomic status, ethnicity, gender, etc. of US students who study abroad. Are their 'voices' being considered in the efforts of HE institutions and national systems to embrace internationalization? No significant evidence exists to demonstrate that this is the case.

In summary, the concept of 'emerging voices' in the new HE landscape should be comprehensive and inclusive in scope. It is not only one single, unified voice, nor does it always come from the same cluster of countries or from the same type of institutions.

Regaining Control of HE Internationalization

For some time, globalization was perceived as an inevitable process, while internationalization could be controlled or steered. This was the case generally in HE as well. 'Internationalisation is seen as something higher education institutions *do* while globalisation is something that is *happening to them*' (Mitchell & Yildiz Nielsen, 2012, p. 3). This is no longer (nor was it perhaps ever) the case. Certainly there are multiple debates, ongoing analysis and numerous critical voices focusing on bringing HE internationalization back into the primarily academic sphere and making room for new perspectives from the less dominant systems or institutions to be heard. The *Affirming Academic Values in Internationalisation of Higher Education: A Call for Action*, adopted by the International Association of Universities (IAU, 2012)[2] is one example, as is the *Nelson Mandela Bay Global Dialogue Declaration on the Future of Internationalisation of Higher Education*, adopted in 2014. Even more recently, in 2015, a newly articulated definition of internationalization offers a strong reminder that internationalization must also fulfil societal purposes. This newly coined definition takes, as its starting point, the classic Knight (2003) definition of internationalization and adds a few key aspects. Internationalization becomes:

> the *intentional* process of integrating an international, intercultural or global dimension into the purpose, functions and delivery of post-secondary education, *in order to enhance the quality of education and research for all students and staff, and to make a meaningful contribution to society.*
>
> (De Wit et al., 2015)

This definition introduces two key ideas into the concept of higher education internationalization: agency or intentionality on the one hand, and clearer purposes, both internal in terms of quality and external, making a meaningful contribution to society, on the other. Both additions are important and help map actions into the future where HE internationalization is assessed against a broader set of measures than predominantly those linked to economic competitiveness, and takes into consideration 'voices' that have so far been somewhat peripheral to the discussion.

There are strong signals that HE institutions are ready for this shift. For example, at the global level, the third most important benefit of internationalization, immediately following benefits directly related to student learning, is enhanced international cooperation and capacity building (Egron-Polak & Hudson, 2014a). Also, the institutional risks in the IAU Survey portray a concern with issues of equity, as institutions fear that international opportunities may be available only to those who can pay. Thus institutional respondents around the world demonstrate a clear will to push back and resist the strong and often inequitable influence of globalizing drivers in internationalization.

Finding an Alternative Global Policy Framework

Transforming Our World: The 2030 Agenda for Sustainable Development, adopted by the United Nations in September 2015, may offer a new framework within which internationalization of HE could thrive, reconnecting with a broader set of purposes, rationales and institutional partners. This new Global Agenda is structured around 17 Sustainable Development Goals (SDGs) to be reached by 2030, with more than 160 related targets and framed by the five Ps as follows: people, planet, prosperity, peace and partnerships. Though HE is rarely mentioned in the texts explicitly, and only one goal speaks directly to the sector and to universities in particular, there is hardly any institution more suitable to play a central role in achieving these goals than the university. Furthermore, the SDGs and targets of the 2030 Agenda are repeatedly characterized as integrated and indivisible, global in nature and universally applicable. This means that the Agenda engages the responsibility of all countries and that achievement of one set of targets is dependent on actions on multiple fronts. This is why, rather than being dispirited with the relatively small recognition given to the academic and research community and to HE institutions of higher education as actors within this action plan, HE institutions must, on the contrary, demonstrate their involvement on multiple levels and in diverse areas, ranging of course from education, to urban studies, the health field, economics, environmental sciences, peace studies, engineering and renewable energies research, agriculture and anthropology, management, law, governance and media studies and so many more.

It is also essential to note that SDG 4, focused on education specifically, clearly notes an important benefit to be drawn from further internationalization of HE and particularly through international mobility and cooperation. The goal's targets specify various aims as follows:

4.3 By 2030, ensure equal access for all women and men to affordable and quality technical, vocational and tertiary education, including university
[...]
4.7 By 2030, ensure that all learners acquire the knowledge and skills needed to promote sustainable development, including, among others, through education for sustainable development and sustainable lifestyles, human rights, gender equality, promotion of a culture of peace and non-violence, global citizenship and appreciation of cultural diversity and of culture's contribution to sustainable development
[...]
4.b By 2020, substantially expand globally the number of scholarships available to developing countries, in particular least developed countries, small island developing States and African countries, for enrolment in higher education, including vocational training and information and communications technology, technical, engineering and scientific programmes, in developed countries and other developing countries
4.c By 2030, substantially increase the supply of qualified teachers, including through international cooperation for teacher training in developing countries, especially least developed countries and small island developing States.
(United Nations, n.d.)

HE institutions already contribute, in a variety of ways to goals such as those of the 2030 Agenda and have done so for decades. They collaborate to build capacity in partner institutions in many disciplines; they internationalize their curriculum with the aim of instilling in graduates a global consciousness; they have focused on developing learning outcomes linked to global citizenship; they undertake research on sustainable lifestyles and alternative economic models, develop new health policies and practices that expand access to treatment, train teachers at home and internationally, etc. However, these valuable activities are often somewhat marginal in the overwhelming focus of internationalization strategies on attracting more international students, on finding partner institutions that enjoy a strong international reputation, on building partnerships according to self-interest due to pressure to show impact at home, focusing on research that has the greatest potential to raise both individual and institutional status, and others.

The global commitment and the global imperative to address the challenges outlined by the SDG Agenda offer both a renewed legitimacy and incentive for the reorientation of internationalization strategies towards these goals and areas of collaboration. They should also stimulate a broadening of partnerships to diverse nations and institutions and serve to encourage institutions from all regions of the world to work together towards the needed changes in behaviour if we are collectively to secure sustainable development around the world. In this context, the economic drivers of globalization must, once again, take a secondary place to make room for the more balanced approach to higher education internationalization where academic and societal (in the broadest sense) interests and needs also have an important place.

Notes

1 AHELO (Assessment of Higher Education Learning Outcomes) is a global project conducted by the OECD intending to assess what students in higher education know and can do upon graduation. Its implementation has been abandoned due to a variety of limitations and challenges, including the active opposition of some OECD member countries.

2 www.iau-aiu.net/sites/all/files/Affirming_Academic_Values_in_Internationalisation_of_Higher_Education.pdf.

Chapter 2

School Internationalization and Its Implications for Higher Education

Fazal Rizvi

Much of the recent literature on the internationalization of higher education has focused on issues that are mostly internal to the systems of higher education. This literature has addressed issues pertaining to student mobility, including the national origins and destinations of international students; the ways in which universities recruit them; and the role that rankings and the perceived status of universities play in their preferences. Also examined are the challenges that students face in cross-cultural settings; the strategies they use to negotiate these challenges; and the approaches that universities adopt to internationalize their curricula, seeking to provide experiences that prepare students, both local and international, for the requirements of global labor markets. Over the years, there has thus been a growing body of literature on international student pathways, their employability and issues of transition from higher education to the world of work.

So while issues internal to higher education are well-researched, seldom explored are the questions of the ways in which the secondary schools prepare students for international higher education, as well as the implications for universities of the attempts by schools to internationalize their policies, programs and practices. This is surprising in view of the rapid growth in recent years in the number of international schools around the world, which are often designed specifically to prepare students for international higher education. In this chapter, I want to discuss the complex relationship between the internationalization processes increasingly taking place in schools and the ways in which internationalization of higher education might now be conceptualized. I argue that higher education researchers and policy-makers can ill afford to overlook the kind of students schools are sending to the universities: that is, they need to address issues of 'input' as they much as they do 'outcomes'.

My discussion is based partly on the findings of a large international research project I have recently completed with a group of researchers from across the world. Funded by the Australian Research Council, the project, 'Elite Schools in Globalizing Circumstances', examined the ways in which elite schools, grounded in the traditions of the British public schools, interpret and negotiate the forces of globalization, develop global connections with other like-minded schools and help their students develop a global imaginary. With case studies of seven such schools in the United Kingdom, Australia, India, Singapore, Hong Kong, Barbados and South Africa, the project was conducted over a period of five years (2010–2014). It produced a diverse range of insights about the ways in which these schools retain their colonial legacy, using it to differentiate themselves from other, more recently established elite schools, but at the same time deliver an education more in line with the global aspirations of their students and parents. In a book emanating from the project (Kenway et al., 2016), we use the phrase 'class choreographies' to show how these schools presume and enact their social privileges in a space that is not only locally embedded but also transnationally extended. The space in which these schools now operate, and also seek to influence, is no longer only national but also global.

Common to each of the seven case-study schools is a commitment to internationalization, though the ways in which this commitment is expressed varies greatly. This variation is grounded in the particular history of each school, as well as the local and national conditions under which it operates. Each school seeks to align its internationalization objectives to the educational priorities of the nation-state, but also draws heavily on a globally circulating discourse (Rizvi & Lingard, 2010) relating to the need for schools to respond to the challenges and opportunities associated with globalization, preparing its students for the requirements of a globally networked labor market. Furthermore, each school is deeply conscious of the fact that it operates in a highly competitive educational market in which new corporate schools have also become increasingly active. To retain its status, each of our case-study schools is convinced that it must embrace internationalization as one of its key objectives if it is to retain the prestige it has enjoyed for more than a century. With the support of parents and alumni, each has therefore developed a whole range of strategies to internationalize most aspects of its work.

Chief among these strategies is a focus on student mobility. Each school claims to be driven by a recognition that the ubiquitous mobility of people and ideas has now become a permanent feature of societies everywhere. These schools therefore regard as highly relevant, and utterly important, programs that enable their students to travel abroad to participate in conferences, study tours and educational exchange, in order not only to have experiences of other cultures but also to develop skills of intercultural communication and global leadership. For most of these elite schools, student-led meetings, such as United Nations youth conferences, have become common. In 2012, for example, the Singapore school in our project coordinated a conference called 'Tiltshift', bringing together students from the Global Alliance of Leading-Edge Schools (GALES), an association of top secondary schools around the world, to participate in a conference that tackled issues as diverse as migration, health care, poverty and the environment. This is not, however, a unique event. Students and their parents at elite schools have now come to expect study tours of global cities and sites of historical or geographical significance as an essential part of 'good education'. Study tours for service learning abroad have become a common feature at these schools, as indeed has the idea of educational exchange that enables students to spend up to a year at a partner school abroad.

Many such conferences, study tours and programs of educational exchange are coordinated under the aegis of various global networks, some of which have existed for quite some time, while others have emerged in recent decades. So, Round Square (RS), for example, is a network of 'innovative' schools founded in 1966. It now boasts 'like-minded' schools in 40 countries across five continents. Inspired by the educational philosophy of Kurt Hahn (Veevers & Pete, 2011), in order to become a member of RS global network, schools need to demonstrate their commitment to six key principles: International Understanding, Democracy, Environmental Awareness, Adventure, Leadership and Service. RS schools are thus carefully selected and membership is keenly sought. GALES similarly aims to bring together groups of students who want to look beyond the parochial concerns of their own schools and national communities. Its aspiration is to forge the next generation of the world's leaders. Another network of schools, G-20, is an association of 20 heads of leading schools who wish to share their experiences and examine the challenges of education in a world that is increasingly becoming interconnected and that requires schools to work across national borders.

Global connections through networking are viewed by many elite schools not only as a challenging imperative but also as an opportunity. It has enabled them to recruit international students at an age as early as 12. At the British school in our study, almost 40% of the students in its senior classes are international students, recruited from the growing wealthy class in China, Korea, the Middle East and Africa. Most of these students view international school education as a preparation for entry into the Ivy League universities in the United States or Oxford or Cambridge in England. Similarly, the Australian school in our project recruits a large number of students from Asia, and barely hides the fact that, apart from enhancing its cultural diversity and providing its students opportunities for productive intercultural exchange, its focus on internationalization represents a source of income for the school. This has made the school more commercially inclined than ever before.

Business considerations have thus become a major factor in elite schools' discourses of internationalization, just as they have been at many universities for more than three decades. And just as some universities, such as Nottingham University, New York University and Monash University, have campuses abroad, some schools, such as Harrow in England and Haileybury in Australia, have also created large campuses in Hong Kong and Tianjin respectively. These campuses exist for local students who are not inclined to travel abroad for their schooling at an early age, but expect nonetheless to be prepared for higher education abroad. In this way, while the interests of students and those of the schools converge, so do the interests of the universities that now recruit, in ever-growing numbers, students from the elite internationalizing schools. A new cultural economy is forged, which clearly needs to be better understood.

Most of the schools in our project offer 'international' qualifications. Their language of instruction is English, the use of which is justified on the assumption that the education they offer is designed primarily to prepare their students for higher education in a high-ranked Anglo-American university. Indeed, parents in countries with fast-growing economies are now prepared to spend large sums of money to educate their children in international schools whose curriculum is often divorced from local agendas. The appeal of international qualifications throughout Asia in particular has grown rapidly in recent years. International Baccalaureate (IB) and Cambridge International (CIS) programs are the most popular. According to a former president of The Association of International Schools in India (TAISI), at least one new international school offering an international curriculum is established in India each week (personal communication). She insists the idea that international programs are not only socially prestigious, but more importantly provide a seamless path to higher education abroad, has now become entrenched in the popular imagination of India's rapidly growing middle class. This was clearly evident in the Indian school in our project, which, when it called for applications to its newly created CIS Examination stream in 2010, was inundated with student interest, with more than 90 applications for 30 available places.

Although they differ markedly in their curricular and pedagogic approaches, international programs such as IB and CIS share a common ideological position on the need to develop in students a global imaginary – to view the world as interconnected and interdependent – so as to develop a cosmopolitan outlook. One of the central values of IB, for example, is 'international-mindedness', an idea that highlights the crucial importance of intercultural understanding for living and succeeding in a world in which contact and exchange across cultures and nationalities have become ubiquitous, and a source of strategic advantage. To achieve such an understanding, IB regards multilingualism and global engagement as essential. Its emphasis on the Learner Profile (LP) is designed to specify ten key attributes that are deemed necessary to become an effective learner in the 21st century.

Furthermore, the notion of 21st-century skills (including life and career skills, learning and innovation skills, information, media and technology skills, along with a focus on global awareness, civic and environmental literacy) is widely supported by global corporations and foundations. Given the links that these organizations often have with leading private schools, it is not surprising that the discourses of international-mindedness and 21st-century skills are widely promoted and often used to mark their elite differentiation.

These discourses are, of course, not entirely confined to elite schools and are slowly making inroads into public schools in lower- and higher-income countries alike. Indeed, whole systems of schools have now begun to embrace the rhetoric of internationalization. In its strategic plan for 2013–2017, for example, the Toronto District School Board in Canada has suggested that 'in an increasingly connected world, supporting student success means bringing the world into our classrooms and opening our schools to the world'. The board encourages schools to recruit and welcome more international students, broaden its pedagogy and contribute to an ever-increasing understanding of global citizenship.

The notion of education for global citizenship can be found in the mission statements of many schools, both private and public, around the world. Singapore, for example, has developed a global citizenship program for all schools, in an effort to provide

> students with a variety of experiences that serves as a key platform for the development of valuable partnerships with several countries, each with its own unique cultures and traditions. This program is designed to engage students' heart (empathy), head (knowledge) and hands (application).
>
> (SST, n.d.)

Globally, this view of global citizenship education in schools is now supported by such powerful and influential organizations as the Asia Society and the Soros Foundation.

What this brief account clearly suggests is that in recent decades there has emerged in schools and school systems around the world a set of globally converging discourses, policies and practices around the idea of internationalization. These discourses underline the importance of helping students to understand how the world is becoming increasingly interconnected, and how cultural, economic and political engagement with this world in the future will be contingent upon the extent to which students are able to negotiate its possibilities. Internationalization has apparently become a key aim of school education. It has not only underlined the importance of initiating students into a world-view that transcends nationally bounded concerns but also created various commercial possibilities for wealthy private schools.

The ability of some schools to generate additional revenue from international students has had the effect of perpetuating their social distinction (Bourdieu, 1979) within an emerging global market of elite schools. In this way, educational experiences of global mobility and networks have become a central characteristic of elite schools with a commitment to provide their students an education that prepares them to enter higher education institutions anywhere in the world. Their students thus leave the schools with a 'global imaginary', a particular view of their academic and work future, a set of expectations and aspirations they eventually take to the institutions of higher education. In this sense, the logic of internationalization in higher education is inextricably linked to what is happening in schools.

Preparing students for higher education has long been a preoccupation of academically oriented schools around the world. The curricular choices that students make at these schools have invariably been shaped by their plans for studies beyond school. As they approach the end of schooling, much of their conversation, both formal and informal, centers on the universities they would like to attend. Traditionally, these students have targeted the leading universities within their own national borders. Our research shows, however, that this is no longer the case. Students at elite schools, in both lower- and higher-income countries, now aim for what they regard as the 'best in the world'. It is here that the relevance of global university rankings often kicks in.

At our research schools in Singapore and Barbados, a large proportion of students find their way into elite universities in North America or the United Kingdom. The international students at our British school expect to be admitted to Ivy League universities in the United States or Oxford or Cambridge in the United Kingdom. Not only do they work hard to realize this ambition, but much of their conversation at school is also about the requirements of admission and the relative status of the various universities. For example, we encountered a student in India, with little prospect of going abroad for higher education, who seemed obsessed with university rankings. He studied them and had developed an encyclopedic knowledge of the boastful information contained on various university websites.

Schools too were keen to provide their students and parents with information and advice about universities abroad, their academic expectations and the kind of campus life the students could expect. The Indian school helped its students prepare the portfolio that many American universities use as a base for student admission decisions. The school in Barbados organized a very popular University Expo at which Canadian, American and British universities provided information about the courses and scholarships they offered. Not that many of the students needed this information, as they had already examined studiously the contents of the university websites, and had also sought out advice from alumni of their university of choice within their own diaspora communities. Of the seven schools in our research project, only the students at the Australian school did not aspire to higher education at a university abroad, but focused instead on Australia's leading universities. At all other schools, the space of possibilities for most students had increasingly become global.

An understanding of the global market in higher education thus appears to have become well developed at elite schools, not only in countries widely regarded as 'developing' but also in 'developed' countries that recruit a growing number of international students from lower-income countries. Within the 'developing' countries, aspirations for higher education abroad seem to have become a point of social differentiation between those schools whose students routinely aspire to international education and those that cannot. Indeed, international education may already have become a fulcrum on which a closer link between centers of economic power and elite institutions of education, both schools and universities, is forged and perpetuated.

If this is so, then higher education researchers are faced with a new set of questions, pertaining to the complex and changing relationship between schools and universities on the global stage. In the early 1990s, policy-makers, educational researchers and university leaders focused largely on the global forces that were reshaping higher education on the ways in which they provided universities a set of new opportunities to raise revenue in the context of declining public funds, and the curricular and pedagogic challenges that ensuing cultural diversity posed for them. The role played by schools in their thinking was largely overlooked. What my argument suggests is that universities can no longer ignore what goes on in the elite schools sectors around the world, since school internationalization has major implications for higher education policies and practices, in relation to international student recruitment, university governance and also curriculum and pedagogy.

With respect to student recruitment, the growth of international schools and programs around the world is partly a reflection of the rapidly increasing level of demand for international higher education. If this trend continues, then recent projections of growth (Ortiz, Li Chang & Fang, 2015, for example) may turn out to have been underestimated. This is so because at old elite and new international schools around the world, most students have now begun to consider international higher education as *normal*. This suggests that the demand for international higher education is likely to continue to grow, even without the help of massive marketing campaigns. These campaigns themselves might have to change, to provide the kind of information and advice that is no longer basic but specific to the needs of particular students. Recruitment agents might need to work more closely with schools, and view their task in terms of providing advice on academic pathways, perhaps becoming educational counselors. The Internet has transformed the world of information, particularly for younger people. They are now able to search for information that was once provided by recruitment agents. Furthermore, social media has enabled them to get advice directly from their various networks, including alumni of their own schools and the universities they are considering. It needs to be noted that the next generation may be the second or third generation of international students, with family members who might have already been to a university abroad. This has implications for both schools and universities.

In the past, the global markets in higher education and secondary schools were often treated as discrete. What recent developments in schools indicate is the need to view the educational market as integrated, with synchronous relationships across secondary schools and higher education sectors. If this is so, then, as de Wit (2015a) has observed,

> higher education has to realise that internationalisation starts not only at the university but before that and they should support and collaborate with the other levels of education, take advantage of this development and build their own strategy on it.

This underlines the need for universities to develop closer and more direct links with schools and school systems around the world, in ways they have traditionally done within their own localities. They might need to become transnationally extended, developing collaborative links not only with universities abroad but also with schools. For researchers, this raises the question of how such an integration might be conceptualized, what barriers still exist across the two sectors and how they might be brought into a conversation with each other, not only within the national space but also across national borders. Researchers might also need to investigate governmental regulations in the receiving countries that continue to prevent student mobility across national borders, and how school authorities in the sending countries might need to make their qualifications internationally transferable. Comparative studies of academic performance at particular universities by students from different countries may reveal much about the curriculum architecture of various systems of education, and how they could be better aligned with each other.

Yet the idea of a globally integrated educational market need not imply global uniformity, a kind of world curriculum. It must rather suggest a qualifications architecture that incorporates local knowledge and cultural traditions but also prepares students for a world of global interconnectivity and mobility. Many school systems are increasingly aware of this imperative, and are shifting their foci toward an internationalized curriculum in a number of non-trivial ways. Over the past two decades, attempts by universities in English-speaking countries at internationalizing their curricula (Leask, 2015a) have been predicated on an assumption that their students have had no or little international experience. This is no longer the case. Institutions of higher education now need to recognize that a large number of their new students are familiar with global issues and have expectations of universities that are shaped by their experiences in schools of global mobility, exchange and learning. The new generation of international students, more frequently than not, can be expected to have attended an international school or have studied for a global program, such as IB and CIS. Many of these students are confident speakers of English, much more so than was the case barely 20 years ago. Universities thus have to develop new pedagogic approaches to internationalization that build on an extensive reservoir of global knowledge, intercultural communication skills and mobility experiences that are now increasingly offered at schools.

This is not to suggest that all students have such academic and cultural backgrounds. Many still hail from traditional sources – students who have had limited access to international programs and global mobility. Many come from public schools in regional towns where English is not widely spoken. For them, access to international higher education is a major achievement in ways that are simply assumed by students from elite private schools in metropolitan cities, with cosmopolitan lifestyles and aspirations. Universities thus cannot overlook the facts of the enormous diversity of class and cultural backgrounds among the students they recruit, often from the same country. For them, national origin is no longer a reliable indicator, if indeed it ever was, of student capabilities, interests and aspirations. Schools have always been a site for producing and reproducing social inequalities (Khan, 2012). In the contemporary era, a focus of internationalization in schools has potentially become an additional component in the cultural logic of social differentiations, visible most clearly in the various mechanisms of access to higher education, of inclusion and exclusion.

Such mechanisms join secondary schools and higher education sectors at the hip, and highlight the importance of universities developing a better understanding of schools not only within their own national context but also in countries from where they recruit their international students. Many of these students now go to universities abroad with a stronger sense of a global imaginary and expectations. Universities can ill afford to overlook the fact that, for these students, 'cosmopolitanism' has become 'ordinary' (Skribic & Woodward, 2013). If this is so, then there are clearly new challenges for internationalization in higher education. Universities need to explore ways of building upon the global awareness that many of their students have already developed, the global experiences they have already encountered and the global aspirations that have already developed. One of their key ethical challenges is to help students realize the nature of their own social privileges and interrogate its sources, some of which lie in the opportunities that they have of the kind of global mobility for higher education that very few are able to enjoy.

Politics, Conflict and Social Issues

Part II

Politics, Conflict
and Social Issues

Chapter 3

Higher Education's Response to the European Refugee Crisis
Challenges, Strategies and Opportunities

Bernhard Streitwieser, Cynthia Miller-Idriss & Hans de Wit

Introduction

This chapter broadly examines higher education's role in responding to refugee crises generally and the Syrian refugee crisis in Europe from 2015 in particular. Our analytic focus is on the range of shifting responses by international and domestic organizations and higher education institutions in Europe. We characterize European country responses as a gradual evolution from emergency-based responses, most clearly illustrated through the funding of limited numbers of competitive fellowships and university slots, to more coordinated efforts that address the large-scale educational needs of displaced university-aged youth.

We argue that universities' reception of refugees ought to be understood within broader higher education internationalization frameworks and global engagements, because receiving countries' efforts to help refugees maintain and acquire high-level skills during periods of crisis and displacement will have a significant and ongoing impact on the recovery and reconstruction efforts of sending regions once the conflict ends. While developing countries are usually the primary senders and receivers of refugees, the crisis that began in Europe in 2015 has changed that pattern once again.

Although we focus on the Syrian refugee flow to Europe as our empirical case, the challenges we analyze and the recommendations we identify have application to refugee situations across national contexts and conflicts more generally. In broad terms, we suggest that the Syrian refugee crisis, which is characterized as the worst refugee crisis in Europe since World War II, offers valuable lessons for ways universities can most comprehensively respond to high-skilled migration during crisis and conflict situations.

As part of the response process, universities must consider not only the impact that migrants have on receiving countries, but also what the broader impacts are and will be for migrants themselves and for the labor market and educational needs in sending countries. The latter two factors highlight why this issue is so relevant to the internationalization of higher education more broadly: receiving countries' efforts to help refugees maintain and acquire high-level skills during periods of crisis and displacement will have a significant and ongoing impact on recovery and reconstruction efforts post-conflict. This approach is consistent with other emergent literature on the topic. In separate reports looking at the Syrian refugee crisis and its relation to higher education by the Brookings Institution and World Education Services, for example, universities' response efforts are characterized as being critical strategic initiatives aimed at wider recovery efforts for Syrian students, academics and their country (Barakat & Milton, 2015a; Magaziner, 2015). We aim here to extend such analyses and explore how the higher education sector's response to refugee crises might be understood in light of broader internationalization initiatives and goals. Additionally, we suggest that as receiving countries begin to develop higher education refugee policies, universities in these countries will take on an increasing role in longer-term reconstruction efforts in sending regions. In other words, opening access to higher education for refugees not only solves an immediate problem for any given individual, but also helps to ensure that as political stability returns to countries in conflict, formerly displaced citizens will be able to return with skills and knowledge, in engineering, medicine, international law, democratic governance, or primary and secondary education, for example, and transition more smoothly back into their society in tandem with reconstruction efforts.

Case Example: The Syrian Refugee Crisis in Europe

The Syrian refugee crisis escalated rapidly in 2015, as the Syrian civil war entered its fifth year and it became increasingly clear that inadequate options for safety and stability in the surrounding region were unlikely to improve. Over the course of 2015, hundreds of thousands of Syrians began making the perilous journey to Europe, arriving on Greek islands and at the Hungarian border and trying with mixed success to move further into the European Union. Of course, Syrians are not the only ones fleeing their country and looking for refuge, safety and economic livelihood in Europe and other industrialized countries. But the scope and intensity of the Syrian refugee crisis has brought the issue of refugees into sharper relief.

Examining the impact of this crisis on higher education policies in receiving countries is particularly critical in light of the fact that research and policy responses to refugee education needs in general by the higher education sector have received insufficient attention (Magaziner, 2015). Educational policies and practices around refugee flows mostly attends to the needs of younger children and adolescents in primary and secondary schooling. The Syrian refugee crisis has displaced millions of its most highly educated citizens and is an ideal case to examine. Perhaps more than any other refugee group, the influx of high numbers of university-educated and university-eligible Syrians into receiving countries means that higher education is being called upon in new ways, compared to previous migration flows. There is a gradual evolution from emergency-based responses, such as common strategies of funding in the form of limited numbers of competitive fellowships and university slots, to more coordinated efforts addressing the large-scale educational needs of university-aged youth, who are seen as a "lost generation" (Watenpaugh, Fricke & King, 2014) and estimated to be around 100,000 currently displaced from Syria (Redden, 2015).

The Refugee Crisis in the Context of Global Immigration Patterns

Migration flows comprise millions of people around the world at any given time, driven to move between and within countries for a variety of reasons both voluntary (for labor, as students) and involuntary (as political or economic refugees). The United Nations (2013) estimates the total number of refugees globally to be 15.7 million, which is approximately 7% of international migrants more generally. However, according to experts at the UNHCR, only 1% are able to access higher education (Lambrechts, 2015). Following a period of decline between 1990 and 2010, the number of refugees has been rising in recent years. Nearly 90% of these refugees live in developing areas of the world; 87% of all refugees worldwide reside in the global South.

Several points from the data on refugees are important as context for this chapter. First, "economic refugees" and "political refugees," two terms with contested distinctions sometimes difficult to discern, constitute only a small proportion of total migration patterns. Second, in periods of relative political calm and economic development, the number of refugees declines. And third, in periods of increased political, social and economic tension, it is in fact developing countries that are ultimately both the primary recipients as well as the primary senders of refugees.

Global Mobility and the Higher Education Sector

In many ways, higher education institutions are better equipped and more flexible than other sectors to handle unanticipated, large enrollments of new international students. Many universities already have well-developed infrastructures in place, from classrooms and libraries to assistance with housing and meal services, along with other key resources and trained support personnel. Universities dealing with a mass influx of refugees may need to augment their existing infrastructures and creatively adapt rather than develop entirely parallel systems devoted only to refugees. The problems are likely more of scale and scope than of substance.

Universities have a long history of receiving international students, and the recent acceleration in globalization has led to even greater mobility by individuals seeking better educational opportunities. Ethnic conflicts, religious strife and economic hardships have been major drivers of educational migration even in periods with smaller refugee flows. Universities also have an incentive to become increasingly global more generally, particularly due to heightened competition driven by advances in information sharing, competitive rankings/league tables and the search for world-class excellence and lucrative partnerships that, it is believed, will lead to new sources of prestige and revenue. These last two rationales appear to drive most of the agenda of higher education and national governments in stimulating mobility, resulting in five million students currently studying in another country than their own, an increase from two million at the turn of the century and expected to increase to eight million in the coming decade. Refugee students are a negligible proportion of these numbers, as they do not generate short-term revenue but rather costs for the receiving institutions and governments.

While diaspora patterns are traditionally from the Southern hemisphere to the Northern (i.e., from Africa into Europe, from Latin America into North America), but also occur laterally (from Asia, the Middle East and Eastern Europe into Western Europe and North America) (ICEF Monitor, 2015a), mobility happens for many reasons today that include but go far beyond forced migration (Agarwal, Said, Sehoole, Sirozi & de Wit, 2008; Altbach, Reisberg & Rumbley, 2010; Deardorff, de Wit, Heyl & Adams, 2012; Knight, 2008a; Streitwieser, 2014). For Syrian refugees heading into Western Europe today, while their migration has unquestionably been forced, one can regard them, because of their added diversity, as a dimension of university internationalization and as connected to broader issues of global stability. Developing and maintaining high skills for refugees also promises to have a significant impact on sending countries once internal conflict has ended and reconstruction and restored stability again makes them viable economic and political partners. Over the years several NGOs and institutions of higher education around the world have promoted and realized the integration of refugees into higher education, but only in very small numbers. The European refugee crisis creates challenges for how to make that happen for much larger numbers.

Despite possible advantages in terms of existing infrastructures in the higher education sector, a large inflow of displaced persons has the potential to strain any economic, social and political system. Integrating new arrivals into European society generally, and into the many receiving countries' higher education institutions specifically, will require a unique combination of thoughtful policy-making, government and institutional funding, and social tolerance and patience. We suggest that there are particular areas that will prove challenging for universities integrating larger numbers of refugee students in particular.

The rapid integration of tens of thousands of refugees into higher education brings particular challenges related to *language training, integration into coursework and credentialing*. Ensuring adequate translation and interpretation of existing university transcripts and credentials will be a large administrative task. European universities are also faced with a rapid need to develop language courses and help new refugee students gain the necessary language skills to transition into the language of their host country. Securing adequate space and instructors for intensive language classes is also a pressing challenge in many already overcrowded institutions.

Broader social context: Universities do not exist in isolation; they must enact policies and practices that are situated within the broader social, political and cultural contexts of their respective communities and nations. Public reaction to the influx of refugees to Europe has been mixed. Initial reactions to the Syrian refugee crisis in general were quite positive in some countries, particularly compared to previous negative reactions to economic and political refugees. However, anti-immigrant and Islamophobic sentiment has grown significantly since the migration crisis began. University decision-making about refugee policies and integration must be made with an understanding of these broader political and social contexts and the ways they may impact all students, whether they are refugees or not.

Competition for Talent

As indicated above, revolutionary advances in technology and communications brought about by globalization over the last quarter-century have led to new workforce needs that young people with IT skills address particularly well, especially for the aging populations of Western Europe and its declining birth rates. Although their studies have been interrupted, the existing skills that university-eligible refugees bring with them into European higher education institutions can enrich those institutions. Rather than being a burden on faculty and curricula, ideally they help to broaden and enrich what is on offer to the entire student body. While political refugees typically eventually return to their sending countries, many thousands will also stay in their receiving countries for a longer period of time, particularly if violent conflict and warfare continues over multiple years and refugees begin to integrate into host communities. Many Syrian refugees arrive with marketable skills, in IT or software development, for example, which position them to meet many workforce needs in countries throughout Europe. Current discussions about how best to recruit and retain high-skilled migrants to Europe, and what role the higher education sector can and should play in this process, are thus quite relevant for the issue of universities' responses to the refugee crisis.

The knowledge economies of the OECD countries face an urgent need for a more highly trained and skilled workforce because of falling birth rates and aging populations in some countries (Germany), struggling economies and partial brain drain in others (Spain and Ireland) and general decline in interest in science and engineering (across the board). Immigrants who arrive with or quickly gain the requisite training and skills are urgently needed to fill these gaps (De Wit & Ripmeester, 2013). De Wit and Ripmeester cite a 2012 McKinsey report, *The World at Work: Jobs, Pay, and Skills for 3.5 Billion People* (Dobbs et al., 2012), which refers to a mismatch between jobs and graduates. The report claims that despite 75 million unemployed young people globally, 39% of employers complain they cannot fill vacancies with skilled labor. De Wit and Ripmeester also cite the 2012 European Commission report, *Employment and Social Developments in Europe*, that documents this skills mismatch. They point out that countries are increasingly aware that skilled migration often fails, thus international students have become an attractive group of prospective skilled migrants because they become trained to local standards and are already integrated into local communities.

The age of arriving migrants is also an important factor that mediates the success of their integration in the host economy over time. Those who arrive as children and young adults and complete their schooling in the host country, compared with those who arrive as adults, "confront few of the barriers experienced by foreign-trained professionals, in terms of host country language ability, qualification recognition, or acculturation. Their productive lives will be longer, given their youth at point of enrolment" (Hawthorne, 2012). According to de Wit and Ripmeester, the percentage of international students who stay after graduation in the country of study, known as the "stay rate," is on average 25% for OECD countries, whereas the regional and local alumni retention rate in general is much higher (60%) for all graduates and even higher for masters and doctoral graduates (70%). Clearly there is room for skilled refugees to stay on and support their host country's economy if prevailing governing policies are supportive, the population is receptive and refugees see an advantage to staying on even after their home countries become stable again.

These arguments, relevant in the case of attracting and increasing the stay rate of international students, are also relevant in the case of refugees who arrive with higher skills developed in their home country or who demonstrate the potential to develop these skills quickly based on previous education. Highly skilled refugees who already have labor experience and secondary or undergraduate education that has prepared them to become highly skilled working members of society are attractive to economies experiencing labor shortages. How the education sector in general, and the higher education sector in particular, will address these obstacles and find innovative pathways for refugees to enter higher education and to utilize their skills to advance their prospects and potentially meet economic needs in receiving countries raises interesting questions.

The obstacles noted above – becoming integrated, learning adequate language skills, facing discrimination and most importantly understanding how to access the local job market – are realistic challenges that face newly arrived refugees. These challenges, however, are only some of the larger issues related to even bigger questions of who gets to be part of upward mobility and why, what adaptation and belonging really means, how to square allegiance to home country and adapting to the new host country, and other very difficult questions that lie beyond the scope of this chapter but must be acknowledged.

Higher Education's Response to the Refugee Crisis

As we suggested above, the current refugee crisis has shed particular light on the role of universities to act as early responders to mass displacement caused by internal conflict. Some 26% of the college-age population in Syria was enrolled in tertiary education in 2010, just prior to the beginning of the civil war (Trading

Economics, n.d.). Approximately half of these are currently displaced, meaning that between 100,000 and 200,000 youth have had university education either interrupted or postponed, among the estimated 12 million Syrians, or roughly half the country's population, who have fled their homes during the crisis (Horn, 2015; Karasapan, 2015). The vast majority of these are in Lebanon, Jordan and Turkey, which together house four million Syrian refugees. Although thousands of Syrian refugees are enrolled in Turkish universities in 2016 (4,600 estimated), this number represents only 1–2% of university-aged refugees in Turkey (IIE, 2014), meaning that there are enormous gaps in educational opportunities for refugee youth (Karasapan, 2015; World Bank, n.d.). In addition, a larger group of young refugees who are now in secondary education will soon be ready to enroll in higher education, and there are already highly skilled older refugees who require support in adapting their education to requirements in receiving countries.

Responding to refugee inflows is thus not only an issue of border control, visa and other restricting measures, but also one primarily related to educational provision. Discussions about controlling or accommodating refugee flows, dealing with resettlement challenges and fostering successful short- and long-term integration need to include education as a central factor. We argue that universities should be seen as essential sites during refugee crises and be able to respond quickly and independently from the red tape that often hampers responses by federal or state-level bodies. Universities have resources that can be deployed to assist traumatized students and their families (de Wit & Altbach, 2015). But if the higher education sector is to fulfill this mandate, universities must go beyond merely offering policy seminars and conference panels on refugee issues and must also implement meaningful pathway programs that go far in addressing the real and pressing needs of newly arrived immigrants.

It is unrealistic to expect universities to fulfill such roles without financial support, however, and here the European Union and its member states have a vital role to play. Although by 2014 the European Union had already pledged over $1.1 billion toward relief efforts that included educational programs both within the Middle East and for those displaced in other areas (European Commission, 2014a), more targeted efforts are needed. Rather than directing billions of euros toward border controls and refugee camps, targeted investments in education create meaningful immediate but also lasting opportunities for refugees resettling elsewhere or eventually returning home to rebuild their countries (de Wit, 2015b). Reducing EU policy red tape can prevent refugees wasting their educational years waiting for resettlement in refugee camps when their real need is for direct and concrete support from international organizations, including the United Nations and the World Bank, which can create massive scholarships and pathway programs for refugees as a potential solution. Other observers of the crisis have also advocated a relaxation of the usual procedures for processing eligible students into higher education and the need to suspend customary rules to relax admissions standards at a time of extreme crisis (Grove, 2015).

Efforts by International and Domestic Organizations

Early responses to the Syrian refugee crisis focused primarily on establishing and funding direct scholarships. As Syrian universities closed down or were the sites of targeted violence during the early years of the civil war, international higher education organizations responded by opening opportunities for Syrians to temporarily relocate to foreign universities. The German Academic Exchange Service launched a direct scholarship program, funding 200 Syrian students to go to Germany; individual German states offered dozens of additional placements at their universities. Organizations like Scholars at Risk have helped to relocate Syrian professors and academics through visiting appointments and fellowships. The Dutch Foundation for Refugee Students (UAF) directly supports 60 refugees on an annual basis in resettling into society in the Netherlands and the transition back into higher education institutions.[1] The British-based Council for At Risk Academics (Cara) has helped 140 refugees and their families, predominantly Syrian academics, relocate to UK universities. Other groups and organizations (such as the Global Platform for Syrian Students, the Institute for International Education's (IIE) Syrian Consortium for Higher Education in Crisis, the IIE Scholar Rescue Fund in partnership with the Alexander von Humboldt Foundation's Phillip Schwartz Initiative) have provided scholarships, fellowships, emergency grants, test preparation courses, mentorship programs and more for Syrian students. The European University Association (EUA) has created an interactive Refugees Welcome Map that highlights how universities across Europe are helping and engaging refugees as they seek to continue their academic careers (EUA, 2016).

However, such efforts to offer scholarships and fellowships to a few hundred Syrian students pale in comparison to the tens of thousands of displaced university students arriving in nearby countries like Lebanon, Jordan, Turkey and elsewhere in the region, which have even fewer resources to offer in response to refugee student needs. The individual scholarship and university placement model that characterized the initial response to the refugee flow by international and national organizations simply could not respond to the scale of the crisis.

As a result, international higher education organizations started to shift their strategy by the latter part of 2015, looking for ways to open up higher education placements for thousands more students. Qatar and Turkey have been collaborating on a plan to establish an independent university for Syrian refugees, which would employ the 400 Syrian academics who are currently refugees in Turkey. At least three Islamic foundations are reported to be building similar universities in Turkey. The German Academic Exchange Service (DAAD) is seeking a more coordinated response by collaborating with government agencies in the UK, the Netherlands and France, and shifting their own strategy to fund language, tutoring and mentoring classes at universities throughout Germany as well as supporting "third-country" scholarships to pay university tuition and living expenses for refugees in Turkey, Lebanon, Jordan and Egypt. The Open University has partnered with the British Council to provide academic programs to Syrian refugees in Jordan and Lebanon; the current plan provides access to 3,000 students, from which 300 of the highest performing will then get access to online degree courses and programs. Each of these efforts reflects a shift in strategy from "helicoptering" in a few thousand Syrian students to select spots at European universities to developing broader, scaled-up approaches that have the potential to reach all university-aged refugee youth within Europe and across the Middle East and North Africa region.

Moving Forward: Crisis, Challenges and Opportunities

The university sector in Europe has been called upon to respond to a refugee crisis that has presented European countries with a diversity of new challenges. The tendency to act only in crisis mode may prevent European universities from more careful reflection and long-term planning. The opportunity to help Syrian academics and displaced students in this war-torn region at this time of need, as well as to foster partnerships between institutions in the Middle East and universities abroad, should not be overlooked.

Despite some laudable programming initiatives noted above, policy statements by leading European and North American organizations, working directly on issues of international higher education, suggest that the rhetoric promoting accommodation of refugees appears to be louder than the current reality of creating actual programming to address their immediate and concrete needs. Calls to integrate refugees without actually providing programs, perhaps mostly because they are expensive and require the kind of funding that only governments and the largest international agencies can provide, carry with them a subtext of urgency and fear: abandoning young men to wallow in resettlement camps for too long may increase the risk that extremist groups will provide a space for marginalized men and women to vent their frustrations, as witnessed in attacks in Madrid in 2004, London in 2005, Paris in 2015 and Brussels in 2016.

There have been some efforts to produce concrete recommendations for the higher education sector. The EUA has urged universities and EU governments to facilitate refugee access to higher education through information, flexible admissions and language help, with the goal of rapidly integrating refugees so they may contribute to the economy and society. They warn that not doing this could result in "resignation, failure, and social marginalization" of current and future generations (CEU, 2015). In its October 23 press release, the EUA issued a number of recommendations, focused on offering language training and foundational courses, waived entrance requirements and expedited or flexible review and credential recognition and funding support (EUA, 2015).

Conclusion

This chapter illustrates that there are many ways that governments, higher education as a sector and individual universities can respond positively to the presence of large numbers of refugees. One cannot ignore the challenges, which are enormous and related not only to structural and institutional issues like language training, accommodation, credentialing and funding, but also to issues like cultural sensitivity, integration, discrimination and adaptation. It is this kind of humanitarian support that governments, institutions and individuals can contribute through means of soft power that is needed most by many international students arriving in their host countries. Indeed, some universities are providing such support. The challenge is partly the rapid increase in numbers but also a broader set of issues facing displaced, and possibly traumatized, people rather than those who have chosen to migrate for study purposes (Stevenson & Willott, 2015). Indeed, there is a world of difference between those who choose educational mobility for reasons of enlightenment and experience in another culture, and those who are forced into it out of desperation and the desire simply to survive.

But one should not ignore the opportunities that education in general and higher education in particular can provide in these times of crisis. If we invest in the further education for this group of newly arrived refugees, as enlightened governments have done with past migration flows, instead of letting them spend years idling in refugee camps or in abandoned housing on the outskirts of Europe, it stands to pay dividends.

European societies that open themselves up to the benefits of multiculturalism will not only gain by accepting and building their economies through the assistance of skilled migrants, but also by taking in and training refugees in need of shelter who will either stay and through their training and expertise fill a skills gap to alleviate the economic needs of their receiving host countries, or else eventually return home, reconstruct their own countries and exhibit their gratitude by helping to build a more stable and peaceful world for generations to come.

We believe the Syrian case has helped to showcase on a grand scale, arguably unprecedented in modern times, how university internationalization can be connected to broader issues of global stability in the short and long term. When universities open up opportunities for newly arrived, university-eligible migrants to develop and maintain high-level skills, they positively impact not just the migrants themselves if and when they are able return to reconstruct, rebuild and restore their civil societies, but they also provide benefits over the long term for host societies. The challenges are indeed vast, but the opportunities are also significant.

Note

1 The 'Additional Resources' list for this chapter includes all Internet-based sources consulted, but not directly quoted, for this chapter.

Additional Resources

www.eaie.org/eaie-resources/essential-reading.html (accessed February 8, 2016).

www.humboldt-foundation.de/web/philipp-schwartz-initiative-en.html (accessed February 6, 2016).

http://cimo.fi/cimo_in_brief (accessed February 11, 2016).

www.resettlement.eu/country/finland (accessed February 11, 2016).

www.resettlement.eu/page/who-we-are (accessed December 8, 2015).

www.resettlement.eu/page/supporting-refugees-access-higher-education (accessed December 8, 2015).

http://bologna-yerevan2015.ehea.info/files/Bologna%20Process%20 Revisited_Future%20of%20the%20EHEA%20Final.pdf (accessed December 8, 2015).

http://ec.europa.eu/education/policy/higher-education/doc/inspiring-practices-refugees_en.pdf; www.refugees-welcome.net (accessed December 7, 2015).

www.nokut.no/en/Foreign-education/Other-recognition-systems/Recognition-Procedure-for-Persons-without-Verifiable-Documentation (accessed December 7, 2015).

www.ph-ludwigsburg.de/9712+M5dd11c9fe2d.html (accessed December 7, 2015).

www.eua.be/activities-services/eua-campaigns/refugees-welcome-map (accessed April 2, 2016).

Chapter 4

Higher Education and Its International Dimensions in Post-Conflict Settings

Savo Heleta

Introduction

From Iraq, Afghanistan, Syria, Somalia to South Sudan, to name only a few countries experiencing violent conflict and war, higher education (HE) systems and institutions are facing devastation and collapse. Barakat and Milton (2015a, p. 1) note that 'higher education is often an unrecognised casualty of war'. When wars finally end, countries face numerous challenges that require human capital and capacity to stabilize, recover, transform and develop. Universities are places where the necessary capacity can be developed, including critical thinkers, administrators, civil servants, technicians, scientists, doctors, teachers and many other professions.

In most war-torn countries, the HE sector and institutions are 'caught in the crossfire of violent conflict, with devastating consequences for the sector and for conflict-affected societies' (York Accord, 2015, p. 2). In the aftermath of war, universities lack academic capacity, infrastructure and funds and often experience repression and threats to academic freedom. Another challenge is the 'forced displacement of higher education communities' due to the fighting. This displacement has 'a long-term [negative] impact on the sector's quality' (Barakat & Milton, 2015a, p. 1). All of this limits the capacity of HE institutions to contribute to the recovery after wars end.

Higher education plays a 'critical role in developing the knowledge-intensive skills and innovation on which future productivity, job creation and competitiveness depend in a globalized world' (UNESCO, 2011, p. 57) and needs to be one of the post-conflict recovery priorities. Despite the importance of higher education for recovery, development and progress, rebuilding of HE systems and institutions continues to be neglected by international donors and local authorities during the rebuilding phase (York Accord, 2015). The main reason for this is the fact that war-torn countries grapple with so many pressing priorities such as stabilization, peace-building, resettlement of displaced people, infrastructure development, recovery in the health care and basic education sectors, livelihood improvements, reconciliation and state-building. In addition, international donors and organizations involved in rebuilding conflict-ridden countries have so far failed to 'appreciate the strategic role of the [higher education] sector in stabilising and promoting the recovery of war-torn communities and states' (Barakat & Milton, 2015a, p. 1).

This chapter will focus on higher education and its international dimensions and explore how these international dimensions – which include partnerships, cooperation, support and research collaboration – can assist in the process of rebuilding HE systems and institutions in the aftermath of violent conflict. The author will argue that despite the enormous challenges facing post-conflict countries, rebuilding and gradual internationalization of higher education need to be considered as priorities by local and international actors. Students in these countries deserve quality and relevant education that prepares them for global engagement and functioning.

The first section of the chapter will briefly conceptualize post-conflict settings and challenges. This will be followed by a discussion about the importance of higher education for post-conflict recovery and development. The next section will explore the relevance of internationalization in post-conflict settings. The fourth section will focus on the role of international partners and local actors in rebuilding higher education. The last section will conclude the chapter.

Post-Conflict Settings and Challenges

In order to engage with and assist war-torn countries, it is crucial to understand their complex realities. Violent conflict leaves behind destruction, displacement and loss of life. Populations are traumatized, social fabric and cohesion are damaged, economies and infrastructure are destroyed and government institutions are dysfunctional and often lack capacity to provide even the most basic services to the citizens. The education sector, institutions, infrastructure and capacity – from primary, secondary to higher education – are partially or completely destroyed (Heleta, 2015, p. 2).

Woodward (2011, p. 106) writes that the immediate post-war period is often a 'continuation of the war to define the new state'. El-Bushra (2006, p. 230) adds that civil wars are almost always fought over power and control. The immediate period after war 'requires redefining how power is exercised and shared'. During this time, warring parties shift from military to political means and compete over political and economic power and distribution of resources.

The main aims of post-conflict reconstruction are to 'reactivate economic and social development' that had been disrupted or destroyed during violent conflict and to 'create a peaceful environment that will prevent a relapse into violence' (Barakat & Zyck, 2009, pp. 1071–1072). Annan (1998, p. 19) stresses that without reconstruction and development, lasting peace and stability are unlikely. According to Collier, Hoeffler and Söderbom (2008, p. 474), there is a 40% chance that post-conflict societies will return to fighting within a decade if countries do not rebuild in the aftermath of war.

While post-conflict reconstruction aims to 'revive a country's economy, to rebuild its society and to restore its polity' (Ali & Matthews, 2004a, p. 6), attempting to rebuild and return to the pre-war socioeconomic and political set-up is not the best option for war-torn societies. Binns, Dixon and Nel (2012, p. 260) write that in most cases, 'return to the "normality" of pre-conflict is not necessarily desirable', adding that if inequalities led to violent conflict, these should not be reintroduced after war. Rather than going back to the pre-war set-up, there is a need to transform and improve socioeconomic, personal and communal relationships in the aftermath of conflict (Karbo, 2008, pp. 114–115). Finally, it is important to highlight that the length and complexity of the rebuilding process will depend on the severity of conflict. The more severe the conflict and destruction, the more complex, difficult and lengthier will be the rebuilding phase.

The Importance – and Neglect – of Higher Education in Post-Conflict Settings

The HE sector plays a crucial 'role in knowledge production, innovation, skills development, cultural preservation and national progress' (York Accord, 2015, p. 4). 'Well-educated, informed and engaged citizenry is the foundation' needed for peace and security, respect for human rights, rule of law and sustainable development (Annan, 2015). Without quality higher education, countries emerging from violent conflict will not be able to improve the living conditions of their citizens and develop (Hoosen et al., 2009, p. 30). According to Kofi Annan (2015, p. 1), 'education is one of the most effective forms of peace-building, a source of hope for each individual and the premise of development and progress in every society'. Thus, higher education has the potential to contribute to recovery, peace-building, better governance and economic development in the aftermath of war (Buckland, 2006, p. 7; Feuer et al., 2013, p. 1).

Well-functioning HE systems and institutions are 'vital when it comes to developing the kind of free-thinking intellectual capital that is necessary to rebuild a war-torn nation's culture and knowledge once it is possible to do so' (Law, 2015). Post-conflict 'reconstruction strategy that places higher education at the centre of knowledge-led development could play a transformative role in leading the transition from conflict to prosperity' (Barakat & Milton, 2015a, p. 10). However, rebuilding HE systems and institutions is not a priority and does not feature in post-conflict planning. The key priorities of the international community are conflict prevention, humanitarian assistance, basic education and democratization (Feuer et al., 2013, p. 2; York Accord, 2015, p. 3). When it comes to local authorities, they often prioritize security, self-enrichment and staying in power by any means, while paying little attention to the delivery of basic services, poverty alleviation, employment and education (Maathai, 2010, pp. 16–17).

It is important to point out that while the primary focus of the international community is on rebuilding basic education as part of the humanitarian response, the total spending on rebuilding the education sector in post-conflict settings – including basic, secondary and higher education – accounts for only 2% of overall humanitarian assistance (UNESCO, 2011, p. 3).

Due to the complexity of post-conflict transition, rebuilding and reform of the HE sector and institutions will always be a challenging process 'marked by high levels of political instability and uncertainty, and low levels of capacity' (UNESCO, 2011, p. 20). In the aftermath of war, education systems and institutions need to be rebuilt and reformed in contexts where funding and capacity are limited and 'political authority and civil administration are weakened, compromised or inexperienced' (Buckland, 2006, p. 7). These challenges require long-term commitment and assistance from the international community, which includes both donors and universities from the developed and emerging world.

The Relevance of Internationalization in Post-Conflict Settings

In today's globalized and interconnected world, where knowledge is a key driver of growth, socioeconomic development and livelihood improvements, countries emerging from violent conflict need substantial and long-term support to rebuild and reform their HE systems and institutions. These countries need to be able to develop university graduates who can contribute to reconstruction, development and the establishment of lasting stability and peace (Heleta, 2015, p. 11).

Despite the challenges on the road to recovery and stability, rebuilding HE sectors and institutions needs to become one of the priorities in the process of reconstruction. Post-conflict countries need to catch up with the rest of the world in terms of production of relevant knowledge. As pointed out by Barakat and Milton (2015a, p. 8), 'the real long-term challenge is not to simply rebuild what existed before the conflict, but to ensure that the sector recovers in a way that leapfrogs years of isolation, decline and destruction'. This includes development of an internationalized outlook of the institutions as well as their research, teaching and learning.

Today's world requires a 'deep awareness of local and regional cultures, perspectives and identities, and how they are responding to each other in an era in which cooperation is a prerequisite for progress' (Oxford Martin School, 2013, p. 11). This applies to every corner of the globe as almost everything today has 'local and global connections. The global impacts the local, but the local also mediates and shapes the global' (Hudzik, 2015, p. 15). Getting institutions, academics and students 'to see themselves and the work that they do in a larger global context' is crucial in light of the challenges facing the world – such as conflict, inequality and environmental degradation – that cross national borders (Rumbley et al., 2012, p. 15). In addition, while international cooperation and collaboration in higher education 'are not guarantees for peace and mutual understanding, they continue to be essential mechanisms for keeping communication open and dialogue active' (Altbach & de Wit, 2015, p. 9).

It is evident from the above that HE internationalization is relevant for any country and any setting, including countries that have experienced violent conflict and are on the road to recovery. However, it is important to remember that post-conflict reconstruction involves a 'triple transition': security transition from war to peace, democratic transition and socioeconomic transition (Ali & Matthews, 2004b, pp. 396–397). While rebuilding higher education *should be* part of every post-conflict reconstruction strategy (York Accord, 2015, p. 4), in most cases, higher education is not going to be anywhere near the top priorities in the first and second phase of the transition from war to peace. During this time, the main priorities will be the establishment of basic security and stability and preparations for democratic and socioeconomic transition. Rebuilding higher education may only become a priority of local actors and the international community at the end of the second and in the third transitional phase. Even during this time the focus may not be on internationalization but on the rebuilding of basic HE structures and institutions. However, through their engagement, international partners can assist in the development of local capacity for integration of international dimensions in the curriculum, teaching, learning and research at universities in conflict-ridden countries.

The Role of International Partners and Local Actors in Rebuilding Higher Education

International donors, organizations and universities need to work with academics, universities, ministries of education and other local actors on rebuilding HE sectors and institutions in the aftermath of war. The engagement by international academic institutions can also contribute to the internationalization of higher education in post-conflict settings. However, this should not be 'a goal in itself, but a way to enhance the quality' of teaching, learning and research (de Wit, 2015c). The following subsections will discuss the role of international and local actors in more detail.

Lobbying for Meaningful Support and Funding

One of the key challenges in the quest to rebuild higher education will be to convince international donors to contribute to these efforts. This will not be easy as there are other pressing priorities in post-conflict settings. Since the end of the Cold War, donors and organizations working in conflict-ridden countries have considered higher education as a 'luxury that war-torn societies can ill afford' (Barakat & Milton, 2015b). Academics, experts and practitioners will have to understand this and find ways to lobby donors and other international partners to provide meaningful support and funding. They will also have to find ways to persuade local authorities, education officials and university leadership that rebuilding higher education should be one of their priorities. Authorities in these countries will be dealing with basic survival issues and recovering from years of fighting, destruction and social and political divisions. Rebuilding higher education is likely to be the last item on their list of priorities in the first few years after the war. Still, as in the case of the donors, convincing local actors that their communities and countries will benefit from quality higher education offered by local institutions is crucial.

Foreign Aid Priorities

When it comes to foreign aid for higher education in developing and post-conflict countries, 'only a small share of aid is currently intended to strengthen higher education systems in recipient countries. About 70% of aid to post-secondary education is intended for scholarships to study in donor countries' (UNESCO, 2015, p. 7). This needs to change. In post-conflict settings, those who benefit from academic mobility are the fortunate few who receive scholarships and external funding as well as the wealthy and the elites who can fund their own mobility. They often study in the developed and emerging world due to the poor quality of higher education in their home countries; many of them never come back. Some use academic mobility as a way to escape hardships, preferring to continue their lives in more stable countries.

Spending foreign aid mainly on academic mobility to the developed world is not helping to build capacity in the HE sector in post-conflict countries. Even if those who have benefited from scholarships to study in donor countries return to their own country when they finish studying, there is no guarantee they will end up at universities and subsequently help in rebuilding efforts. Instead of funding outgoing mobility and (intentionally or not) significantly contributing to brain drain, foreign aid needs to assist with the rebuilding and development of local HE systems, institutions and academic capacity.

Meaningful Assistance from International Partners

Rebuilding higher education in the aftermath of violent conflict 'is a major challenge that requires a collective effort between a range of national, regional and international educational actors' (Barakat & Milton, 2015b). Universities from around the world can play a key role in this endeavour through collaboration and provision of assistance. International partners can assist universities in post-conflict settings through staff exchange, joint research, student exchange and development of mechanisms for accreditation and quality assurance. Financial assistance from international donors will be crucial in this process as most universities from the developed and emerging world cannot embark on extensive projects and assist post-conflict countries to build capacity in the HE sector without external funding (Heleta, 2015, p. 13).

Apart from assisting post-conflict countries and their HE institutions for reasons of academic solidarity and engagement, international partners stand to gain from this involvement. International travel, teaching and research opportunities will help internationalize their own academics and staff, who will develop new knowledge, experience, perspectives and competence that can be utilised in work with students in their home institutions (Heleta, 2015, p. 13).

Locally Driven Reform and Recovery

In many countries around the world, education has been/is 'actively used to reinforce political domination, the subordination of marginalised groups and ethnic segregation' (UNESCO, 2011, p. 17). This, in turn, often leads to animosity and violence. After violent conflict, it is crucial to reform systems and prevent the emergence of HE structures that reproduce inequality and divisions and promote prejudice, segregation or superiority of certain groups (Heleta, 2015, pp. 14–15). The end of war provides 'opportunities to build back better rather than to restore the ills of social and economic systems' (Barakat & Milton, 2015a, p. 9) in the education sector and society at large.

International donors, universities, experts and practitioners can play a crucial role in the process of rebuilding higher education. However, even though external actors are in a position to 'influence the trajectory' of the reform and reconstruction due to their geopolitical standing, influence and/or provision of funding (Feuer et al., 2013, pp. 4–5), it is very important that international partners do not impose their own ideas, models, ideological underpinnings and worldviews onto the institutions and systems they are trying to assist. Rebuilding and reforming processes need to be locally driven and owned. Universities in post-conflict settings need to attend 'to the unique needs and aspirations of their particular institutions, local communities, and regional or national contexts' (Rumbley et al., 2012, p. 3). Choices, priorities and strategies for HE systems and institutions must be locally decided. International partners need to support this process without impositions.

Short- vs Long-Run Engagement and Assistance

Due to the destruction and lack of capacity in many post-conflict settings, it may take years to rebuild local HE institutions. In the short run, international donors and partners can consider establishing satellite campuses where education is delivered by universities and academics from the developed and emerging world (Heleta, 2015, p. 11). In such instances, it will be important to safeguard war-torn countries from exploitative and predatory transnational education practices. Involvement by external actors must be guided by 'core principles of ethical engagement,' which include transparency, accountability, quality and respect for local cultures (Rumbley et al., 2012, p. 6). In the medium to long run, the focus needs to shift to meaningful assistance and rebuilding of physical infrastructure, institutional capacity and the overall HE systems. This is the only way post-conflict countries can establish universities capable of delivering quality higher education to their populations instead of remaining dependent on outside assistance (Heleta, 2015, p. 12).

Incentives for Local Academics

The inability to pay academics well is one of the many challenges facing war-torn societies. In many countries, salaries in the HE sector are so low that academics must have at least one other job to survive. This leaves them with limited time to focus on academic work and undermines the quality of teaching, learning and research at universities (Tobenkin, 2014, p. 25). HE institutions in post-conflict settings need to find ways to provide incentives to keep academics and attract back those who left when the fighting broke out. In particular, bringing back local academics who have lived and worked abroad can add important international capacity, experience and knowledge. However, this may not be easy as the countries and institutions often lack funding and academics may have other opportunities for work, at home and abroad (Heleta, 2015, p. 13). Better use of the above-mentioned foreign aid can play a positive role in retention and remuneration of academic staff.

Internationalization at Home and Curriculum Reform

Internationalization at home needs to be one of the key priorities in the process of rebuilding higher education in post-conflict settings. According to Beelen and Jones (2015a, p. 69), 'internationalization at home is the purposeful integration of international and intercultural dimensions into the formal and informal curriculum for all students within domestic learning environments'. Due to funding constraints, the large majority of students in war-torn countries will not be able to afford to study in another country, even for a semester. Purposeful integration of international and intercultural aspects into the curriculum can help all students in all programmes gain knowledge about regional and global issues and develop global competence.

It is important to remember that higher education 'does not automatically impart good values, attitudes and norms to students ... education is a multi-faceted process that can just as easily regress to nationalistic and exclusionary content' (Feuer et al., 2013, p. 14). Key in this process is the curriculum. The curriculum needs to be reformed to be inclusive and balanced and promote peace, reconciliation and social cohesion (Heleta, 2015, p. 15). At the same time, it is important to incorporate into the curriculum 'international and comparative perspectives throughout the teaching, research and service missions of higher education' (Hudzik & McCarthy, 2012, p. iv). Clifford (2009, p. 135) defines internationalized curriculum as:

> Curricula, pedagogies and assessments that foster: understanding of global perspectives and how these intersect and interact with the local and the personal; intercultural capabilities in terms of actively engaging with other cultures; and responsible citizenship in terms of addressing differing value systems and subsequent actions.

While the above attributes are relevant for students in any country, some are particularly relevant for students in countries that have experienced instability and conflict. Specifically, in post-conflict countries where populations are traumatized, disillusioned and divided along ethnic, religious or other lines (Heleta, 2015, p. 2), intercultural competence and responsible citizenship could assist in peace-building among students and formerly divided communities. In addition, understanding of global perspectives and learning about similar processes in other countries could help academics and students come up with new ideas and approaches to overcome their own challenges. This is in line with Hudzik's argument that curriculum internationalization can lead to the development of 'knowledge of differences and similarities in practices and ideas' as well as 'critical thinking and learning through the several lenses of different cultures and world views' (2015, p. 16).

Development Opportunities for Staff and Academics

Clifford (2009, p. 141) writes that 'development opportunities for [university officials and] staff to work with colleagues overseas … and the availability of international resources are all essential ingredients of a change programme' and successful reform and internationalization at universities. Funding and commitment by the international donors and partners will be crucial in this process. International partners need to identify local university officials interested in and passionate about HE management and its international dimensions, provide them with opportunities to expand their knowledge in this field and support their efforts on the ground.

When internationalization becomes one of the priorities at universities in post-conflict settings, the main issue will be the 'availability and willingness of academics to adopt and develop' international perspectives and use them in their classes (van der Wende, 1996, p. 190). According to Hudzik (2015, p. 67), 'without active involvement of academic departments and their faculty and the substance of ideas embedded therein, internationalisation risks becoming an intellectually vacuous process'. To actively engage, academics will need to have international knowledge, experience and perspectives to meaningfully contribute to the development of globally competent graduates. Many academics will need to be given opportunities to spend time at partner universities abroad and work with colleagues on research and development of new teaching methods and curricula. In addition, technologies such as video conferencing can be used – if the infrastructure in post-conflict countries allows it – for collaboration between academics from different countries.

Conclusion

Despite the numerous challenges facing war-torn countries, rebuilding higher education needs to become one of the priorities of the international community and local actors. Post-conflict societies will struggle to stabilize, rebuild, improve living conditions and develop without quality HE institutions that can build much-needed capacity and human and intellectual capital.

International dimensions of higher education can contribute in the process of rebuilding HE systems and institutions. Universities from the developed and emerging world need to play a crucial role in this through collaboration and provision of assistance. International support can help universities in post-conflict countries rebuild physical infrastructure and improve the quality of education.

Universities in post-conflict settings do not have a choice but to integrate international dimensions into the curriculum, teaching, learning and research in order to prepare their students for global engagement. Students in any country deserve quality and relevant education that develops them into globally competent graduates capable of functioning in the complex and constantly changing world. Ultimately, this is crucial both for the graduates and their countries. Whatever the graduates decide to do when they complete their studies, they will need to be globally competent. Similarly, the countries need graduates who possess the knowledge and skills to engage with the rest of the world and deal with local, national, regional and global challenges and opportunities.

Chapter 5

Internationalization Strategies and Social Inclusion

The Experience of Women Entrepreneurs in Rural Areas of the Region of Valparaiso, Chile

Carlos Ramírez Sánchez, César Cáceres Seguel & Carolina Pinto Baleisan

Background

The incorporation of an inclusive approach in the development of internationalization strategies emerges as a way to respond to structural inequalities in emerging countries. In Latin America and the Caribbean, universities have a strategic role in formal education and in particular against the processes of social connectedness, which have gained an increasing role in the strategic guidelines of higher education institutions, shifting from a "peripheral" context to a strategic one. Thus, these institutions can provide training opportunities and international transfer of knowledge not only to students and scholars, but also to marginalized or excluded groups from tertiary educational systems.

From a case study in the Region of Valparaiso in Chile, this chapter explores the experience of a group of women entrepreneurs from rural areas who participated in internationalization projects led by the Viña del Mar University (UVM). The text suggests consideration, from the viewpoint of its protagonists, of the contributions of an international experience aimed at disadvantaged groups. The results obtained indicate some lessons and recommendations for the design of internationalization projects with an inclusive approach.

Regional diagnostics indicate a consolidation trend in the process of internationalization in Latin American and Caribbean universities, even if its transformative potential has been limited by the implementation of short-term actions (Gacel-Ávila, 2012) and by the difficulties of adding evaluation processes (Siufi, 2009, p. 136). According to this literature, advances in internationalization in these regions are distinguished from other regions of the world by the early development of student mobility (UNESCO–UIS, 2012), the demands of the private sector as an external factor driving internationalization (Egron-Polak & Hudson, 2014a) and the strategic role of universities in local production processes and knowledge transfer (Oregioni, 2013). The transfer of knowledge is a process of social interaction geared toward the production and circulation of knowledge that generate learning externalities. This cannot be analyzed outside the specific social context in which it takes place; rather, the environmental conditions facilitate or hinder knowledge-transfer relations (Bayona & González, 2010). In this sense, we affirm that certain internationalization strategies that pursue knowledge transfer can promote socially equitable systems through coordinated efforts of third parties beyond the university community. Internationalization experiences are key in supporting three aspects: training, specifically applied transfer of knowledge, and joint-venture projects and programs in collaboration with the public and private sector.

Literature on globalization insists on the production of new economic and social inequalities based on the limited access to mobility by certain groups and knowledge of other countries (Wagner, 2007). The upper classes are distinguished by having privileged access to internationalization: "the great families of the aristocracy and the petty bourgeoisie are characterized by an ancient affiliation with cosmopolitanism" (Wagner, 2007, p. 6). However, the middle and lower classes view their positions as further weakened due to the alienation of the decision-making centers. Access to international experiences is then highly selective and uneven, as much for the costs involved (for example, legalization of documents, visas, transport and accommodation) as for the cognitive and social skills that are required at the individual level. In this scenario, universities can contribute substantially to local development, promoting an inclusive approach in their internationalization programs.

The concept of comprehensive internationalization helps create a transversal outlook integrating international and intercultural dimensions in the substantive functions of higher education, thus overcoming the traditional notion of international cooperation (Gacel-Ávila, 2012). This approach can extend the design of internationalization strategies for the university, for example, by considering other different groups of students and scholars, and catering for the cultural, social and economic specificities of a local space. The engagement between universities and communities has drawn great attention through the so-called third mission. This goal emerges as a complement to the classic missions of teaching and research. According to Laredo (2007), the interaction of universities with societal demands occurs both with civil society (projects), policy-makers, as well as private economic actors (consultancy). Even though the third mission approach has been discussed over two decades, it still remains a vague concept associated with several agendas, from entrepreneurial activities to cooperation with NGOs.

Based on *ex post* interviews with beneficiaries of two internationalization projects of the UVM, this research explores how the experiences of internationalization facilitate individual subjective change and effectively foster the transfer of knowledge. This chapter seeks to answer the following questions: (1) What processes of subjective change did the internationalization experience promote? and (2) How do individuals value the content and techniques presented during the international experience? Given the theme of the study, a semi-structured interview was chosen as the appropriate technique to explore social and personal representations associated with international experience. The methodological assumption has to do with the existence of an individual who has a stock of knowledge about a milestone in their life, which is reconstructed during the interview process.

The text is divided into three sections. The following section describes the entrepreneurial projects and territories in which these women operate, the next deals with the interview process and key findings, and finally the main results and conclusions are discussed.

The focus of interactionist sociology can address the question of subjective change that international experience may or may not cause. The study of the subjective construction of the subject seeks to understand the idiosyncratic meanings of people as basic elements in their way of constructing reality and acting on it (Castro et al., 2015). Subjective change can be explained as the transformation of personal representations of a semantic nature involving changes in the modes of interpretation of people on certain aspects of their environment and their lives (Castro et al., 2015, p. 366). For Catalán (2010; Castro et al., 2015, p. 365), the notion of subjectivity assumes that the meanings people give to their representation of the world have a single organization that dialogues with the social, both in its origin and training, and its use. In this context, subjective theories study how individuals understand and build their daily lives, therefore being a valid approach to investigate how the training experience and internationalization generated, in women entrepreneurs, an individual reflexive process about themselves and their environment.

The experience of otherness, of something different, that occurs in international experiences can cause individual reflexive processes in itself and its environment. Thus, the returning individual is not the same as when they left. Alfred Schütz notes that the man who returns to his country "is not the same, neither for him nor for those who have awaited his return" (1999 [1944], p. 64). The inner transformation of the individual in their choices and their personal positions emerges with respect to the physical and social distance from the society of origin. This hypothesis invites us to explore a retrospective view. After an international experience, what changes occur at the individual level?

The research is based on an analysis of projects supporting entrepreneurship in which a stay abroad component was incorporated as a way to strengthen the educational process of the beneficiaries. UVM was awarded two projects during 2013 from the Innovation and Competitiveness Fund of the Regional Government of Valparaiso. These projects sought to establish a network of liaison and support for small and medium manufacturers in the Region of Valparaiso. The initiatives were as follows:

1   Technical support for the Botanical Garden of medicinal herbs located in Hijuelas (a commune of 19,132 inhabitants (2012), located in the Region of Valparaiso). The project's goal is to deliver knowledge on crop-cultivation techniques, conservation, fertilization techniques and marketing of flowers and medicinal plants to Hijuelas florists, as well as municipal professionals, in order to develop expertise in the commune. The Hijuelas commune is home

to about 180 groups of florists who are central to the local economy, 20 of which have specialized in the cultivation of flowers and medicinal plants.

In recognition of the market potential of alternative medicine, the plan was to train 180 entrepreneurs in production techniques and diversification of medicinal products. The design provided a ten-day training for three entrepreneurs at the Botanical Garden of Medicinal Plants in Gombrèn, Catalonia, Spain. It is important to highlight that such a garden does not exist in Latin America. There are botanical gardens that have engaged in medicinal culture, as is the case with Peru and Colombia; however, in collaboration with the UVM, Hijuelas would become the first in Chile. Since 1996, this garden has specialized in the production and conservation of medicinal plants and flowers of the Pyrenees, supplying them to various pharmaceutical companies in Spain and Andorra. The training experience aimed to improve production and conservation techniques of valuable species, as well as improve competitiveness and innovation of partnerships dedicated to the cultivation of flowers. These producers were supported by the Schools of Agronomy and Design, which contributed both in production techniques and in developing the brand image of the products.

2   A second project aimed to strengthen the competitiveness and innovation of women dedicated to loom textiles in the municipalities of Limache (45,277 inhabitants in 2002) and Quilpué (167,938 inhabitants in 2014), both located in the Region of Valparaiso. In connection with the city of Arequipa, it focused on small producers seeking to start a new textile business. Thus, these three groups of women entrepreneurs, *Hilanderas de Colliguay, Artesanas del Telar de los Laureles, Limache* and *Tejedoras de la Comuna Nogales*, were involved. The lack of consolidated marketing strategies and little innovation in its products (hats, dresses, ponchos, home decor) profiled a target group to be supported by UVM. The university's internationalization program enabled training opportunities and transfer of experience with a group of entrepreneurs in Arequipa, Peru, who already had international sales channels, primarily focused on production and exportation to the European market.

The International Dimension of Entrepreneurial Projects for Women in Rural Areas in the Region of Valparaiso, Chile

The two internationalization experiences analyzed were developed by the UVM with a dual objective: to contribute to the productive development of the Valparaiso Region and contribute to the comprehensive education of undergraduates. The development of both projects incorporated the participation of teachers and students from different career tracks related to entrepreneurship. The projects sought to directly benefit local low-income women entrepreneurs.

The entrepreneurial experience in Spain was aimed at learning how to manage the Botanical Garden of Medicinal Plants in Gombrèn, Catalonia, with more than 20 years of operation. The entrepreneurs were trained in new applications and uses of medicinal plants, to generate knowledge for new products in Chile. These themes were supplemented by a Female Leadership and Entrepreneurship Module, led by experts from the University of Girona, Catalonia. Participants were trained by experts from these centers in issues related to the management of botanical gardens, in order to share their new knowledge with entrepreneurs in Chile.

In the case of the Women Weavers Project, the international experience took place in Peru and sought to share *in situ* the consolidated experience of women involved in associated work and exporting their products to the European market. It sought to display the partnership model and certain techniques allowing them to transfer this experience to their own context. In addition, it aimed to better assess those critical factors that allow the creation of new business models, generating changes in their production processes and drawing on international experience.

Results

The interviews demonstrated, in the case of the entrepreneurial group *Artisanas del Telar de los Laureles*, that their specialization on the loom followed a pragmatic approach as it was a technique dominated by a significant group of women. In the case of Rosana, one of the participants, her group of women weavers began their work in 2002 as an initiative that sought to generate a second household income. With the municipality's support, they started a training process that gave them the knowledge and basic capital to start their work:

> The training was not complicated, but marketing was difficult. At that time there were very few people weaving on traditional loom ... the main difficulties were human, it was difficult to lead a group of people with different concerns, that was the most complicated.

International experience allowed some of these women to understand their level of productive sophistication regarding entrepreneurial experiences in other countries. The international perspective is then valued as an opportunity to identify areas for improvement in their ventures:

> I was struck by the contrast, as it is a backward town in many things, construction, education ... but, on the other hand, with technological advances in production and marketing. They have rooms with one hundred percent technologized processes, and are exporting to various parts of the world ... We thought we were doing things well, but we are years apart in terms of training and the doors they have opened. They make a more industrialized

weave with very fine wool, ours is more rustic. They commercialize! To commercialize you need much more production.

Two key elements are presented as positive contributions of the international experience. The first has to do with strengthening the effects of reproduction that began after the experience abroad. One respondent confirms:

> We got the most of the experience by learning the shades they use, we learned new drawing and design techniques ... what has been learned has been replicated. I train 35 people per year in loom weaving techniques, other people have done the same.

The learning achieved throughout the training period is implicitly considered unique because of the international dimension. This characteristic allowed a few of the entrepreneurs to train other weavers in the field.

The second contribution has to do with achieving a differentiated positioning against other similar projects:

> The experience in Arequipa took entrepreneurship to another level, a status that benefits the curriculum, as a presentation ... The entrepreneurs who have gone, who have had experience with such projects, have greater knowledge.

In this regard, the international dimension of training involved the creation of new knowledge: a greater understanding of their own cultural and social environment, which has a strong impact on the development of enterprises. Some interviewees indicate their surprise at seeing their own community and country with new eyes. The interview with Ana María Campos offers a clue regarding this aspect when she expresses her perception of the difficulties that exist in Chile:

> Here, there are people who know a lot but do not share their knowledge ... it's difficult to associate. I had to explain to my partners how the trip was, explain what they achieved by associating [in Peru], people here are very scared to work together. I think it's because Chileans are mischievous, they do not have much faith in societies. But that's the basis of transparency, if we have a problem we talk about it. They viewed us as strange creatures when we started to associate.

In terms of the individual subjective change, some respondents described their experience as a milestone marking a new stage in their entrepreneurship. The experiences of these women, in a more complex socioeconomic context, produced in the interviewees a desire for power and self-affirmation as entrepreneurs. This is reflected in Ana Maria's discussion of what changed for her after her trip to Arequipa:

I felt that I was a housewife before the trip, without discrediting it, weaving and selling their products and trying to be an entrepreneur. After the trip, I consider myself a textile artisan. I learned to appreciate what I do and what I enjoy doing. I used to do a little of everything, weaving, jewelry making ... very scattered. It was not such a big production, there was little selling. Now I have focused on one thing, I feel I do it well. Now, I'm convinced, I value my abilities much more.

In this sense, international experience does not produce a radical subjective change in itself, but rather facilitates a transformation that was already under way, giving it greater legitimacy and stimulating individual motivation and perseverance:

What has been experienced is unforgettable, it gives you a greater desire to continue working. It's enriching to witness what they have now achieved with just the bare minimum.

Discussion and Conclusion

The research indicates that lived international experience of women entrepreneurs generated change at the individual level, promoting self-representation as an entrepreneur. On a collective level, the internationalization program enabled this group of women to access a higher "level" or status by collaborating with international networks. In their own words, this differentiates them from their local peers. Moreover, international experience allowed a clearer visualization of certain outstanding areas for improvement, such as marketing and product quality. On another level, the analysis provides precise ways in which universities can utilize their international resources to strengthen social inclusion processes in their territories.

Internationalization is a process that needs to be cross-disciplinary to generate relevant impacts at both societal and individual levels. Using the notion of "comprehensive internationalization" in developing countries allows an opportunity to reflect upon incorporating strategies to overcome social inequality as an essential goal of universities. The gathered experience further highlights four outstanding tasks in the field of internationalization:

1   the need to systematize the experiences of Chile and other Latin American universities in terms of their relationship with communities and vulnerable groups, particularly those who have incorporated internationalization strategies;

2   the importance of progressing in the design of a national policy on university internationalization, allowing for increased training and development opportunities for disadvantaged groups;

3   the need for coordination among internationalization projects of universities and local government initiatives aimed at supporting local entrepreneurs;
4   the necessity to encourage the participation of students and professors as consultants for local entrepreneurs who have participated in internationalization programs.

Thus, incorporating the axis of social inclusion should be seen as part of the plans and policies for internationalization in higher education institutions in the country. Addressing this dimension holistically, not in a fragmented way, incorporating the participation of various parties in addition to the institutions themselves, is a substantial part of the new challenges that the environment demands of its universities.

Part III

Regional Examples of Internationalization in the Emerging and Developing World

Chapter 6

Student Mobility in Latin America and the Caribbean

Latest Trends and Innovative Programs

Jocelyne Gacel-Ávila, Magdalena Bustos-Aguirre & Jose Celso Freire Jr.

1 Introduction

This chapter intends to describe some of the latest trends in student mobility in Latin America and the Caribbean as well as to analyze some of the region's most innovative mobility programs, stressing the distinction between short-term and degree-seeking mobility. Degree-seeking mobility has been continuously expanded in the region during the last 40 years through national policies to train highly skilled human resources for national development as well as to strengthen research and innovation capacity. Short-term mobility is a more innovative and recent strategy that has been gaining importance in the past 15 years. To illustrate the regional situation, five short-term mobility programs are described and critically analyzed: Red Macro, Montevideo Group of Universities, Pacific Alliance, Science without Borders and FOBESII – Proyecta 100,000. While the Brazilian Science without Borders is the largest and most comprehensive national scholarship program in the region, the Pacific Alliance, Red Macro and Montevideo Group mobility programs are cases of good practices to further regional integration. FOBESII – Proyecta 100,000 has, on the other hand, room for improvement to become a more effective internationalization program.

2 Main Trends in the Internationalization Process of Tertiary Education in Latin America and the Caribbean

Internationalization has become a key strategy for all tertiary education (TE) systems in the world, and Latin America and the Caribbean (LAC) is no exception. It is a means to improve educational quality, a strategy to educate graduates with the competencies demanded by the 21st century, an instrument for the updating of academic programs and a powerful tool to enrich the relevance of research.

The region is generally lacking information on its internationalization process, as countries do not collect comprehensive data on the topic, which in the end results in limited planning and long-term policies. Because of poor and unsystematic institutional sources of information and databanks, the few existing reports usually have limited reliability. This is a deficiency that might be overcome through the recently launched Observatory on Internationalization and Networks in Latin America and the Caribbean (OBIRET) by UNESCO/IESALC,[1] since one of its main lines of activity is to build up data on regional internationalization processes.

Therefore, the present analysis is mainly based on data collected by UNESCO and OECD, the World Bank (De Wit, Gacel-Ávila, Jaramillo & Knight, 2005) and the Global Surveys of the International Association of Universities (IAU) (Egron-Polak & Hudson, 2010, 2014a). All these reports allow comparisons among different regions of the world and thus enable an objective appreciation of LAC's positioning, advancement and progress.

Reports coincide in the view that internationalization is definitely gaining importance in the TE agenda in LAC. Governmental funding and support have increased in the region, although it is still one of the lowest in the world. There is greater awareness among decision-makers and educational stakeholders of the benefits of internationalization for students, faculty and research, and therefore of the need to implement broader internationalization strategies. Up to now, LAC has been one of the world regions with the lowest level of institutionalized organizational structures for internationalization, but is now reported to be the one with the highest percentage of institutions currently preparing internationalization policies and strategies. Nevertheless, there is the perception that international opportunities are mainly accessible to students with financial resources, and that internationalization is provoking a growing gap among institutions within countries.

Regarding regional priorities for partnerships, the most recent IAU survey showed that LAC ranked in joint first place both Europe and North America, second the region itself and third Asia. LAC was chosen as second in importance by North America, and was not among any of the top three priorities of Europeans. Importantly, it was not chosen as first priority by any region, including LAC itself (Egron-Polak & Hudson, 2014a).

Among leading internationalization activities are mobility for students, both short-term and degree-seeking modalities, and international research collaboration, in which LAC reaches 36.05% in SCImago's International Collaboration Index, a percentage close to that of Western Europe (40.14%) and North America (33.21%), but far from Africa (50.94%), the leading region (SCIMAGO, 2015).

Furthermore, faculty mobility is also gaining importance as international networking for faculty and researchers is perceived as the main benefit of internationalization. Nevertheless, LAC has not yet implemented either regional or national strategies to attract international scholars, and institutions have very few guest professors as part of the strategy of curriculum internationalization (Brunner & Ferrada, 2011; Gacel-Ávila, 2012).

Language proficiency still remains one of the most important barriers to internationalization and consequently language learning is reported as the main activity for internationalization of the curriculum.

To sum up, the region has made progress in terms of governmental funding, the improvement of organizational structures and the extent of student and faculty mobility programs. Nevertheless, there is room for improvement regarding funding, planning, design of long-term and comprehensive strategies, as well as mobility numbers for students and faculty.

Given the rising importance of student mobility in the region, the present work will focus, in the following sections, on the analysis of its main characteristics, latest trends and developments.

3 Main Trends of Student Mobility in LAC

Student mobility is a key strategy for academic, individual and social enrichment. It improves students' international profile and boosts their employability; it fosters the development of soft skills such as adaptability, openness, decision-making and empathy; and also contributes to a deeper knowledge of foreign languages and cultures. All these aspects are of the utmost relevance to function efficiently in today's global context. Student mobility gives dynamism to the job market providing qualified and competitive human capital. It also contributes to international dialogue, and allows for comparisons between institutions, countries and regions (European Commission, 2014b; Hénard, Diamond & Roseveare, 2012).

Since the objective of this chapter is to elaborate on the latest trends and most innovative student mobility programs in LAC, it is important to state that most statistical information available worldwide often makes no difference between the two forms of student mobility: short-term credit mobility and long-term degree-seeking mobility. Therefore, each is examined separately in the following sections.

3.1 Degree-Seeking Student Mobility

Almost every country in the region launched study abroad scholarship programs in the late 1970s, thanks to the resources of the oil boom and favorable international commodity prices, in order to provide the region with highly trained human capital to boost scientific, economic and social development. Generally speaking, these programs have been administered through education ministries or national organisms devoted to the promotion of science, technology and innovation, such as CONACYT in Mexico, COLCIENCIAS in Colombia, CONICYT in Chile and CNPq in Brazil.[2] These national organizations report a constant increase in the number of scholarships granted in recent years. In Brazil's case the numbers of bursaries went from 1,262 in 2001 to 3,750 in 2015 (CNPq, 2016); for Colombia from 175 in 2009 to 400 in 2014 (COLCIENCIAS, 2016); for Mexico from 3,045 in 2007 to 4,384 in 2014 (CONACYT, 2016); and for Chile the increase went from 13 scholarships granted in 2001 to a total of 5,364 between 2008 and 2014 through the "Becas Chile" program (CONICYT, 2016).

As a response to this rising demand, many countries, especially English-speaking ones like Australia, Canada, the United Kingdom and the United States, as well as European countries such as France, Germany and Spain, among others, set up aggressive strategies to recruit LAC students, particularly from Argentina, Brazil, Chile, Colombia and Mexico. Due to low LAC economic and social development, as well as reduced funding for tertiary education and research, this modality has unfortunately contributed to brain drain over the past four decades. It is estimated that there is one Mexican PhD-holder in the United States for every three living in Mexico (Fundación Bancomer, 2010). Studies on migration of the highly skilled calculate a world average expatriate rate of 5.4%, which is 7.4% in the case of LAC. Countries with the lowest emigration rates of tertiary educated individuals are Brazil (2.6%), Peru (5%) and Mexico (5.4%), while the highest rates are observed in the Caribbean (Barbados (90.4%), Guyana (77.8%), Haiti (70.4%), Trinidad and Tobago (66.6%) and Jamaica (46.1%)) (United Nations & OECD, 2013).

According to UNESCO (2015), the total number of LAC students abroad almost doubled in recent years, growing from 109,642 in 1999 to 203,355 in 2012. Nearly 40% of them are nationals of Brazil (30,729), Mexico (26,866) and Colombia (23,602); followed by Peru (14,844), Venezuela (11,720), Ecuador (10,926), Bolivia (9,096), Chile (8,814), Argentina (8,084) and Guatemala (7,032). The United States is the top destination, receiving more than 31%, followed by Spain, France, Germany, Portugal, the United Kingdom, Canada and Italy. Nevertheless, LAC is still the region of the developing world with the lowest number of students abroad (6.1%), behind Africa (11.6%) and Asia (52.7%) (OECD, 2013). It is also the region receiving the lowest number of international students (1.8%), as well as having the world's lowest outbound mobility ratio (0.9%) (UNESCO–UIS, 2012). In this regard, regional and national strategies to increase international visibility of TE systems to attract more international students and scholars are urgently required.

As far as intraregional mobility is concerned, the percentage of LAC nationals studying within the region increased from 15% in 2001 to 23% in 2008, but decreased to 20% by 2010 (UNESCO-UIS, 2015). Cuba, Brazil and Chile are the leading LAC destinations, with Cuba receiving more than 7%. Intraregional mobility is usually based on neighboring countries, because of reduced costs and common language. These are the cases of Brazil receiving students from Uruguay, Paraguay and Argentina; of Chile receiving students from Peru; and Argentina, from Uruguay, Paraguay and Bolivia.

As a conclusion, despite the evident growth of LAC degree-seeking students abroad, a global comparison is not favorable and LAC governments have to increase their investment in the years to come.

3.2 Short-Term Student Mobility

This modality started to gain importance at the end of the 1990s, and is a key strategy to enhance the region's competitiveness, as its impact is on undergraduate students. One of the first short-term mobility programs in LAC was the Inter-Campus Program, created in 1994 by the Spanish International Cooperation Agency, whose aim was to foster student, faculty and staff mobility for the creation of an Ibero-American higher education space. It was followed by other programs such as ALFA of the European Commission and PROMESAN, neither of which is now available.

For statistics on short-term mobility, there is a general claim that global trend information does not reflect actual numbers. In the case of LAC, this problem is even more acute, with national statistics practically nonexistent. To overcome this lack of data, Project Atlas was launched in 2001, a global initiative involving key national bodies and non-governmental organizations, whose aim is to compute global numbers on both short-term and degree-seeking student mobility (Institute of International Education, 2015). Nevertheless, the project has not yet met these expectations, at least in the case of LAC, since reporting is limited to Mexico and Chile.

Nevertheless, most LAC institutions do have short-term mobility programs established through bilateral agreements or international networks, whose funding almost entirely relies on institutional or personal resources with very limited governmental support. Given the economic fragility of the region and the low levels of institutional and public funding, students from the lowest quintiles tend to be excluded from international mobility. Consequently, the majority of students who can enjoy an international experience come from a socioeconomic elite; a situation that might contribute to the growth of inequality, already one of the highest of the world (Economic Commission for Latin America and the Caribbean, 2015). Likewise, the IAU 4th Global Survey reports "international opportunities accessible only to students with financial resources" as one of the main risks of internationalization (Egron-Polak & Hudson, 2014a).

In the following sections a critical analysis will be made of some of the most relevant and innovative programs in the region.

4 Innovative Short-Term Regional Mobility Programs

4.1 "Red Macro": A University Initiative with External Funding

The Network of Latin-American Macro Public Universities (Red Macro) was created in 2002 through an initiative of the National Autonomous University of Mexico and the Central University of Venezuela, under the auspices of IESALC. The main objective of this highly exclusive network of the largest, traditional, public, autonomous and comprehensive universities of the region is to promote a Latin American identity through education. By March 2015, the network had 34 member institutions: Brazil (4), Caribe (4), Central America (7), Southern Cone (5), Mexico (8) and Andean Region (6).

Red Macro grants around 100 scholarships per year for postgraduate courses or research projects in an institution belonging to the network. The program has had six editions between 2005 and 2014 and funded a total of 704 scholarships mainly for masters (67%) and PhD students (32%) (Red Macro, 2015). Red Macro's remit is to foster intraregional mobility for postgraduate students, an almost nonexistent modality, with full financial support. Nevertheless, the program's main challenge is that it relies exclusively on the availability of funds from Santander Bank, thus resulting in years with no calls. Consequently, the program's sustainability depends heavily on the goodwill, interest and negotiation capacity of participating institutions.

4.2 The Association of Universities of the Montevideo Group (AUGM): A University Initiative with Institutional Funding

AUGM was created in 1991 and presently encompasses 31 public universities from MERCOSUR countries: Argentina (11), Bolivia (2), Brazil (11), Chile (3), Paraguay (3) and Uruguay (1). It organizes four annual mobility programs for undergraduate and postgraduate students, faculty and non-academic staff, entirely funded by participating institutions. The sending universities pay transportation costs, and the receiving ones cover board and lodging (Asociación de Universidades Grupo Montevideo, 2016).

Faculty mobility was the first program launched offering 7- to 15-day stays in an institution belonging to the network to participate in activities such as postgraduate courses, teacher training, development of new research areas, policymaking and institution capacity building. The undergraduate mobility program created in 1998 is based on institutional reciprocity and to date has involved more than 4,600 students. The postgraduate mobility program, created in 2011, has seen 224 mobile students and offers opportunities to stay between 15 days and 6 months. Non-academic staff mobility, the most recent program, had its first edition in 2015 and allows mobility periods of one week.

AUGM mobility programs have several merits: they offer a large variety of mobility modalities; the commitment of participating institutions to finance and coordinate the programs; and faculty mobility, which is crucial for the sustainability of long-term collaboration and institutional capacity building for the improvement of regional research and innovation. Their main weakness is the lack of external funding, which, in part, explains the low mobility numbers. Nevertheless, AUGM remains one of the best examples of regional academic integration for LAC.

4.3 The Pacific Alliance: A Regional Intergovernmental Initiative

The Pacific Alliance is an innovative initiative for regional integration promoted in 2012 by the governments of Chile, Colombia, Mexico and Peru, with the objective of creating a free trade agreement and fostering regional capacity for entrepreneurship, innovation, small and medium enterprises, environmental protection, youth volunteering and cultural cooperation. Additionally, this initiative aims at strengthening the relationship with the Asiatic block (Pacific Alliance, 2015).

This agreement also has a human capital development component, promoting a mobility program coordinated by the foreign affairs ministries, cooperation agencies and other focal entities in the member countries, and has had six calls between 2013 and 2015 with a total budget of US$4.7 million. Each country is committed to grant 100 stipends per year for 75 undergraduate students and 25 doctoral students, researchers and faculty. The program has so far granted 1,040 scholarships for 160 doctoral students, researchers or faculty members, and 880 undergraduate students. Mexico has the highest mobility with 315 participants, followed by Colombia and Peru, with 277 and 275 respectively, and Chile has the lowest mobility with 173.

The program's strengths are many: it stems from a governmental will for economic and political integration, so far assuring continuity in timing and funding; it builds on existing partnerships among participating institutions, has the role of publishing calls, selecting candidates and administering scholarships; participation is open to both public and private institutions; and finally, it involves faculty members, thus strengthening the internationalization process in the long term. Nevertheless, there is still room for improvement in terms of numbers.

5 Innovative National Mobility Programs

In the region some national mobility programs have been launched recently and are worth analyzing for their differences in focus and scope: the Brazilian program, Science without Borders (SwB), and the Mexican Proyecta 100,000.

5.1 Science without Borders: A Most Innovative Governmental Program

The rationales behind this program have been the need to train highly skilled human capital to support Brazilian economic and social development, and to transform its R&D system to cope with the challenges of a knowledge-based economy. It is innovative for the large diversity of modalities offered and for its funding model, with one-quarter of the scholarships subsidized by the private sector and the rest by the Brazilian government.

The goal is for 101,000 mobile students and researchers between 2012 and 2015 in the following priority areas: engineering and technology; pure and natural sciences; health and biomedical sciences; information and communication technologies; aerospace; pharmaceuticals; sustainable agricultural production; oil, gas and coal production; renewable energies; minerals; biotechnology; nanotechnology and new materials; technology for prevention and mitigation of natural disasters; biodiversity and bioprospection; marine sciences; creative industry; and new technologies for constructive engineering (CAPES, 2016).

Besides human capital development, the potential of SwB to further TE internationalization was soon realized and was consequently reframed by the

government. New objectives were defined such as the internationalization of
R&D, science and technology in tertiary education and industry; the enhancement of Brazilian postgraduates' competitiveness through international mobility
in world universities; and the presence of young talents and international highly
qualified researchers in Brazilian universities.

International agencies or institutions such as Institute for International Education
(IIE), Campus France and the University of Bologna were in charge of student
placements. Candidates were first selected by home institutions and then by the
Ministry of Education and CNPq. The distribution of grants is detailed in Table 6.1.

Table 6.1 Science without Borders scholarships

Modality	Goal	Effective
Undergraduate mobility	64,000	78,980
Postgraduate mobility (PhD)	15,000	9,288
Postgraduate degree-seeking mobility (PhD)	4,500	3,365
Postdoctoral stays	6,440	6,243
Expert training	7,060	0
Guest young researchers	2,000	2,971
Guest scientists	2,000	
Professional masters	0	599
Total	101,000	101,446

Source: CAPES (www.capes.gov.br).

The number of scholarships available for postgraduate mobility (short-term
and degree-seeking) exceeded demand, which could be partially explained by
the broad national offer. The opportunity for receiving guest researchers and
scientists was underutilized; nevertheless, this modality could increase in future
thanks to the development of interinstitutional collaboration. Expert training
programs were strangely reported as vacant, but its budget was partially used for
professional masters studies.

With regard to destinations, and following a global trend, English-speaking
countries attracted the majority of students, with the top five destinations being
the United States, United Kingdom, Canada, France and Australia. Among them,
only France, which has developed fruitful and sustainable cooperation with Brazil
for decades, is a non-English-speaking country.

The five fields of study with highest student mobility were: engineering
(45,141), health and biomedical sciences (18,304), creative industries (8,363),
natural sciences (8,303) and information technology (6,225). These figures show
that the program's main goal, to supply highly skilled engineers and technicians,
has been fulfilled.

The 48 destinations offered, combined with a variety of highly renowned
research centers and international companies, will provide Brazil with a large

number of globally competent researchers, professionals and company leaders with a strong command of a second language and broad multicultural knowledge, thus giving the country a definitive competitive edge in the regional and global market.

Although a thorough governmental evaluation of the program is still pending, a preliminary analysis can be done. On a macro level, one of the most relevant achievements has been the international visibility of the Brazilian TE system, and the good academic performance of students and scholars. Furthermore, SwB helped institutions at an incipient stage of internationalization as well as those at an advanced stage, giving the latter opportunities to develop new partnerships in areas and countries where they had little cooperation. Another collateral positive aspect of SwB has been the creation of a program for the teaching and training of foreign languages due to students' linguistic deficiency. The program, Languages without Borders, began with English, but was soon expanded to other foreign languages (French, Spanish and German, and also Portuguese as a foreign language). Federal and state universities affiliated to the program have established language centers offering face-to-face and online language courses. A further positive outcome was public funding for internationalization of federal universities.

A negative aspect of the program has been the large number of foreign delegations visiting Brazilian institutions to recruit students and associated resources, with little knowledge of the program and of the Brazilian education, science and technology system. The challenge ahead is to transform the newly established relations among participating institutions into long-term sustainable international partnerships. One major criticism of the program is the exclusion of social sciences and humanities, especially in a global context where the advancement of knowledge requires an inter- and multidisciplinary approach. Therefore, the inclusion of this field should be taken into account for future phases.

Due to Brazil's current economic and social situation, the next phase of the program has been delayed until October 2016. For this new edition, Brazilian institutions demand control of their students' placements abroad as a way to strengthen their own international partnerships. This could transform the program into a most effective tool for the sustainability of international partnerships and the further internationalization of Brazilian tertiary education. Nevertheless, it could limit the potential of institutions with few international collaborations. This situation could be solved through the creation of consortia of more and less developed institutions to collaborate in the exchange of information and experiences, for the benefit of the least developed.

The two most significant challenges of the program remain, on the one hand, its transformation from a governmental program into a state policy, which will assure its continuity, and on the other, implementation of a broad national internationalization strategy for the TE sector in order to realize the full potential of SwB.

5.2 Proyecta 100,000: An Innovative Governmental Program?

Because academic cooperation between Mexico and the United States by no means reaches the level and scope of their bilateral trade, both countries jointly announced in May 2013 the creation of the Bilateral Forum on Higher Education, Innovation and Research (FOBESII), whose mission is:

> to help both countries develop a 21st century workforce for mutual economic prosperity and sustainable social development; as well as to bring together government, higher education community, private sector, and civil society to promote educational and research cooperation and to increase access to quality post-secondary education especially for traditionally underserved demographic groups in the science, technology, engineering, and mathematics (STEM) fields.
>
> (US Department of State, 2015)

This initiative professes to broaden the limited bilateral academic cooperation existing between the two countries despite their neighborhood, cultural, economic and social ties. Notwithstanding the existence of the North American Free Trade Agreement, signed in 1991, the imbalance in academic bilateral cooperation has grown. Indeed, while the number of Mexican students in the United States has steadily increased, from 9,000 in 1996 to 16,000 in 2013, the number of US students in Mexico has decreased from 6,000 to 4,000 in the same period.

Proyecta 100,000 was established in Mexico in 2013 as an executive platform to put into action political statements with the objectives of increasing academic mobility and networks, as well as promoting English language learning. The goal is to send 100,000 Mexican students to the United States and to receive 50,000 US students by 2018. This Mexican initiative was planned as a counterpart to the US "100,000 Strong in the Americas", whose aim is to increase the number of US students in Latin American countries.

So far, Proyecta 100,000 has only implemented a five-week language program for Mexicans in the United States with two editions (2014 and 2015). In 2014, 7,500 scholarships were granted to students from public TE institutions with a budget of over US$34 million. In 2015, the program's funding decreased by more than 75%, and granted 1,500 scholarships (1,365 to US institutions and 135 to Canadian institutions). If these changes in budgeting continue, attaining the original goal of increasing the number of Mexican students in the United States to 100,000 by 2018 is most unlikely.

The decision of the Mexican government to start with short language programs was justified by the need to improve Mexican students' English proficiency. Nevertheless, it is a very short, non-credit course having students travel in the middle of the semester, thus interrupting their studies at their home institution for five weeks. The program's main weakness is that it is doubtful a five-week program will be enough to solve a long-standing deficiency of the country's education system. Another regional initiative could serve as an example of a better-planned and more cost-effective strategy: the Ecuadorian SENESCYT "Teach English" scholarship program, whose goal is to train ESL teachers by sending them to English-speaking countries for nine months to improve linguistic proficiency and teaching skills (SENESCYT, 2016).

The program has several deficiencies: it is a unilateral non-credit short-term language training course, very lucrative for US institutions charging full tuition and associated services to the Mexican government and institutions, despite the fact that FOBESII was thought to increase bilateral collaboration; the Mexican effort was not matched by the United States, whose contribution was 0.2% (US$100,000) of the budget allocated by Mexico; the program is not tied to an internationalization strategy for the TE sector; all placements were done by the Mexican government at the margin of existing interinstitutional agreements; as language programs are being generally operated in US institutions through entrepreneurial schemes, the establishment of future academic collaborative projects is most unlikely; the inconsistency of Mexican government funding; and the apparent US lack of interest to increase the number of students in Mexico.

Therefore, the goal of Proyecta 100,000 has proven to be unrealistic, and the five-week language course can be considered a politically short-sighted program with no long-lasting impact on the TE system. Consequently, bilateral cooperation between Mexico and the United States remains highly unbalanced.

For the future, the Mexican government and institutions should negotiate better terms with international partners and link programs to a broader national policy for human capital development and internationalization of tertiary education.

Conclusions

Both short-term and degree-seeking student mobility schemes have greatly increased in LAC over the past decades. National governments have steadily increased their funding for study abroad scholarship programs in order to prepare the required highly skilled human capital to support national development. Nevertheless, if compared with other developing regions, LAC still has the lowest numbers of students abroad and of incoming students (the majority being from the region itself), and the lowest outbound mobility ratio.

At the institutional level, short-term mobility has now grown into the most important internationalization activity. New and innovative student mobility schemes for regional integration like Red Macro, AUGM and the Pacific Alliance have been launched. However, the numbers of participating students are still too low. It is key for the region to encourage intraregional mobility based on the establishment of university hubs of excellence. National, broad and diverse mobility schemes, fully funded by governmental and private sectors, are an exception, especially for undergraduate studies, SwB being the unique case. Nevertheless, even this excellent model still needs to be integrated in a broader state policy for internationalization. Proyecta 100,000, another example of a national program, has shown limited impact in regard to human capital development and institutional capacity building, and can be characterized as a traditional scheme of unbalanced cooperation between peripheral and central countries.

In all cases, even the best, fragility in funding and continuity, as well as limited impact on the improvement of the TE sector, are constant and common features among LAC mobility programs. Furthermore, mobility schemes are disconnected from broader national and institutional internationalization strategies. So, an increase in funding of international mobility is urgent for the region, and needs to be carefully planned to prevent further brain drain. It must be connected to broader and long-term internationalization strategies, within the framework of national development plans and corresponding long-term state policies for education.

Notes

1 UNESCO's Latin American Institute for Higher Education (www.iesalc.unesco.org.ve).
2 CONACYT (National Council on Science and Technology): www.conacyt.mx; COLCIENCIAS (Colombian Administrative Department for Science and Technology): www.colciencias.gov.co; CONICYT (National Commission on Scientific and Technological Research): www.conicyt.cl; CNPq (National Council of Technological and Scientific Development): www.cnpq.br.

Chapter 7

Internationalization in the MENA Region

A Case Study of Higher Education

Kamal Abouchedid & Maria Bou Zeid

Introduction

Higher education in the Middle East and North Africa (MENA) region is in the throes of a major change propelled by political, demographic and economic transformations. Until recently these would have been considered nearly inconceivable and include the shift from state-sponsored education in post-independent populist countries to massive privatization.

The ascendency of the neoliberal economy and global economic competitiveness have exercised considerable pressure on Arab governments, compelling them to revamp their domestic economic policies in order to adapt themselves to the functional requisites of the open-market economy through opting for privatization as a determinant for better economic performance. As such, privatization policies adopted by Arab governments over the last two decades and incentivized by the World Bank (WB) and the International Monetary Fund (IMF) have led to an unprecedented boom in private higher educational institutions (HEIs), auguring a shift in policy from insularity to openness. Part of the increase was to accommodate the increasing number of students seeking higher education as a result of population growth and raising awareness of higher education as leverage for social and economic upward mobility.

Student enrolment in higher education has been growing rapidly since the late 1990s (see Figure 7.1). This increase was also accompanied by a concomitant increase in the number of institutions involved from 174 universities in 1998 to 467 in 2008, i.e. 2.7 times as many.[1] The majority of the newly established universities were either privately owned by local providers or branches of foreign universities managed externally. Recent laws allowing for the establishment of private HEIs were adopted by Arab governments as a measure to circumvent dealing with the deteriorating quality of education in the public sector resulting from a lack of governmental oversight, influx of students through open admissions and meagre budgetary allocations to this sector.

The increase in enrolment in the region is redolent of the dramatic widening participation rates in higher education worldwide as estimated by the UNESCO Institute for Statistics (UIS), where about 32.5 million students enrolled in

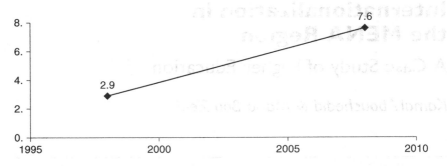

Figure 7.1 Student enrolment in higher education from 1998 to 2008 (in millions) (Source: http://unesdoc.unesco.org/images/0018/001892/189272m.pdf (accessed 13 December 2015)).

higher education worldwide in 2012. But a distinctive feature pertaining to the growth of higher education in the MENA region is reflected in the excessive influx of cross-border international branch campuses as the region became hospitable to international investment in higher education through hosting foreign universities mainly from the United States, United Kingdom and Australia. Statistics provided by the Observatory on Borderless Higher Education (OBHE, 2011) showed that the Middle East hosted 34% of all international branch campuses worldwide in 2009, with additional foreign universities branching out to the region. These cross-border international branch campuses (such as Carnegie Mellon, Texas A&M, Weill Cornell, Sorbonne and many others) are ubiquitous in wealthy hydrocarbon- and oil-rich monarchies or so-called rentier Gulf states (Ross, 2011, cited in Davidson, 2015), where land is rented out to foreign investors allowing for the promotion of international higher education activity.

The unprecedented growth of private higher education in the MENA region, juxtaposed with public HEIs, has resulted in a rather untidy conglomeration. According to UNESCO's (2009) regional report on education in the Arab world, HEIs can be distinguished by the following:

- sector (public, non-public/non-profit, non-public/for-profit);
- affiliation (to the Ministry of Higher Education, other ministries);
- status (universities, independent colleges, technical institutes, community colleges);
- type (traditional, open, virtual);
- nationality (national, regional, international institutions or branches of them);
- model (American, French, German, etc.);
- cultural reference (Islamic, Christian, non-religious institutions);
- orientation (profession-oriented, academic-oriented);

- recognition from respective authorities (licensed, accredited, assured institutions); and
- degree pattern (BA/BS–MA/MS–PhD).

The vast array of HEIs in the MENA region, in terms of providers and provisions, reflects recent structural reforms that have taken place in the wake of privatization. Buncker (2011) outlined a typology of higher educational reform in the MENA region, namely quality assurance, internationalization and distance education. Since the late 1990s, these three-tier reform areas have been placed on the agenda of Arab governments for implementation. Regarding quality assurance, since the late 1990s, Arab governments have requested that HEIs should be accredited, and even went beyond this to establish their own national agencies for quality assurance and accreditation.

As for distance education, and as a result of the recent reforms in the region, the Arab Open University (AOU), patterned on the British Open University, was established in 1996 through the initiative of and funding from Prince Talal Bin Abdulaziz, president of the Arab Gulf Development Program (AGFUND). At present, the AOU has branches in Kuwait, Saudi Arabia, Bahrain, Oman, Jordan, Lebanon and Egypt.[2] While distance education is not well-established in the region due to strict ministerial regulations that seek to curb the flow of diploma mills issued by distance education institutions from outside the region, many HEIs incorporate blended learning into their face-to-face instruction.

A review of the extant literature shows remarkably little attention given to the internationalization of higher education in a region undergoing significant change and reform. This chapter is concerned with higher education internationalization as a consequence of globalization characterized by the flow of information technology, open market economy and increasing cultural openness (Knight & de Wit, 1997), often crossing national borders and creating a favourable context sociologists term cultural osmosis (Flamboltz & Randle, 2011). But although higher education internationalization is conceived of as one means of globalization (Ralyk, 2008), there are conceptual differences between the two. In this chapter we adopt Knight's (2003, p. 2) definition, according to which internationalization is seen as "the process of integrating an international, intercultural or global dimension into the purpose, functions or delivery of post-secondary education". We use the term higher education institutions (HEIs) as a commonly agreed-upon terminology in the higher education discourse in the region and also to avoid confusing post-secondary education with vocational education and training institutions that are also post-secondary in nature in the wider MENA region.

According to Kehm and Teichler (2007), studies on internationalization in higher education are mapped out along seven levels of classification. These being:

1   mobility;
2   mutual influence of higher education systems;

3   internationalization of the substance of teaching and learning;
4   institutional strategies;
5   knowledge transfer;
6   cooperation and competition;
7   national and supranational policies.

In this chapter, we use ten indicators to measure the strengths and weaknesses of internationalization in 310 HEIs in Lebanon, Qatar, the United Arab Emirates (UAE), Morocco, Saudi Arabia, Tunisia and Jordan (see Table 7.1). The objective is to contribute to the burgeoning scholarly discussions on the internationalization of higher education as an international educational priority by sharing original data from the MENA region. This region represents a unique context in the transformation of higher education and, as such, it ushers in research aiming at analysing aspects of internationalization.

Table 7.1 List of indicators

Indicators	Source
Inbound international students	U-Map
Outbound students	UNESCO
International agreements	U-Map
International sources of income	LAES
International faculty	U-Map
Twinning (institutional, programme)	LAES
Accreditation (institutional, programmatic)	LAES
Mission statement	LAES
International admission tests	LAES
Internationalization at home	LAES

Methodology

A main challenge for researchers lies in dealing with the multiplicity of terms relating to internationalization in higher education. De Wit (2002, p. 103) provides subdivisions of the field, including "academic mobility, international cooperation, study abroad, and international exchange". We used ten indicators (see Table 7.1) to measure the strengths and weaknesses of higher education internationalization.

Questionnaire

A questionnaire classifying HEIs was administered in 310 institutions in Lebanon, Qatar, the UAE, Morocco, Saudi Arabia, Tunisia and Jordan as part of a pilot project dealing with the classification of HEIs in the MENA region conducted in

2009–2011 by the Lebanese Association for Educational Studies (LAES) and the Institute of International Education (IIE) (Bhandari and El-Amine, 2012). The questionnaire was developed by a Scientific Committee comprising LAES members and experts in higher education. It comprised 11 separate dimensions adapted from the Carnegie Foundation for the Advancement of Teaching (McCormick et al., 2008), the European Classification of Higher Educational Institutions (U-MAP) and dimensions added by LAES. The dimension on internationalization, used in this chapter, consisted of ten indicators as shown in Table 7.1.

Sample

The total number of HEIs surveyed was 310, drawn from seven Arab countries, divided between public (50.6%) and non-public (49.4%), the latter comprising private independent institutes, community colleges and private cross-border international branch campuses.

Procedure

LAES commissioned one National Coordinator for each country involved, who filled out the questionnaires covering HEIs in the country. The completed questionnaires were sent back to each institution involved in the study to verify and cross-check the accuracy of information about the institution. The final dataset was submitted to the Scientific Committee of LAES for additional review and verification. The final version of the questionnaire data was entered into the Statistical Package for the Social Sciences (SPSS-Version 20) and was made available to LAES members for analysis. Additional sources of data were obtained by the authors from the UNESCO database to augment analyses of internationalization in the MENA region.

Results

Inbound International Students

Data obtained from UNESCO[3] for the seven countries involved showed consistently that Qatar and UAE had the largest inbound mobility rate of international students for both sexes from 2011 to 2014 respectively (see Table 7.2).[4]

The current survey data were consistent with UNESCO's statistics on ratios of international students. Moreover, our data show that the pattern of student nationality, i.e. citizen students, constitute the majority (88–98%), with only a relatively insignificant number of foreign students attending higher education in the region. This applies to all countries except Qatar and the UAE, which have less than 40%. In Qatar and the UAE international students constitute a quarter of all students while Arab students constitute more than one-third (37–38%), as shown in Table 7.3.

Table 7.2 Inbound mobility rate of international students from both sexes in the seven countries surveyed (%)

Country	1999	2000	2001	2002	2003	2004	2005	2006	2007	2008	2009	2010	2011	2012	2013	2014
Jordan	–	8.5	–	–	8.5	10.9	9.9	9.8	9.7	10.5	10.4	11.1	9.9	9.1	–	–
Lebanon	13.8	12.1	11.0	10.6	8.5	9.0	8.5	9.9	12.1	–	–	15.0	15.3	12.8	–	7.6
Morocco	1.5	1.5	1.4	–	1.5	1.9	1.3	1.6	1.9	1.9	1.9	1.9	–	–	–	–
Qatar	0.0	0.0	20.7	21.0	20.9	12.6	24.5	–	–	36.2	36.5	39.1	40.3	41.4	40.7	39.9
Saudi Arabia	1.6	1.9	–	–	4.1	2.1	2.2	2.2	2.6	2.6	2.6	3.0	3.4	3.9	4.6	4.8
Tunisia	1.8	1.5	1.2	1.1	0.8	0.8	–	–	–	0.7	0.7	0.6	0.6	0.5	1.8	–
UAE	–	–	–	–	–	–	–	–	–	–	–	–	42.8	44.5	44.6	44.8

Source: http://data.uis.unesco.org/?queryid=142 (accessed 10 January 2016).

Table 7.3 Inbound international students by country and by number of institutions per category

Country	Foreign students by higher education institution			Total
	Low percentage of foreign students	Medium percentage of foreign students	High percentage of foreign students	
Jordan	9	0	0	9
	100%	0%	0%	100%
Lebanon	16	1	0	17
	94.1%	5.9%	0%	100%
Morocco	12	0	0	12
	100.0%	0%	0%	100.0%
Saudi Arabia	9	0	0	9
	100%	0%	0%	100%
Tunisia	15	4	2	21
	71.4%	19%	9.5%	100%
Qatar	3	4	2	9
	33.3%	44.4%	22.2%	100%
UAE	22	9	12	43
	51.2%	20.9%	27.9%	100%
Total	86	18	16	120
	71.7%	15%	13.3%	100%

Among the HEIs characterized by a high percentage of international students, there was one where all students were international, namely the Institute of Management and Technology, UAE. The HEIs in the UAE were highest in percentage of foreign students (28% of HEIs), followed by Qatar (22.2%), as shown in Table 7.4. In Morocco, Saudi Arabia and Tunisia, the high share of foreign students at graduate level was above average while, in other countries, foreign students were found mainly at the undergraduate level.

Outbound Students

The percentage of outbound students in selected countries shows inequitable numbers (see Table 7.5).[5] Clearly, outbound statistics gleaned from the UNESCO database show that Qatar had the largest ratio of outbound activity, followed by Morocco.

International Agreements

Another indicator used for measuring internationalization was the number of international agreements signed by the HEIs involved in the study. Data revealed that the total number of agreements was 2,288, of which 1,712 were international

Table 7.4 Country by foreign students – undergraduate vs graduate – and by number of institutions per category

Country	High share of graduate foreign students	High share of undergraduate foreign students	Total
Jordan	2	7	9
	22.2%	77.8%	100%
Lebanon	4	12	16
	25%	75%	100%
Morocco	4	6	10
	40%	60%	100%
Saudi Arabia	5	3	8
	62.5%	37.5%	100%
Tunisia	7	6	13
	53.8%	46.2%	100%
Qatar	2	4	6
	33.3%	66.7%	100%
UAE	10	31	41
	24.4%	75.6%	100%
Total	34	69	103
	33%	67%	100%

cooperation agreements as opposed to 289 with Arab countries and 287 within-country agreements. These results should be approached cautiously since little information existed as to whether the agreements were active and included international or regional exchange of faculty and students. However, this finding remains a positive indicator of internationalization in the MENA region.

Regarding the total number of international agreements, the highest mean was observed in Morocco followed by Lebanon, while the lowest mean was in Tunisia, as shown in Figure 7.2.

International Sources of Income

Only a meagre 90 out of 310 HEIs provided information about external gifts and grants, reflecting issues of institutional transparency when it comes to divulging financial figures. The average of these gifts and grants out of total revenue was 2.27%. Local sources constituted 1.51% and international sources only 0.45%, i.e. lower than local sources and other sources. These figures provide a dismal picture of the lack of external gifts or grants received by HEIs, which tend to rely heavily on student tuition fees as the main source of income in the private sector, and as an additional fiscal burden on the public sector, which provides free education to local citizens who pay only nominal registration fees.

International Faculty

According to the survey data, 66% of faculty members were indigenous citizens or faculty from other Arab states, while the other 34% were non-citizens. Also 44.2% of faculty members were returning expatriates; local talent numbers ranged from 85% to 98% compared to [...] the 34% of foreign students, except for Qatar and the UAE, which had 22.2% and 27% of foreign students respectively, since these two countries do not [...] numbers of expatriate foreign workers and foreign lecturers. Qatar and the UAE were highly oriented towards recruiting foreign faculty, while other countries were highly reliant on expatriate recruiting locals, particularly in public [...] institutions.

Twinning Programmes

Only 67 HEIs reported that they had twinning arrangements with other HEIs. The total number of programmes [...] with [...] in which 17 were oriented towards Arab countries (72.3%) and 227 towards international partners (92.9%), indicating an equal engagement in international [...]. It is worth noting that 13 (14.6%) of the 63 HEIs had all their twinning programmes with international partners. The majority of international twinning arrangements were the ones found in Qatar, the UAE and Algeria [...] numbers of programmes were also run [...] data and faculty with opportunities to have a more international experience [...] little information existed as to whether or not [...] programmes that derived faculty student and faculty exchange were provided along with more traditional [...] and cross-institution learning.

Accreditation: Institutional and Programmatic

Institutional Accreditation

Only 39.1% of HEIs surveyed said that they were accredited locally and fewer said they had received an international institutional accreditation (18%) in addition to 8.7% that reported that their accreditation is "in process", as shown in Table 7.6.

Table 7.5 Percentage of outbound mobility by country

Country	1999	2000	2001	2002	2003	2004	2005	2006	2007	2008	2009	2010	2011	2012	2013
Jordan	–	8.5	–	7.8	6.7	5.8	5.8	5.8	5.7	5.3	5.5	6.1	6.3	5.4	–
Lebanon	7.5	7.6	7.4	8.2	9.1	8.8	8.1	7.9	7.3	7.2	7.0	6.5	6.1	5.9	5.2
Morocco	14	15.5	14.8	16.7	16.8	14.3	12.5	11.4	11	10.4	10.1	9.6	8.6	–	–
Qatar	12.9	–	16	16.4	17.0	14.6	18.9	17.8	18	17.3	18.5	20.4	18.6	20.8	24.1
Saudi Arabia	2.8	2.6	2.6	2.7	2.2	2.0	2.1	2.2	3	3.5	4.1	4.7	5.1	5.3	5.4
Tunisia	6.0	5.7	5.4	5.6	–	–	–	–	–	–	–	–	5.4	5.3	5.0
UAE	–	–	–	–	–	–	–	–	7.7	7.8	7.7	7.9	7.4	6.9	6.4

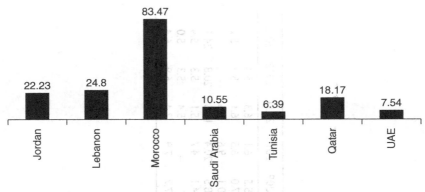

Figure 7.2 Mean distribution of international agreements.

International Faculty

According to the survey data, 66% of faculty members were either local citizens or faculty from other Arab states, while the other 34% were foreign faculty. Also, 44.9% of faculty members were national citizens. Local citizen students ranged from 88% to 98% compared to a meagre number of foreign students, except for Qatar and the UAE, which had 22.2% and 27.9% of foreign students respectively, since these two countries accommodate large numbers of expatriate foreign workers and foreign investors. Qatar and the UAE were highly oriented towards recruiting foreign faculty, while all other countries were highly oriented towards recruiting locals, particularly in public universities.

Twinning Programmes

Only 65 HEIs reported that they had twinning programmes with other HEIs. The total number of programmes in these HEIs was 238, out of which 17 were oriented towards Arab countries (7.1%) and 221 towards international partners (92.9%), indicating an explicit engagement in internationalization. It is worth noting that 55 (84.6%) of the 65 HEIs had all their twinning programmes with international partners. The majority of international twinning programmes were mostly found in Qatar, the UAE and Morocco. Although twinning programmes provide students and faculty with opportunities to have a more cross-cultural experience, little information existed as to whether these programmes have allowed for student and faculty exchange or provided them with international and cross-cultural learning.

Accreditation: Institutional and Programmatic

Institutional Accreditation

Only 39.1% of HEIs surveyed said they were accredited locally, and fewer said they had received an international institutional accreditation (9%), in addition to 8.7% that reported that their accreditation is "in process", as shown in Table 7.6.

Table 7.6 Accreditation

Responses	Local/national accreditation		International institutional accreditation	
	N	%	N	%
No	146	53.3	228	82.3
Yes	107	39.1	25	9
In process	21	7.7	24	8.7
Total	274	100	277	100
Missing cases	37	11.9	34	10.9
Total	311	100	311	100

Table 7.7 Country by programmatic accreditation

Country	Does not have international accreditation	Has international accreditation	Total
Jordan	44	1	45
	97.8%	2.2%	100%
Lebanon	33	8	41
	80.5%	19.5%	100%
Morocco	62	5	67
	92.5%	7.5%	100%
Saudi Arabia	10	6	16
	62.5%	37.5%	100%
Tunisia	30	5	35
	85.7%	14.3%	100%
Qatar	4	3	7
	57.1%	42.9%	100%
UAE	33	18	51
	64.7%	35.3%	100%
Total	216	46	262
	82.4%	17.6%	100%

Within country statistics, HEIs in Saudi Arabia, Qatar and the UAE were more involved in institutional accreditation than other countries in the sample.

Programmatic Accreditation

Forty-six HEIs (17.6% of 216 that answered the question) said they had obtained or were in the process of obtaining programmatic international accreditation. Saudi Arabia, Qatar and the UAE were the countries most involved in accreditation, while Jordan appeared to have the lowest engagement in programmatic accreditation (Table 7.7).

The Accreditation Board for Engineering and Technology (ABET) came first on the list in 12 HEIs, and the United States in general was involved 36 times out of 77 in programmatic accreditation in the seven countries surveyed.

Mission Statements

The mission statements of 310 institutions were analysed through searching keywords that signify the international orientation of each university as posted on their websites. Only 12.9% of the institutions surveyed contained keywords that signified internationalization, while 87.1% of them did not. HEIs in Qatar, Jordan, and UAE had the highest percentage of keywords accenting internationalization in their mission statements (see Table 7.8).

International Admissions Tests

Out of the 310 HEIs, 230 provided information about international admissions tests: 153 (66.5%) said they did not employ international tests for admissions as opposed to 77 (33.5%) that reported that they used such tests. The most common of these were TOEFL and IELTS. The majority of the HEIs surveyed reported using a combination of two or more admissions tests such as TOEFL, IELTS, SAT and ACT.

The average use of such tests is 33%, climbing to 90% and beyond in Qatar and the UAE and 41% in Lebanon, which accommodate a large number of private HEIs. Judging by the data provided, Jordan, Morocco, Saudi Arabia and Tunisia did not report using international admissions tests.

"Internationalization at Home"

We adopted Beelen and Jones' (2015a, p. 69) definition, which states that "Internationalization at Home is the purposeful integration of international and intercultural dimensions into the formal and informal curriculum for all students within domestic learning environments". The survey data showed that 26.1% of the HEIs surveyed used English as the main medium of instruction in all degree programmes, followed by French (24.4%) and Arabic (14.7%). The rest used a combination of Arabic and English or Arabic, English and French. We further inquired into possible exposure of students to aspects of internationalization in a liberal arts curriculum and free elective courses. Qatar registered a high percentage of free electives. As for liberal arts, HEIs that follow the pattern of the American higher education system provided a range of 25–30% of liberal arts courses. Jones (2013a, p. 113) has rightly argued that the literature contains only a limited number of studies into the fulfilment of internationalized learning outcomes, and notices a "relative lack of research into the outcomes of an internationalized curriculum for all students". Our findings were challenged by the distinct paucity of literature on the outcomes of an internationalized curriculum in the MENA region. We attempted to overcome this limitation, partly at least, by presenting unpublished discourse analysis data derived from an ongoing research project on civic responsibility in higher education in 15 Arab countries carried out by one of the authors of the present study under the auspices of

Table 7.8 Country by presence of international dimensions in mission statement

Country		No international dimension	With international dimension	Total
Jordan	n	35	14	49
	% within country	71.4%	28.6%	100%
	% of total	11.3%	4.5%	15.8%
Lebanon	n	41	0	41
	% within country	100%	0%	100%
	% of total	13.2%	0%	13.2%
Morocco	n	68	0	68
	% within country	100%	0%	100%
	% of total	21.9%	0%	21.9%
Saudi Arabia	n	19	0	19
	% within country	100%	0%	100%
	% of total	6.1%	0%	6.1%
Tunisia	n	71	0	71
	% within country	100%	0%	100%
	% of total	22.9%	0%	22.9%
Qatar	n	6	5	11
	% within country	54.5%	45.5%	100%
	% of total	1.9%	1.6%	3.5%
UAE	n	30	21	51
	% within country	58.8%	41.2%	100%
	% of total	9.7%	6.8%	16.5%

LAES. Part of the data deals with the pedagogy of inquiry and deliberation in the discourse of 36 universities as posted on their websites.

The discourse analysis of the 36 universities in 15 countries surveyed generated a number of significant results. The word count pronouncing the five meanings devised for the study (cooperative learning, critical thinking, problem-solving, applying knowledge and discussion/debate) was 9,258, constituting only 1.7% of the total discourse. Of the total statements comprising these five meanings, only 3.25% on cooperative learning appeared in only six universities, being Qatar University, the American University of Beirut (AUB), Canal Suez University in Egypt, King Saud University in Saudi Arabia, Ain Shams University in Egypt and the University of Bahrain. Cooperative learning in the classroom did indeed occupy a narrow space in the discourse.

Both problem-solving and critical thinking were fairly pronounced in the discourse by universities, despite 31% scoring zero on problem-solving and another

33.4% scoring zero on critical thinking, such as Sana'a University in Yemen, universities in Tunisia (three public and one private) and two public universities in Morocco. Debate/discussion in the classroom was very narrow (5% of the total) and was pronounced by only 12 universities with the highest number of statements being four, at the American University of Beirut in Lebanon. Whether pedagogy of inquiry and deliberation in the universities surveyed sought to inculcate students with international, intercultural or global aspects of learning is unclear since classroom observations, analysis of syllabi and evidence of hands-on activities have not been conducted, suggesting the need for further research in this vital area of internationalization in higher education.

Discussion

Ten indicators were used to examine aspects of internationalization in HEIs in the wider MENA region. The present results have shown a remarkably lacklustre performance in internationalization of higher education in the wider MENA region, seen at least from the perspective of the HEIs surveyed and the indicators used. Moreover, the notion that asserts that the evolution of internationalization as part of the reform attempts in the region has stimulated institutional change, such as changes in managerial attitudes and cultures (Deem & Brehony, 2005), needs to be taken with caution in light of the results discussed below.

The results show that Qatar and the UAE attracted international students not necessarily through exchange programmes but as part of providing education to expatriate communities working in these two countries. Save Qatar and the UAE, the lack of student mobility in the region could be attributed to security reasons and political unrest. Bureaucracy involved in exchange could also be a factor chiefly responsible for the lack of international student and faculty presence in the region. In connection with this, higher education academic calendars in the region could be different from those in other countries, limiting the prospects of student and faculty exchange. This is evident in the multiplicity and diversity of educational providers in the region coupled with the absence of a Regional Qualifications Framework that would facilitate the recognition of credit transfer across institutions and thereby encourage student mobility. In addition, the relatively low number of foreign faculty in most countries surveyed is attributed to the priority given to employing national citizens or citizens from the Arab world. Exceptions were found in both Qatar and the UAE, which have, over the years, received increasing numbers of cross-border international universities that tend to recruit foreign faculty.

It is common knowledge that HEIs expand the scope of their scholarly activities beyond national borders through international agreements. Thus, activities of HEIs have become increasingly more international in terms of cooperation (Horta, 2009). This has partly reflected the number of agreements signed by the HEIs surveyed. However, the present results should be taken cautiously in light of the lack of information about the nature of these agreements, the scope of their activities and the extent to which HEIs are actively engaged in implementing such agreements. However, a positive sign suggested by the data from the HEIs surveyed is the number of twinning programmes mainly found in Qatar, the UAE and Morocco. In our experience, twinning with international universities is a manifestation of the need to promote quality in the region where local university standards see improved quality through twinning with accredited universities from outside the region.

In terms of mobility, the contribution of public HEIs to social mobility is lower than it is in the private sector. This conclusion may be explained by issues of quality and type of specialization. For instance, specializations in humanities such as literature, social and political sciences make little contribution to mobility, unlike other fields of study such as engineering and medicine. This inequitable contribution of disciplines to mobility in the framework of internationalization remains a challenge to be addressed in the region.

According to Romani (2009), it is very unlikely that the deluge of international campuses in the region can proceed without resulting in a conflict between local cultural traditions and the requisites of internationalization. Thus, despite the proliferation of international branch campuses, their contribution to the promotion of internationalization is yet to be seen in light of the intersection of foreign and local cultures. Also, there are contradictions between legal regulations in host countries and governance systems and structures followed by the newly implanted international branch campuses, let alone issues of academic freedom in host countries that might contradict the value systems of the hosted HEIs.

Concluding Remarks

This study is not without limitations, the most significant of which is the reluctance of many HEIs to answer all the survey questions, often resulting in empty cells and large standard deviations. Realizing that it is difficult to generalize the present results to the entire MENA region, we nonetheless conclude that internationalization of higher education in the seven countries surveyed provide valuable lessons for policy-makers and researchers.

First, internationalization requires the allocation of immense physical and financial resources that many institutions in the region lack. In particular, public universities have inadequate governmental funding and private ones primarily generate their revenues from student tuition fees in the absence of external grants and funding.

Second, internationalization requires a commitment from leaders in higher education that must be reflected in policies, mission statements and strategic plans. As it stands, only a few universities surveyed pronounced internationalization in their mission statements as official guiding strategic documents.

Third, the organizational frameworks of the ministries of higher education in the region do not include legislation that could govern and ensure supporting and developing cooperation between HEIs and civic society, or between institutions and the labour market. Despite the promising numbers of international cooperative agreements, cooperation exists only in an advisory capacity or as piecemeal initiatives taken by some HEIs on individual basis.

Fourth, the region lacks a Regional Qualification Framework that would facilitate transferability of credits and mobility of students across the diverse HEI institutions characterizing the region today. Although not supported by the data discussed in this chapter, one can conclude that student mobility is also challenged by security problems and political instability in the wider MENA region, and the outbound flow of students is curbed by visa problems with Europe and the United States due to fear of terrorism and illegal immigration, which have started to pose serious threats to the Western world in the wake of the Syrian crisis.

Fifth, privatization policies that allow the establishment of HEIs, specializations and branch campuses are motivated sometimes by political and commercial considerations at the expense of standards, educational quality and professional preparation in terms of curricula, faculty qualifications, research output (Abouchedid & Abdelnour, 2015), buildings and facilities, placing limitations on HEI engagement with internationalization.

As Altbach and Knight (2007, p. 303) argue, "Internationalism will remain a central force in higher education, though its contours are unclear". In fact, the MENA region can no longer afford to lose its competitive edge in both regional and international markets, and higher education remains a public plaza for potentially promoting internationalization.

Notes

1 Source: http://unesdoc.unesco.org/images/0018/001892/189272m.pdf (accessed 13 December 2015).
2 www.aou.edu.lb/index.html (accessed 7 January 2016).
3 http://data.uis.unesco.org/?queryid=142 (accessed 10 January 2016).
4 Inbound mobility rate = 100 × [Total number of students from abroad studying in a given country (inbound students)] / [Total tertiary enrolment in that country].
5 Number of students going abroad (exchange or just pursuing their education) × 100/number of higher education students in the country.

Chapter 8

The Internationalization of Higher Education in the Caribbean

David Rampersad

I Introduction

Given the historical, linguistic and geographical diversity of the Caribbean, especially the insular Caribbean, any endeavour to analyse the status and prospects of the internationalization of its higher education system is not a straightforward undertaking. This chapter highlights some of the characteristics of the internationalization strategies of regional higher education institutions (HEIs) as well as public policy responses. It focuses on the strategy of the University of the West Indies (UWI), an institution serving 17 territories, to illustrate how one HEI is making maximum use of its multinational reach to take advantage of the opportunities provided by internationalization in order to serve its constituents more effectively.

The Caribbean includes independent countries, overseas territories and countries of the EU member states and territories of the United States. The mainland countries of Belize, Guyana and Suriname are traditionally classified as part of the Caribbean. Most independent Caribbean countries are former dependencies of the United Kingdom, Spain, France or the Netherlands. More recently, their economic and migration links with the United States and Canada have expanded considerably. The higher education system reflects the impact of these relationships, especially in its governance structures, curricula and partnerships (EUCARINET, 2015, p. 7).

Public universities have existed for a considerable period of time, including some in Cuba and the Dominican Republic that have been active for several centuries. The UWI was established in 1948 to remedy the paucity of technical capacity in the British territories. Given the heterogeneity of the region and consequently its higher education system, emphasis is placed in this chapter on the English-speaking Commonwealth Caribbean and, in particular, the UWI that serves 17 independent countries and British overseas territories. During the past half-century, the growth in the number of national, publicly funded HEIs has been marked as governments have recognized their role as drivers of economic development and innovation. These HEIs include, among others, the University of Guyana (established in 1963), the Anton de Kom University of Suriname

(1968), the University of Technology in Jamaica (1995), the University of Belize (2000) and the University of Trinidad and Tobago (2004).

While public HEIs respond primarily to national demand, they are increasingly cognisant of the dynamic education environment that includes opportunities provided by growing overseas student demand and by information and communications technologies (ICTs). This demand and the proximity of the Caribbean to the North American market have also led considerable numbers of offshore private HEIs to establish operations in the English-speaking countries. In large part, they offer professional degree programmes either in a residential setting or using distance modalities. As a result of these activities, the Caribbean has become a net exporter of higher education services (Rochester-King, 2015, p. 1).

Individual Caribbean HEIs and associations of HEIs, such as the Association of Caribbean Universities and Research Institutions (UNICA), have traditionally played a leadership role in regional and international associations of higher education, including, among others, the Association of Commonwealth Universities. They also participate in associations with a focus on Latin America and the Caribbean that address common concerns such as research, accreditation, mobility and funding. They do so to ensure that Caribbean priorities and peculiarities are taken into account when regional and international policies and strategies in education are considered, as well as to gain new insights into ways of addressing institutional challenges.

2 Principal Characteristics of Internationalization of Higher Education in the Caribbean

With the exception of UWI, a regional institution, most public HEIs are national institutions that rely to a considerable extent on public funding. In light of difficult economic conditions, some HEIs have devised internationalization strategies, policies and initiatives to assist in accomplishing their mission of spearheading knowledge creation. Since their aim is to build capacity among staff and students to ensure greater engagement in research and outreach, many participate in international consortia, partly to gain greater access to international funding that helps develop their research strengths. They engage in student mobility programmes, inward and outward, facilitated mainly by schemes supported by multilateral development agencies and foreign governments. Many also seek accreditation for professional programmes, including those in engineering (UWI, n.d.c) and medical sciences (CAAM-HP, n.d.), from international accreditation bodies not only for purposes of quality assurance but also to attract extra-regional students whose fees are generally higher than those paid by national students.

Since graduates require the appropriate qualifications to gain access to the international employment market as well as to undertake postgraduate education, the curricula of both public and private HEIs are designed to equip them with the knowledge and skills to satisfy market requirements and to advance their careers. Curricula, particularly those of professional degree programmes, are therefore formulated to meet international standards. The participation of HEIs in international partnerships and the mobility of staff to and from partner institutions also have an impact on curriculum design and content. During the past half-century, as most countries in the region have become independent, national and regional perspectives have been included in curricula together with the traditional emphasis on global perspectives.

3 Public Policy Support

The economic difficulties facing many Caribbean countries, resulting partly from the impact of the financial crisis of 2008 and the end of preferential access to some major overseas markets, have been a significant driver of the internationalization of higher education. Governments have recognized that higher education provides opportunities as well as benefits, including innovation, that propel economic development. They have therefore begun to introduce national systems and processes designed to increase international student recruitment. These include, among others, steps to facilitate the issuing of student visas, boosting security measures and incentives to private providers of student housing (St. Augustine Education City, n.d.).

Public agencies are also reinforcing the infrastructure that helps generate synergies among the relevant parties to create a marketable proposition. The Trinidad and Tobago Coalition of Service Industries, for example, has established a Committee for the Export of Education Services, comprising a variety of stakeholders, to design and implement a strategy for encouraging the export of such services and to advocate for streamlined administrative and regulatory frameworks related to immigration, security and housing.

At the regional level, the Caribbean Export Development Agency (CEDA) has identified the higher education services sector as a significant source of growth and investment and included it as one of three priority sectors in the CARIFORUM–EU Business Forum in April 2015 (CARIFORUM consists of the 15 members of the Caribbean Community and the Dominican Republic). It commissioned studies that assessed the potential of the sector to exploit opportunities in selected markets, especially in Europe and Africa, such as *Towards a Strategy for the CARIFORUM Higher Education Sector*. The recommendations of those studies included:

1 the incorporation in national development and foreign policies of a strategy for attracting international students, educators and researchers to the region;
2 the rationalization of national administrative, legal and regulatory frameworks; and
3 the definition and promotion of national and regional brands.

(Rochester-King, 2015, p. 7)

CEDA has established an Advisory Group on Higher Education Services, consisting of policy experts, representatives of HEIs and public agencies responsible for trade and investment promotion, to recommend solutions to the challenges facing the sector including those that inhibit regional HEIs from gaining access to new markets. The group will also engage in advocacy with other regional institutions and donor agencies on behalf of the sector.

4 Taking Advantage of New Opportunities

In response to the increasingly competitive higher education environment and the opportunities for growth and development that internationalization presents, public HEIs have begun to strengthen their internal administrative systems and processes. Moreover, members of staff responsible for internationalization are beginning to make a stronger case for internationalization both internally and nationally and to engage their counterparts in a more concerted fashion. This is especially important since it is not uncommon for knowledge of, and participation in, internationalization strategy to be limited to a relatively small group within an HEI, thereby resulting in less than adequate institutional support. Moreover, despite the efforts of governments and public agencies, the significance of higher education as a service for export is not always appreciated by the national community. A concerted policy of public sensitization is thus required.

Offshore private HEIs, including more than 30 private offshore medical schools, have been particularly agile in responding to buoyant demand. Their international student recruitment and marketing strategies are centred on specific markets while the fact that many of their programmes are accredited in the United States makes them particularly attractive. Some national private HEIs have been equally prompt in taking advantage of opportunities. The Kenson School of Production Technology, a private HEI in Trinidad and Tobago that specializes in training in the energy sector, has been marketing its programmes in regions as diverse as West Africa and the Falkland Islands (Kenson, n.d.). Other national private HEIs offer programmes franchised from international HEIs, principally in professional fields such as business, law and ICT, among others. Those programmes, normally delivered on-site after working hours and partly through online systems, have found a ready market, especially among the working population. Focused marketing strategies and comprehensive support services are a hallmark of many of the private HEIs.

In this regard, it should be borne in mind that the Caribbean and its HEIs are attractive partners for international counterparts that are seeking to conclude partnerships. In addition to their proximity to the Americas and to EU overseas territories, they enjoy historical links to EU member states, Asia and Africa. The diversity of intellectual activities, including interdisciplinary research related to Small Island Developing States (SIDS) and the experience of HEIs in obtaining external funding and of working in consortia, attracts both international students and research partners. Despite these advantages, a comprehensive marketing thrust is required to emphasize the strengths of the higher education sector and to help position it more successfully in the international education community.

4.1 Maximizing the Use of ICTs to Create Market Demand: A Case Study of the UWI Open Campus

The innovative approaches of HEIs include the offering of programmes through distance modalities to facilitate access by external populations (Hosein et al., 2004). In this regard, a significant agent in the strategy of internationalization of the UWI is the Open Campus (OC), which was established in 2008 to expand services in multi-mode teaching and learning from both physical and virtual sites in the 17 contributing countries of the UWI. Its student population totals 5,500, constituting approximately 10% of the UWI student population, and ICT is the primary tool in reaching them (UWI, n.d.b).

Building on the expertise of the UWI in matters relating to the Caribbean and the interest in Caribbean Cultural Studies shown by scholars from international HEIs and maximizing the use of its state-of-the art ICT infrastructure, the OC proposes to develop new programmes in response to overseas demand for Caribbean Studies. It expects to expand its services to other territories in the Caribbean that are not members of the UWI as well as to Latin America, Asia and Africa by leveraging existing partnerships with HEIs in these regions for the delivery of new programmes. Among other things, it intends to promote joint teaching and research, student exchange and training and share technical and administrative expertise.

The possibility of establishing a physical presence overseas is also under consideration. The concentration of a considerable proportion of the Caribbean diaspora in North America and the United Kingdom makes these locations the most desirable for this initiative. As a first step, the OC is contemplating providing services in the New York area to individuals with Caribbean antecedents and links. It will employ the UWI Single Virtual University Space, which provides a seamless environment that uses technology, to coordinate the resources of all campuses to facilitate programme delivery. In order to encourage greater interest in its online programmes, the OC is also considering the design of a Massive Online Open Course (MOOC) on the Caribbean. In essence, the UWI is making maximum use of technology to meet international standards, enter new markets and engender demand for programmes in which it enjoys a strong reputation.

5 Partnerships and Collaboration

International partnerships and collaborations that provide added value form the core of the internationalization strategy of many HEIs. Some of the selection criteria that guide HEIs include the following:

- Potential partner HEIs must be recognized as leaders with a track record of achievement in research;
- They should be based in countries where funding is available to promote partnerships, joint research and student mobility;
- Their policies for collaboration, including student mobility, and administrative support systems must be geared to supporting institutional collaboration; and
- Agreements must be clear and targets capable of being achieved.

Cuban HEIs, for instance, have established relationships with universities in Latin America, Canada and Europe, among others, particularly since the 1990s, in response to changing geopolitical conditions. They have joined international networks, such as the Ibero-American Programme of Science and Technology for Development (CYTED), the Latin America Academic Training (ALFA) programme and INCO-DEV, a sub-programme of the Research and Development Framework Programme of the European Union. Apart from enhancing their participation in the international research community, such activities have helped build postgraduate capacity (Perez, 2005).

The priority for the Université des Antilles that serves Martinique and Guadeloupe is the identification of strategically important partners for long-term relationships, including cooperation in research and joint programmes, staff and student mobility as well as participation in associations of higher education. On the other hand, the University of Belize participates in international consortia that facilitate access to resources for capacity building in areas such as curriculum development, administrative training, scholarships and joint programmes, among others. The strategy of the Arthur Lok Jack Graduate School of Business in Trinidad and Tobago (affiliated to UWI) is based on collaborative research, student exchange and the delivery of executive education. It is currently working with partners in Central America to deliver executive education programmes in several countries in that sub-region (UWI, n.d.a).

5.1 Partnerships as a Strategic Tool: The Example of the UWI

The University of the West Indies, which was established in 1948 under the tutelage of the University of London, has built on the experience of that foundational relationship to craft partnerships with international HEIs, participate actively in research consortia and attract international students. Its *Strategic Plan 2012–2017*, which has identified Outreach as one of seven priorities, calls for the UWI to be, by 2017, "a regionally integrated, innovative, internationally competitive university, deeply rooted in all aspects of Caribbean development and committed to serving the diverse people of the region and beyond" (UWI, 2012). Consequently, the UWI has reinforced its administrative infrastructure by establishing the Office of the Pro Vice-Chancellor for Global Affairs and the Central Office for Regional and International Affairs. Their responsibilities encompass strengthening and managing relationships with external institutions, including HEIs and education organizations, as well as regional and international funding agencies, in order to attract support for major research and other capacity-building projects. Campus International Offices are responsible for specific Campus internationalization strategies, especially student mobility.

Perhaps the most significant aspect of the internationalization strategy of the UWI is the expansion in the number of research partnerships. During the last decade, more than 100 partnerships have been established with other HEIs and research institutions on all continents, an initiative that has raised the profile of the UWI in the international research community, especially on matters relating to SIDS. This strategy also embraces alliances with other Caribbean HEIs that are designed to help them build their own research capacity and several of the latter have been included as partners in UWI proposals for external funding. Both Central and Campus research offices play a vital role in overseeing resource mobilization and research management.

As part of its thrust to strengthen research in the region as a prelude to increasing regional participation in international research projects, the UWI is spearheading the effort to create a multinational Caribbean Research and Innovation Funding Agency to facilitate collaboration among HEIs in Spanish-, English-, Dutch- and French-speaking territories. This agency is expected to extend the capacity of HEIs to carry out groundbreaking research relevant to the Caribbean as well as to support innovation. By strengthening regional research output that will help lead to greater collaboration with international partners, the agency will increase the research capacity of HEIs, thus assisting them in participating effectively in international consortia.

6 Mobility Initiatives

Mobility programmes, especially those funded by international development agencies, which enable students from the region to spend time at HEIs in other regions and vice versa, are another noteworthy component of the internationalization strategy of HEIs and are particularly important given the dearth of such support at the national level. They include, among others, the Caribbean–Pacific Island Mobility Scheme (CARPIMS, n.d.) for staff and students that, based on its emphasis on research and postgraduate education, is designed to increase capacity in Caribbean and Pacific countries. The ANGLE (Academic Networking, a Gate for Learning Experiences, n.d.) and DREAM (Dynamizing Research and Education for All through Mobility in ACP, n.d.) programmes have also expanded the opportunities available for mobility. HEIs also intend to continue taking advantage of similar EU programmes including Erasmus+ (European Commission, 2015).

In addition to participating in the design and implementation of mobility programmes, Caribbean HEIs have established internal support systems to help prepare students for the selection process of highly competitive international mobility programmes. These include the Commonwealth Scholarships, Rhodes Scholarships, Fulbright Awards, Organization of American States (OAS) Awards and the Emerging Leaders of the Americas Programme, funded by the Government of Canada, that enables staff and researchers to gain access to expertise and facilities not available in their own institution (Government of Canada, n.d.).

7 New Horizons: HEIs and the Wider World

While Europe and North America have traditionally been the focus of attention for student mobility and research partnerships, changing international geopolitical and economic realities, as well as a growing recognition of the value of relationships with counterparts in regions offering new opportunities for growth and development, have caused HEIs to look further afield, especially where they can leverage historical and cultural links. The proximity of Latin America, the increasing interest shown by Asian countries in the region, awareness of the growing potential of the African continent as well as the size of the diasporic populations in North America and Europe, among other things, have alerted HEIs to significant opportunities for greater student mobility and research partnerships.

7.1 The UWI: Maximizing the Impact of International Relationships

The UWI has reinforced existing, and created new, links with Asia. Its longstanding relationships with Indian HEIs build on historical, population and linguistic links between the Caribbean and the subcontinent. For many years, the government of India has provided support for academic posts, especially in Indian history and Hindi and, more recently, Ayurvedic medicine. It also offers scholarships for the study of music, film, history and Hindi, among other subjects, at Indian HEIs. A renewed effort on strengthening this relationship is expected to result in stronger research and mobility partnerships with HEIs in this emerging Asian economic power.

In light of the growing presence of China in the Caribbean, efforts to establish relationships with Chinese HEIs are being pursued energetically, especially in the areas of research and capacity development. Of particular note is the agreement between the UWI, the Chongqing College of Humanities, Science and Technology and Suzhou Global University of Software Technology for the establishment of the Suzhou UWI Global University. This is intended to strengthen the UWI presence in China and create the Suzhou UWI Global Institute for Software Technology. In addition to encouraging research, this initiative will contribute to national and regional capacity building in areas that are important for long-term development. In another strategic move, the UWI is collaborating with the China Agricultural University in a major agriculture project in Trinidad and Tobago. Confucius Institutes that provide instruction in Chinese language and culture, to prepare students to respond effectively to opportunities provided by growing links with China, have been established on the UWI Campuses in Barbados, Jamaica and Trinidad and Tobago.

Given the proximity of Latin America and the long tradition of staff and student mobility with the Caribbean, the strengthening of relationships with HEIs in that region, especially through increased levels of staff and student mobility as well as joint research projects, is a priority. This initiative is linked to the wider engagement between HEIs in Latin America and the Caribbean and the EU and, in this connection, the UWI brings to bear its long experience of relations with EU HEIs and EU funding programmes. The teaching of English as a Second Language is an area in which a number of Caribbean HEIs have leveraged their geographic position and historical links to meet the demand from non-English-speaking countries for competitively priced language programmes.

8 Obstacles to the Implementation of Long-Term Internationalization Strategies

While offshore private HEIs recruit considerable numbers of international students, most public HEIs have not been as successful, partly because their marketing strategies are not as focused and their student support systems not as comprehensive. Moreover, while many public HEIs have enunciated internationalization strategies that include international student recruitment, participation in mobility programmes and research partnerships, they do not always recognize the importance of ensuring synergies with other strategic priorities or of mainstreaming those strategies. The degree of priority to be afforded to the various components of those strategies is not always appreciated.

Offices responsible for internationalization may not be funded at the level essential to achieve the maximum level of results or staffed with the requisite numbers of professionally trained individuals or those who can operate with the appropriate level of authority. In times of financial stringency, especially when pressures exist for an emphasis on the core business of teaching, internationalization strategies do not necessarily receive the required prominence. Furthermore, the dependence on external sources of support for student mobility and research, which may not be available when needed, is a matter for concern given limited national and regional support for activities of this nature.

9 Conclusion

The internationalization of higher education in the Caribbean is based on a conventional approach aimed at strengthening institutional capacity including research, attracting international students to read subjects in high demand and sending local students overseas to take advantage of opportunities and state-of-the art facilities that are not available at home. Given that the history and culture of the Caribbean have been influenced largely by Europe and North America, it is not surprising that internationalization strategies adhere to the practice in those regions.

Public HEIs have come to appreciate that a focused strategy, based on meeting national and regional priorities and strengthening their international culture, is required to maximize the opportunities available through international higher education. Their emphasis on strengthening research as well as research management capacity and of seeking external funds to underwrite that research has increased national and regional awareness of the significance of research and its impact on economic and social development. On the other hand, private HEIs have been able to attract significant numbers of international students by offering competitive professional programmes, implementing a comprehensive marketing strategy and providing robust student support services, and have had a significant economic impact in the territories in which they are domiciled.

The UWI has taken full advantage of its regional mandate and presence, its long-standing international reputation and relationships and its ties of population and culture to several regions that are growing in geopolitical importance to position itself as a significant actor in creating partnerships with leading HEIs and in attracting international students. The establishment of partnerships is designed to strengthen its research capacity to enable it to participate successfully in the international research sphere. It is also maximizing the use of ICTs to reach new constituents and respond to new demands. It has taken a conscious decision to strengthen its administrative infrastructure to achieve these goals.

Despite these positive developments, internationalization efforts continue to be ad hoc and take place mainly at the national level, thereby circumscribing their impact. A comprehensive, regional approach that focuses and deploys limited resources effectively, that is based on attracting greater numbers of international students in subject areas in which public HEIs have a good reputation and that leverages the results of research and the considerable technical expertise of HEIs, will strengthen the reputation of the region in the international higher education sphere and enable it to forge its peculiar brand of internationalization.

Chapter 9

Internationalization of Universities in the Peripheries

Manja Klemenčič

I Introduction

There are countries that are considered centres of civilizational and economic attraction. These 'centres' typically possess a combination of favourable living and working conditions such as a high standard of living, political stability, personal freedom, safety and security, being inclusive, taking care of their environment, nurturing arts and culture, making significant public investments in education and health, promoting entrepreneurship and possibly even being blessed with a pleasant climate. There are also 'centres' within countries: for example, capital cities tend to draw in people from other regions. What makes a particular country, region or city attractive to non-locals lies, of course, in the eye of the beholder. Hall and Lamont define a 'successful society' as 'one that enhances the capabilities of people to pursue the goals important to their own lives, whether through individual or collective action' (Hall & Lamont, 2009, p. 2). Different people value different issues and measures of prosperity and attractiveness. Students tend to be attracted to 'centres' in search of a good education and employment opportunities thereafter. Also, the language makes certain countries, especially English-speaking locations, more attractive than equally or even more 'successful' societies of, say, Northern Europe or Japan.

There are other countries that do not have this combination of favourable living and working conditions and are thus less attractive for immigration. These might be called 'peripheries', places with a less flattering depiction of wellbeing for their own citizens and, therefore, less attractive to non-citizens. These may relate to economic downturn, poverty, armed conflicts, income inequality, undermined personal freedoms, intolerance, low educational opportunities and so on. In peripheries, emigration is widespread; more people move away than move in. Of course, given the complexity of personal aspiration, no objective division of countries into centres and peripheries exists, with most countries drawing people in from less-developed or poorer countries.

The attractiveness of countries, regions or cities where universities are located certainly plays a role in institutional capacity to attract talented students, academic staff, researchers and higher education professionals, especially from abroad. Studies exploring the attractiveness of universities to foreign students reveal that higher education system conditions and broader social, economic and political conditions play an important role in attracting foreign talent (Kolster, 2014). In the models that try to explain why students migrate, study abroad decisions are presented as a series of 'push and pull factors', among which host country reputation is one important pull and, conversely, economic and social conditions at home can present significant push factors (Mazzarol & Soutar, 2002). While broad macroeconomic, social and political conditions are difficult to control in raising the attractiveness of study locations, more feasible options exist through collaboration for cities and universities to attract foreign students and researchers (for examples, see van Winden, 2014). In short, collaboration between universities and cities, along with favourable policy interventions from governments, can resolve the predicaments of peripheral locations with regard to internationalization.

This chapter addresses the imperatives for and the approaches to internationalization of universities in peripheral locations. The first section sets the scene by rehearsing the imperatives that exist for all universities, but are magnified in the case of institutions in peripheral locations. The following two sections discuss the approaches to internationalization of universities in peripheral locations from two perspectives. The first focuses on institutional approaches to internationalization and highlights the four 'internationalization gears' (Klemenčič, 2015): international profiling, international institutional cooperation, international mobility and international recruitment. These gear functions help strengthen internationalization of the core functions, teaching, research and third mission. The second perspective considers university collaboration with the cities and regions in which they are located, and the need for these to jointly develop an integrated approach to internationalization. The key message being that universities, cities and regions (and national governments) all have a stake in developing an internationalized environment attractive to foreign talent, and so need to collaborate to achieve this. The chapter concludes with a discussion on the role of national governments and the challenges to internationalization of universities in peripheral locations.

2 Imperatives for Internationalization

The internationalization of higher education is important for all countries and regions and an increasing number of national governments develop national internationalization strategies, in addition to the strategies of universities (de Wit et al., 2015). Internationalization is recognized as a proxy for quality. Attracting foreign students, researchers and teaching staff increases selectivity and contributes to the quality of teaching and research. Such concentration of talent lends prestige to the institutions, national systems and communities where they are located. It also helps to re-reproduce prestige, because talent attracts more talent and, in turn, financial resources (for example, by attracting fee-paying students). Involvement in global knowledge networks enhances the quality of research and knowledge-transfer capacity. Talent also feeds social development and economic growth through knowledge exchange (Pinheiro et al., 2015). In other words, internationalization of universities can have a spillover effect on other sectors.

In pursuit of internationalization, universities in the centres tend to have certain advantages over those in the periphery. Since societies in the centres tend to be more internationally diverse, this is reflected in more internationally diverse students and staff, whereas institutions in the periphery must work purposefully to achieve this. International knowledge networks may also be rare or less well-developed in peripheral locations. Talent is drawn to more prosperous locations with better prospects for jobs, higher earnings and other aspects contributing to individual wellbeing. The chances are that more capable people will be recruited if the selection draws in international candidates. Institutions in peripheral locations need to put a lot more effort into international branding to attract foreign talent. They cannot build their internationalization strategy on the attractiveness of their country or region if it is not a realistic selling-point.

In sum, for universities in peripheral locations, the imperatives for internationalization are magnified by the limited 'organic' intake of talent and the high salience of international networks and graduates with international competences to aid economic development and growth. As Scott (1998, p. 122) suggests, 'not all universities are (particularly) international, but all are subject to the same process of globalisation – partly as objects, victims even, of these processes, but partly as subjects, or key agents, of globalisation'. For institutions in peripheral locations, a deliberate internationalization strategy is indeed a necessary ingredient of their own modernization and institutional capacity building (Klemenčič & Zgaga, 2013), and the same imperative holds for national internationalization strategies by national governments (de Wit et al., 2015). At the same time, universities are key public institutions to drive internationalization in the society and economy in which they are embedded. With mobility programmes they enable students and staff to network internationally and develop international social capital. Helping students develop international competences (including foreign-language skills) prepares them for international engagements once employed, and so forth. While universities in peripheral locations cannot rely on the attractiveness of their countries to boost international activities, they have the potential, and indeed responsibility, to support internationalization of other economic, governmental and non-governmental sectors in their region and country. These institutions need to be 'reinventing their management structures and institutional systems in ways that place internationalisation as a key strategic priority' (Gao et al., 2015, p. 301).

3 Developing an Integrated Institutional Approach to Internationalization

In practice, one finds great diversity in institutional approaches to internationalization with, as de Wit (2013a) states, no single model that fits all, since both external and internal context needs to frame the appropriate approach. This chapter focuses on peripheral location as one of the key conditions influencing institutional approaches to internationalization and explicates characteristics that work for institutions in such locations.

Institutional approaches to internationalization range from simply add-on, marginal activity to others where internationalization is central to institutional existence, guided by a comprehensive process that permeates all aspects of institutional operations and functions (de Wit, 2002). In this respect institutions go through several stages of maturity in internationalization functions. Many authors have argued in favour of an integrated institutional approach as being the most developed (e.g. Knight, 2008b; Middlehurst, 2009; Taylor, 2010; Jones, 2013b). The more internationalization is integrated across institutional structures, processes and operations, the more likely synergistic effects of activities and processes will follow.

Such synergistic effects are especially called for in peripheral university locations because of the imperatives described above. To achieve this, 'internationalization gears' need to be developed as part of the internationalization strategy. These have been identified as *international profiling, international institutional cooperation, international mobility* and *international recruitment* (Klemenčič, 2015). In machines, gears are used for transmitting power from one part of a machine to another. In universities, these internationalization gears create more power or speed within core functions of teaching, research and third mission. For institutions in peripheral locations, the four gear functions of internationalization are paramount in light of limited resources and limited international visibility of their locations; yet their development depends greatly on institutional climate and higher education system conditions and whether these enable and support internationalization.

Profiling means that universities focus on their relative strengths and use investment, reorganization of existing resources and cooperation strategies to foster excellence and competitive advantages in selected areas of teaching, research and third mission. International profiling implies international orientation in selecting flagship study or research areas of knowledge-transfer programmes around which they build global recognition. Profiling is directly linked to institutional positioning, the process through which institutions locate themselves in specific niches and develop specific relationships within the higher education markets (Fumasoli & Huisman, 2013). In an era of globalization, both institutional profiling and institutional positioning are necessarily international. As flagships those programmes are selected that are world leading or show potential for comparative advantages in international contexts. Similarly, institutional positioning strategies target niches and relationships in international higher education markets. Consequently, international profiling and positioning strategies require sharpening distinctions between various international engagements and choosing those engagements that help strengthen the international profile of the selected flagship programmes. In turn, these programmes help build the international visibility of the entire university.

Higher education system conditions enabling of internationalization

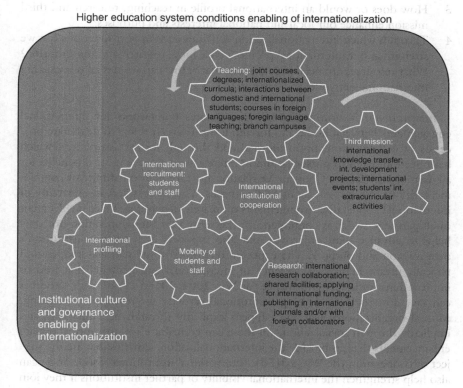

Figure 9.1 **The effect of internationalization gears.**
(Source: Klemenčič, 2015).

International profiling is challenging due to competing views within the institutions themselves (and in discussions with their funding bodies) on which areas of core functions to privilege with more resources and which to cut back. The least contentious decisions are those where additional external funding is obtained to boost flagship programmes. More frequently, however, profiling involves some rationalizing measures, cutting the cost of less well-performing programmes by closing them down, reducing them or reorganizing programmes through mergers. These decisions are politically difficult, especially in universities governed by principles of collegiate consensus. The following are some possible questions to guide decisions on international profiling:

1   What are our areas of strength, our international competitive advantages or areas of international visibility?
2   In which areas would we like to develop international competitiveness and visibility?

3   How does or would an international profile in teaching, research and third mission enhance our local and national interests and purposes?

4   Through which internationalization activities and support functions can we strengthen our international profiles in teaching, research and third mission? What resources are needed to achieve that? How can we utilize our existing international networks and partners?

International institutional cooperation creates frameworks for international engagements between home and foreign institutions. It refers to deliberate processes of collaboration, both informal and through formal association, which have been initiated to pursue common interests and achieve mutual benefits for all partner institutions. Cooperative relationships are built on affinity or complementarity of interests, missions and purposes. The success and sustainability of international cooperative arrangements ultimately depend on active involvement of all partners, which is contingent on the sense that the cooperation not only helps to advance joint objectives, but also supports each partner institution's own mission and purpose. The expected outcome of international cooperation typically means improved efficiency of international engagements that lead to improved institutional performance (de Wit, 2004, 2015d). Pooling of resources can save costs or help develop institutional capacity for research or teaching. Mutual organizational learning happens explicitly through benchmarking and implicitly through socialization. All these can contribute to institutional quality enhancements that go beyond the internationalization activities that are the subject of cooperation (de Wit, 2015d). International institutional cooperation can also help strengthen the international visibility of partner institutions if they join their activities in branding and international positioning.

For cooperation it is not necessary that all partner institutions have the same capacities, in the sense of resources or reputational capital. However, asymmetry in resources or reputation decisively impacts the purposes and the terms of cooperation. For example, if a world-class university in a developed economy forms an international partnership with a flagship university in a periphery location, which does not rank highly in global league tables, it can be expected that international development will be a part – if not the overarching framework – of such cooperation. International development implies that partner institutions have complementary purposes, yet expect different outcomes from and have different objectives in the partnership. The less-developed partners seek capacity building and access to international knowledge networks via their partners from more advanced countries. Those from developed countries seek access to indigenous knowledge and indigenous social networks. Again, both partners benefit, but the benefits are different. When two world-class universities of a similar reputational standing and resources build a partnership, they do so out of complementary purposes and objectives, such as to make teaching more international through joint study programmes, or to create a joint research centre. The objectives are the same and the partnership helps both institutions advance mutual interests, even with potentially competing institutions.

Decisions on institutional cooperation are complex and demanding. The following are some possible questions that can guide such decisions:

1   Why should we develop institutional cooperation and what can we gain from it? What can we offer partners? What are the potential risks of such cooperative arrangements?
2   Who can be our preferred partners? Who can help us develop? Whom can we help develop? With whom do we have an affinity or common interests, mission and purposes?
3   What type of international cooperative arrangement in terms of scope and depth makes most sense for us?
4   How much will such an arrangement cost? What and how many resources will we need to invest in the cooperation?

For institutions in peripheral locations, regional cooperation is a particularly desirable option, since it potentially helps strengthen regional relevance of the partner institutions and their collective international status and visibility. Regional cooperation refers specifically to cooperation built among universities in neighbouring countries and/or within the same region within a country. Universities in peripheral countries may not be the most desired international partners of institutions in the educational hot spots, but they are often preferred partners to other institutions in the peripheral neighbouring countries. Indeed, geographical proximity and cultural closeness are important factors in formation of partnerships in all sectors, including higher education (Klemenčič & Zgaga, 2013).

Regional cooperation among institutions from peripheral countries can successfully combine the logic of cooperation and competition to raise visibility and build higher education capacity in the region, yet it is also subject to tensions similar to those in other international institutional cooperation arrangements. On the one hand, regional partners cooperate to promote the visibility and attractiveness of their region and enhance the quality of educational provision. Jointly, they can be more successful in attracting research funding and can pool resources in collaborative research. Through cooperation they benchmark, enhance understanding of each institution and experience social and organizational learning. On the other hand, regional partners (like those in any other international cooperative arrangement) inevitably also compete against each other to attract talent and resources. Geographic proximity and cultural similarities may create even fiercer competition between regional partners than in other international partnerships. In addition to the questions listed above, the following are some possible questions that can guide specifically decisions on regional institutional cooperation:

5   What are the specific regional interests we have in common and how can advancing those interests help us advance our national and local interests?
6   In which areas do our institutions directly compete and how can we offset potential conflicts of interest?

Mobility of students and staff members helps these crucial actors develop international competences and social networks abroad and are important drivers of internationalization within their home institutions. International competences not only benefit the individuals on a personal level, but also contribute to furthering the internationalization objectives of their institution. Studies on the impact of the Erasmus+ Programme on university internationalization show, for example, that returning Erasmus students can contribute to the internationalization of teaching and that mobile staff are more willing and able to support student exchanges (Klemenčič & Flander, 2014).

International recruitment of talent, including students, academics, research and professional staff, is both essential for boosting internationalization activities of universities and contributing to institutional quality. International candidates bring with them knowledge, cultural and social capital and former institutional associations that can boost international engagements.

In sum, the internationalization gears described above help offset the natural disadvantages of universities that are located in the periphery and should be part of an integrated approach to internationalization, desirable for every university, but imperative for institutions in peripheral locations. The four internationalization gears help bring speed or power to internationalization activities within core institutional functions, especially teaching and research.

4 Universities Working with Cities and Regions and National Government towards Integrated Municipal, Regional and National Approaches to Internationalization

In this section, a proposition is made that the integrated institutional approach described above using 'internationalization gears' should be developed as part of a broader city or regional and national approach to internationalization. In other words, at the same time as developing their own internationalization strategy, universities should reach out to city, regional and national governments to collaboratively work towards enhancing internationalization. This section looks specifically into the third mission of universities and how universities, with city and regional partners, can jointly further internationalization. The role of government is addressed in the Conclusion.

In analysing joint efforts between universities and cities to co-create more attractive cities, van Winden (2014, p. 3) makes a convincing observation:

> Both city and university have a stake in developing an 'attractive city' ...
> For a university, the attractiveness and quality of life of the host city matters: it affects their current students and staff, and being in a more attractive city helps the university to attract the best mobile (foreign) students and researchers. For the city government, enhancing attractiveness is a core business, because it is a key factor in attracting (and keeping) higher educated inhabitants, knowledge based companies, tourists and investors. The

university is a key asset in this respect: it is a magnet for young, dynamic and talented young people, and increasingly also for companies. The university is also a source of cultural, social, intellectual and political life in the city ... Student life has become part of a marketable urban lifestyle brand.

The literature on cooperation between universities, cities and regions is part of two larger and interlinked discussions. One is on the social mission and public role of the university and its academic inhabitants, which falls into the literature on universities' third mission (for an overview, see Pinheiro et al., 2015). The other revolves around development of innovation systems as part of the knowledge economy and knowledge society discourse (Cooke, 2001). In both discussions, universities feature as one of the key knowledge producers, which are in globalized network society 'increasingly interconnected and interdependent with a variety of external constituencies at the local, national and international levels' (Pinheiro et al., 2015, p. 235).

This situation calls for expanded university–community partnerships as well as for increased cooperation between universities, government and industry through a 'triple-helix' association (Watermeyer, 2015). The third mission engagements vary between social (such as open public lectures, public events in promotion of science, arts, literature, innovation, opening classrooms to pupils from schools, etc.) and economic (knowledge transfer via commissioned research, spin-offs, the use of research facilities, consultancies, etc.) (Pinheiro et al., 2015). In a similar vein as the collaboration between cities and universities has been advocated to build regional innovation systems, such collaboration can also pursue internationalization objectives. Universities could be guided by some of the following questions:

1   How can campus and urban life be connected to make the city more attractive for students and knowledge workers? For example, what is needed in urban planning, use of public space and collaboration between different public and private institutions to strengthen internationalization of the city and its universities?
2   How can universities' and cities' (or regions' or countries') internationalization objectives, approaches and measures be connected or integrated to achieve synergistic effects on the internationalization of entire communities? Where are the mutual or complementary interests and possibilities for pooling resources or joining efforts?
3   Who are the key persons within universities, city and local governments and other institutions – businesses and non-profit organizations – who can develop and monitor implementation of a common approach to internationalization?
4   What, if any, governing structures or institutions are needed to facilitate development and implementation of an integrated city, regional or national approach to internationalization?
5   How can international orientation be developed in the social aspects of universities' third mission?

6   How can international orientation be developed in the economic aspects, knowledge transfer, of universities' third mission?

The key is for internationalization efforts of each individual societal actor within a given community to be connected to and integrated with others to reinforce each other's efforts and support those lagging behind. The expectation of spillovers is based on the logic of diffusion of ideas and knowledge in a public space: internationalization practices seen as advantageous for performance are imitated by others prompted by competitive pressures (imitation among same-sector institutions) or the pursuit of creativity and innovation (among institutions from different sectors). Internationalization practices here mean any activities conducted as internationalization gears, mentioned above, or within core university functions.

Horizontal spillovers lead to capacity building through imitation among different sector institutions within the same community (city, region or nation). Note that social learning was discussed above as one of the intended or accompanying outcomes of international engagements between two or more partner institutions. Such social learning can also lead to imitation of internationalization practices and qualifies as *vertical spillovers*, that is, between partner institutions engaged in international cooperation. There is a clear difference between horizontal and vertical spillovers. Vertical spillovers can be an intended outcome of internationalization and are to some degree always an accompanying effect of international engagements. Horizontal spillovers, however, typically occur due to competition unless facilitated, as advocated here, by a deliberate effort to create an integrated and collaborative approach to internationalization among several social partners within the same city, region or country.

5   Conclusion

There are cities and regions within countries or countries themselves that are considered 'centres' of civilizational and economic attraction, and other places less attractive to non-citizens, considered as 'peripheries'. Universities in the centres have a natural advantage and a better starting point to internationalize; their countries or central regions attract talent, which attracts more talent and in turn financial resources. Lacking these natural advantages, institutions in peripheral locations need deliberate internationalization strategies. This chapter advocates an integrated institutional approach to internationalization that rests on four internationalization gears. Furthermore, universities in peripheral locations need to collaborate with cities, regions and national governments to strengthen the internationalization of their entire communities and achieve knowledge and idea spillovers in internationalization.

In universities, it is the academics, researchers and students who initiate international engagements in alignment with their intrinsic academic and professional interests. Institutional leadership and administration needs to create an enabling and supportive environment for internationalization, with objectives that reinforce institutional purposes and mission, connected to and integrated with the internationalization objectives and efforts of cities, regions and the country in which they are embedded. Finally, the government has to support universities and other societal actors in their efforts to internationalize and to gain international visibility.

Government legal, policy, regulatory and financial frameworks can have a significant effect on institutional internationalization behaviour. Governments face the difficult policy challenge of either concentrating resources in a few world-class universities (centres of excellence) or trying to pursue a world-class system of quality across the entire higher education system (van der Wende, 2001) along with regional development. Internationalization can be seen as a key driver to achieve either objective, but the internationalization strategy plays out differently in each case. In the case of selected world-class universities, internationalization focuses on research collaboration and recruitment of foreign staff and student talent for positional advantage (Marginson, 2006). For a world-class system, internationalization of study at home, international mobility and institutional cooperation are also emphasized.

Faced with the imperatives of internationalization, universities in peripheral locations, like those elsewhere, experience tension between competing in global league tables and maintaining national relevance and national character (Marginson, 2011; Douglass, 2016). Yet, for universities in peripheral locations, the choices they make are even more significant. By imitating world-class universities, they risk losing sight of local and national educational needs and priorities (Marginson, 2011; Douglass, 2016). For them, the internationalization of higher education is often associated with modernization, or catching up with more internationalized peers in more developed higher education hubs. This sense of catching up is precisely the one that can prompt universities into uncritical imitation, thus losing sight of activities that are more meaningful and relevant to the needs and demands of those societies that gave them life and purpose (Douglass, 2016). Finally, universities in peripheries are also susceptible to misconceptions about internationalization, including striving for too many agreements, teaching in English and seeing internationalization as a goal in itself instead of as an instrument to increase the quality of teaching, research and service to society (de Wit, 2011).

Chapter 10

Regional Partnership and Integration

Key to the Improvement of Internationalization
of Higher Education in Latin America

Carlos Alberto Vigil Taquechel

Internationalization has become a kind of mantra for the higher education (HE) sector. This trend has increasingly strengthened globally and there is almost no rector or university leader who does not openly defend the importance of internationalization. However, it is one thing to utter politically correct speech about internationalization and quite another to work on it consistently.

What is the positioning of Latin American universities in the current international context of higher education? While other regions and countries are widely represented in the main international HE rankings, only a few Latin American universities are referenced, almost always at the bottom of the lists. Furthermore, none of its main higher education institutions (HEIs) are considered world-class universities. These are irrefutable facts but they are not reasons in themselves for worry. League tables and global reputation labels should not be the indicators for measuring Latin American universities' quality and pertinence. The region has to identify new internationalization paradigms that aim to ensure critical contribution of HEIs to the main development issues.

Unfortunately, other facts have to be added to this scenario. When compared to other regions, especially those representing developed and emerging economies, Latin America appears significantly behindhand in terms of grade, dimension, quality and maturity of internationalization processes. Based on this comparative lag of key internationalization indicators, it must be recognized, with some regret, that Latin America's positioning in the growing and competitive market of international higher education is still very poor.

This chapter analyses some of the main barriers that hamper HE internationalization and integration in the region and proposes some initiatives that can be implemented with the aim to palliate the lack of policies and the deficient organizational structures at the institutional level.

Organizational and Structural Hurdles for Internationalization

Latin America exhibits a wide variety of universities. Even within the same country, universities differ greatly with regard to their strategies, policies, approaches and missions. This level of heterogeneity is also found when organizational structures, procedures and cultures associated with the management of international processes are analysed. However, there is also a number of common realities that can be classified as general characteristics and that reveal the weaknesses of a large segment of HEIs in the region. An overview of some of the most relevant characteristics is provided below:

- Tendency for highly bureaucratic university governance bodies, with autocratic centralized models, which constitute a great barrier to the engagement of university communities in international initiatives.
- Lack of internationalization strategies. International actions are conducted through passive/reactive management models mainly focused on academic mobility. University comprehensive approaches for internationalization are unusual.
- Financial constraints deeply associated with the lack of internationalization strategies. Many of the region's universities do not have their own budget for implementing international actions, which leads to an enormous dependency on external funding programmes.
- Wide disparities and significant gaps in the internationalization processes for conducting education, research and innovation. Collaboration with local governments and industries for internationalization purposes is minimal.
- Most of the HEIs manage international activities through traditional and obsolete models of international relations offices (IRO). In general, these units have precarious structures, with very limited human resources and significant financial and infrastructural constraints in operation. In addition, as referred by Gacel-Ávila (2012, p. 503), "senior international officers, as well as staff are subject to a high turnover produced by the recurrent changes in institutional management, which is a trait of Latin American Institutions".
- In many cases, the level of professionalization (expressed as the professional capacity, qualification, group of skills or level of specialization to properly conduct the international strategy of the organization) of IRO staff is low (Gacel-Ávila, 2012). This reinforces the lack of autonomy of these units in the internationalization decision-making process.

Obviously, there are more components that hinder the progress of internationalization in Latin America. In general, a lot of other key barriers are found in most of the countries and HEIs. Some such hurdles include language skills of faculty members, staff and students and the official recognition or approval of study plans, degrees, diplomas or credits obtained abroad. Also, a lot of work needs to be done to better adapt curricula to the requirements of the labour market and make it more flexible. Governments should also adopt legislation with more flexible immigration policies and promote incentive policies to attract students and young scientists from other countries and regions.

Another very important obstacle refers to the policy for hiring foreign academics and researchers to integrate them as faculty members. Most Latin American HEIs face legal and financial constraints to hire personnel abroad. However, a procedure that favours the hiring of foreign academics, researchers and staff is essential to reduce the high rate of endogamy that seems to be a common characteristic in a large number of regional universities. As has been recognized in previous studies, the "universities that rely principally on their own undergraduates to continue into graduate programs or that hire principally their own graduates to join the teaching staff are not likely to be at the leading edge of intellectual development" (Salmi, 2009, p. 21). There is, therefore, an inverse correlation between endogamy and teaching and research performances, which is the same as saying that internationalization is a cornerstone for improving university quality and enhancing academic and scientific indicators.

The above-mentioned components are also key drivers to foster the so-called "internationalization at home" approach, considered to be one of the most effective types of internationalization. This approach ensures an inclusive and less elitist internationalization as it has the potential to impact the whole university community and not only the small segment that can take advantage of mobility actions. Taking into account that Latin America is considered the most unequal region of the world as well as the one showing the poorest number of internationalization indicators, it is highly recommended that HEIs and governments embrace "internationalization of the curriculum at home" as one of the core components of their strategies for the improvement and development of higher education in the region. With the same purpose, Latin American universities should make better use of technologies in order to foster digital learning and online collaboration platforms as an effective way to ensure equal access to internationalization opportunities for the whole university community (Beelen & Jones, 2015a).

Regionalization: The Cornerstone for Successful Internationalization

As has been noted by Rumbley and Altbach (2015, p. 9), "a significant element of internationalisation is regionalisation". Latin America is particularly weak in this criterion if it is considered that a common strategy towards the strengthening of higher education remains a pending issue. The last edition of the global survey by the International Association of Universities (IAU) underlined this fact once again (Egron-Polak & Hudson, 2014b). While regional cooperation is prioritized in Europe, Asia and the Pacific and even Africa, Latin America sees it as more important to cooperate with Europe and North America, so relegating to a second level cooperation within its own regional HE space. This and other data addressed by the survey evidence the lack of integration, both at a national and regional level.

This has been a major concern for many sectors of Latin American higher education. In 2008, the declaration of the Regional Conference of Higher Education in Latin America and the Caribbean in Cartagena, Colombia (known as CRES) concluded by stressing the importance of regional integration as a key strategy for building a university model that could respond to the characteristics and needs of Latin American society. As a consequence, and inspired by the Bologna Process, the Latin American and Caribbean Higher Education Area (known as ENLACES) was created. This has been the most ambitious project of regional integration in the HE sector so far. Unfortunately, this initiative, developed with the aim of bringing together governments, associations, universities and a large sector of the Latin American university community in the pursuit of common goals, has not found very fertile ground to succeed.

The enormous institutional diversity, the large disparities and asymmetries among the national educational systems, the lack of financial and infrastructural resources, the lack of a real commitment by the national governments of the continent to promote a common regional agenda of higher education and the absence of a supranational institution that can properly articulate the work at a regional level, have all been obstacles impossible to overcome. It has to be mentioned that some initiatives have been developed recently with the leadership of two of the main regional associations (UDUAL and the Montevideo Group) to revitalize ENLACES (UDUAL, 2014). Nevertheless, considering its institutional representation, impact and scope, the outcomes are still very limited as regards making this initiative a feasible platform for regional integration in the field of higher education.

In order to reverse this damaging situation, Latin America cannot postpone any longer the launching of its own HE cooperation scheme. A programme is needed that will grow intraregional exchange of students, academics, researchers and staff with the aim of boosting an autochthonous academic and scientific cooperation framework, as Europe has done through Erasmus since the programme was launched in the mid-1980s. This seems to be a *sine qua non* condition to reinforce HE internationalization in the region in a relatively short period of time.

In this regard, there are many forums in which Latin American leaders have advocated and supported the need for and importance of higher education. The Organization of American States (OAS), the Organization of Ibero-American States (OEI), summits with leaders of the European Union and, more recently, the Community of Latin American and Caribbean States (CELAC) are just some of the most representative. In all these forums they have announced the launch of different initiatives to promote mobility as well as academic and scientific exchanges within the regional space. In addition, these scenarios have served as witnesses of statements and programmatic documents that could be roadmaps for driving higher education in the region, together with science, technology and innovation towards success. However, these attempts have failed over and again and only some progress with limited success has been capitalized upon so far. It is clear that very little can be done to move this area forward without the willingness and real political commitment of its leaders to invest seriously in the quality of universities and in the internationalization of higher education.

Among all these scenarios, the most significant progress in promoting regional academic and scientific exchange has occurred in the Ibero-American context through various programmes financed by the Spanish Agency for International Development Cooperation (AECID) or by private institutions such as Banco Santander. An increasingly dynamic role has been played by the Ibero-American General Secretariat (SEGIB), especially since 2014 when Rebeca Grynspan began her mandate. The Secretary General has made higher education, and especially the creation of an Alliance for Academic Mobility, one of the organization's priorities for the coming years. This alliance, led by SEGIB, implies the development of public–private partnerships for financing the 200,000 scholarships that the organization is expecting to implement up to 2020. With this purpose, it was announced that Banco Santander has already committed, but the involvement of a great number of institutions on the Latin American side will be necessary to achieve this goal (Marcos, 2015).

As stated in the recent study on internationalization of higher education conducted by a group of experts at the request of the European Parliament, internationalization is a very complex process, "driven by a dynamic and constantly evolving combination of political, economic, sociocultural and academic rationales" (de Wit et al., 2015, p. 273). The last decade was defined by prosperity and high rates of GDP growth in most of the economies in the region. This would have been the ideal period to invest and work in a concerted manner to promote actions that ensure more quality of its universities and a more significant presence of its national HE systems globally. Regrettably, this was not the case and with the new economic outlook characterized by modest growth rates and downward revisions in medium-term growth projections, the region will certainly find great barriers to giving higher education a leading role as a critical driver for the improvement of Latin American society.

While this happened at a regional level, some interesting experiences have taken place at the national level, with some countries carrying out initiatives that deserve recognition. Obviously, the Brazilian programme, Science without Borders, which rapidly emerged as one of the most significant government-funded mobility initiatives in the world, is the most renowned reference. Moreover, valuable initiatives have been undertaken in other Latin American countries such as Ecuador, Mexico, Colombia, Chile and Peru. However, a sign of the influence of the current economic situation is reflected in the slowing down or reduction of some of these programmes. Science without Borders itself shows the weaknesses and vulnerabilities of Latin American programmes. The current crisis in the Brazilian economy has seriously affected the programme due to substantial budget cuts introduced by the government for 2016 (ICEF Monitor, 2015b). In addition, it should be highlighted that a characteristic of most of these programmes is the financing of outbound mobility to universities in the United States, Canada and Europe. Their impact in reinforcing cooperation dynamics within the region has been minimal.

Innovative Partnerships for Internationalizing Higher Education Institutions

As noted in the above-mentioned study (de Wit et al., 2015), there is an evident shift from cooperation to competition in higher education. Nevertheless, Latin American HEIs should avoid such trends because trying to beat their counterparts from developed and bigger emerging economies in a dispute of global dimensions will probably be a very difficult enterprise. Taking that into consideration, it is practically an imperative that Latin American universities work together with the aim of finding their own innovative ways for internationalizing higher education.

Undoubtedly, the reinforcement of integration and partnership within national HE systems seems to be a very effective way of being competitive in this global contest. Nonetheless, the lack of will and agreements of regional governments to develop a common policy promoting HE internationalization at both national and regional levels, as well as the scarcity of funds available for financing internationalization actions, make integration and institutional cooperation in the sector more difficult to achieve for HEIs.

Consequently, universities in Latin America should not wait any longer for supranational solutions. They have to be capable of transforming the adversity of this environment into a fruitful scenario, adopting new and innovative initiatives that ensure implementation of the most appropriate and suitable modes for conducting their specific internationalization goals.

As most universities have major limitations in carrying out autonomous initiatives to promote internationalization, this situation seems to be an excellent opportunity to explore joint concerted actions, at national and regional levels. Such actions could foster the promotion of integration while significantly contributing to diversifying and multiplying the region's options globally.

Would not degree, masters and PhD programmes be more competitive and attractive if they were developed jointly by a number of universities in the region? Would there not be more impact if research projects were conducted by academics and scientists from different universities in the region? The University of Sao Paulo (USP), for instance, is considered the best Latin American university in the main rankings worldwide. The institution has reasons to rejoice in that fact, but it should not be satisfied with residual benefits left by world-class universities, especially if it can go further. Would not a collaborative framework with the State University of Campinas (UNICAMP) and the Sao Paulo State University (UNESP) make Sao Paulo a much more attractive and highly competitive academic and scientific hub? This is probably the most notable and illustrative example, but this simple formula based on the concentration of potentialities and

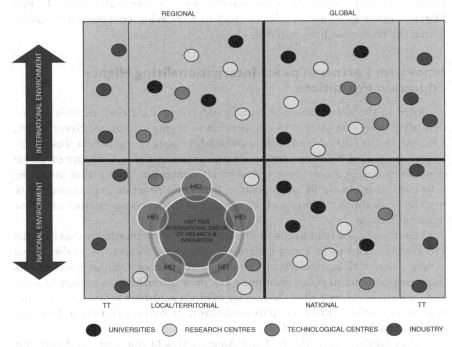

Figure 10.1 Strategic partnerships developed by a highly professional unit of a given territory to foster comprehensive internationalization actions in various higher education institutions through a collaborative approach.
(Source: Vigil Taquechel, 2015).

talent could be applied in other Latin American cities, states or provinces and should be perfectly feasible for international collaborations among HEIs of different countries in the region.

Such a collaborative scheme is not only feasible for developing academic and research activities. Universities should and can go further in their pursuit of successful internationalization. Universities can explore sustainable business models to support internationalization processes within HEIs. Collaboration could serve as a reference point for institutions of a given territory to share different types of essential services that are difficult to develop independently. Figure 10.1 describes this idea as a prototype of a specialized unit providing service to various HEIs of the same region or city to comprehensively promote internationalization in science, technology, innovation and entrepreneurship by building dynamic partnership networks in local, national, regional and global environments (Vigil Taquechel, 2015).

There are no formulas that fit all institutions. Each university has the obligation to find the most suitable approaches and tools. However, in territories where universities do not have the conditions to set up solid units for the management of key university processes such as internationalization, technology transfer, innovation or collaboration with industry, the foundation of these highly professionalized units that provide support to various HEIs in different critical areas seems to be a major asset for improving the mission of universities.

The adoption of this type of collaborative unit can produce a great variety of benefits. Among the most important are the structuring of a common internationalization strategy based on the main sectors of the local economy; reinforcement of cooperation bonds among the universities themselves; building of a strategic network for university–industry cooperation; engagement of other public and private stakeholders in internationalization processes; and the implementation of different initiatives generated by universities with public–private financing. Another benefit this type of unit can offer is the improvement of innovation through hybridization processes, assuming they will be able to recruit professionals from different sectors, disciplines and cultural backgrounds, building multidisciplinary and multicultural teams where academic leadership and managerial skills may be combined.

In principle, there is no doubt about the impact this kind of unit can also produce in enhancing university contributions to the knowledge-based economy. Depending on the particular circumstances of each territory, these units can be established exclusively with funds from partner universities or in association with local governments and corporations. The implementation of this model can catalyse the process of universities based in the same location bringing their own DNA to internationalization in order to differentiate themselves from other institutions worldwide and ensure better positioning in the global and competitive market of higher education.

Conclusions

So that the internationalization of higher education can be effective there must be a comprehensive process with consistent planning for the medium and long term and adequate provision of financial resources. At this very moment, the core activity of Latin American universities in internationalization remains at the mercy of individual initiatives by faculty members and staff as well as of financial resources offered by programmes and organizations from other regions of the world. These are the foundations that need to be removed and changed if the region wants to move forward in its integration and improve its positioning in the global context of higher education.

Latin America cannot remain lagging behind in this regard for much longer, ignoring trends and rationales for internationalizing higher education. There is no time to waste waiting for the materialization of supranational understandings that enable cooperation and regional integration. In each context there are enormous sets of opportunities that can be capitalized upon. In most cases it is a matter of flexibility and creativity in finding and achieving the right solutions for our problems. There is too much at stake and the only thing that should be avoided is prolonging the status quo.

We must be aware that the challenge of building quality education demands the reinforcement of cooperation schemes within the regional common space. As long as the region is unable to progress in this common objective, both national and institutional, the internationalization of Latin American universities will remain spontaneous, dispersed, reactive and dependent on the external entities agenda and funding. Integration is not only critical, it is a *sine qua non* condition. Integration seems to be the best way to raise our voice in global landscapes to maintain our own identity.

Part IV

National Policies for Internationalization

Chapter 11

Internationalization in a Non-Market Environment
The Case of Russia

Olga Ustyuzhantseva

Introduction

Internationalization processes have become one of the most popular topics of public discourse in Russia, in which internationalization is perceived as a part of globalization processes and a tool to achieve competitiveness with universities throughout the world. There are two main centers that study internationalization of higher education in Russia, both funded by the government: the National Research University Higher School of Economics, and the non-profit organization established by the government, the National Training Foundation. The research themes covered by these institutions and a range of other scholars include the competitiveness of the Russian educational system, models of export of education services, problems and prospects of participation in the GATS (General Agreement on Trade in Services) and the Bologna Process (Baidenko, 2009; Kupriyanova-Ashina & Chang Zhu, 2013; Larionova et al., 2010; Nikolaev & Suslova, 2010; Sheregi et al., 2006). At the same time, an obvious gap in the analysis of internationalization processes within the Russian political and economic context after the end of the USSR provoked a deep transformation of education policy and the system of higher education itself. This chapter aims at filling this gap and examining the transformation of the rationales and roles of internationalization stakeholders (the state and higher education institutions (HEIs)) induced by the changing political and economic environment from 1991 to 2015.

The research is based on the analysis of various sets of data: national policy programs and regulations; official statistical data; programs and reports of universities; and analytical reports of research institutions such as the Institute of Sociology (Russian Academy of Science) and the Center of Social Forecasting and Marketing.

The First Period of Internationalization: Liberalization and the Market Environment

Unlike in Europe, higher education in Russia was imported (by Tsar Peter the First) and did not arise as a result of the development of society. Therefore, historically, higher education in Russia had neither autonomy nor liberality. The main purpose was the utilitarian servicing of state interests. This explains the intense and extensive development of technical and vocational education in the Soviet Union. It was necessary for the country to achieve industrialization and technical excellence in the confrontation with the West. The USSR's collapse opened an era of political and economic liberalization. The Soviet state, which had been a dominating stakeholder, ceased to exist and the nation entered a transition period. This resulted in a reconfiguration of the roles and rationales of the state and HEIs in internationalization processes.

The key document governing the educational sector in this period was the law "On Education," enacted in 1992. This law established the main principles of the education system, which can be generalized as decentralization, democratization and humanization. The HEIs got autonomy in decision-making on teaching programs, employment, economic activity and academic cooperation. Administration of the universities at all levels became elected. Two articles of the law set rules for the international activity of HEIs, according to which they had full freedom in fulfilling international activity and receiving and disposing of profit from it (On Education Law, 2002). This was the first document to provide a legal base for internationalization in the post-Soviet period. For the first time, it established HEIs as independent and fully functional stakeholders in international academic activity. The only regulations they had to follow were the general legislation of the Russian Federation, basic protocols of the Ministry of International Affairs and routine regulations of the Federal Revenue Agency.

The reverse of this process was the drastic decrease in state funding for education: 3.57% of GDP in 1991, with a low point in 2000 of 2.94% of GDP, and a high point of 4.54% in 1997 (HSE, 2005). HEIs entered the free market environment, not protected by the state, and had to diversify their funding sources. One of their main profit sources became paid educational services, which universities were allowed to provide after 1992. By 2000–2001, the share of paying students of all HEIs was 40.9% (Federal Statistics, 2015).

Since that time, HEIs have sought profit and expanded international connections aimed at getting access to advanced knowledge, facilities and financial resources through various international programs such as ERASMUS, TASIS, the Soros Foundation and others. The presence of international connections (joint educational programs, student exchanges) improved institutional reputation in the national market for education services. Because the main goal of HEIs at that time was survival, providing modern and highly competitive education became essential. Thus, internationalization was not a target but rather the means of being competitive.

The tensest period for the restructuring of HEIs and their adaptation to the new environment was the first decade after 1992. We can see this by the decrease in the number of international students studying at Russian HEIs from 896,000 to 724,000 (see Table 11.1). This was a time of heavy economic shocks for

Table 11.1 International students at HEIs in Russia

Years	Number of international students studying at HEIs in Russia, thousands	Total number of students studying at HEIs in Russia, thousands	Share of international students in the total number of students studying at HEIs in Russia (%)
1980/1981	64.5	3,045.8	2.12
1990/1991	89.6	2,824.5	3.17
2000/2001	72.4	4,741.4	1.53
2005/2006	113.8	7,064.6	1.61
2006/2007	126.2	7,341.4	1.72

Source: Adopted from Statistical Collection (2015a).

Russia, such as hyperinflation, devaluation of the ruble, the bank crisis and "Black Tuesday" (1994), with a 27% reduction in the value of the ruble.

After this period we see slow but stable growth in the number of international students. By 2006–2007, Russian HEIs reached the former Soviet level of the number of international students and even exceeded it by three times through the export of education services. In 2005–2006, aggregate education export income reached 16.4 billion rubles (US$608.1 million): 41.8% from tuition, the rest from living expenditure during the period of study (Statistical Collection, 2015b).

At the policy level, the main goal of internationalization was declared to be ensuring the geopolitical and socioeconomic interests of Russia and participation in the global process of education development to provide high-quality education and competitiveness of Russian graduates on the global market (Concept, 2002). This was supported by the programs and regulations instituted in this period. The first set was devoted to state higher education standards, licensing and accreditation. In 2003 Russia joined the Bologna Process and initiated implementation of a two-tier system of education through decrees and decisions (Eurydice, 2007).

The most important phenomena of this period were the changed roles of the state and HEIs and the appearance of a market environment for HEI activity. The government removed itself from its dominant position in the higher education sector and became the facilitator of the sector. Historically this was unusual for the government of Russia. The governance of higher education was decentralized, the universities achieved autonomy and their financing was diversified. Along with general economic liberalization in the country during this period, this created a market environment for university activity. Thus, economic and academic rationales for internationalization were the predominant rationales both for the government and the universities.

The Second Period of Internationalization:
The Changing Environment

The free market stimulated universities to adapt actively to the new environment and they did so successfully, given the years of economic shocks in Russia. That the number of international students and the total revenue from education exports reached Soviet levels is an indicator of that success. But the early 2000s were marked by the beginning of power centralization in Russia. For the higher education sector this meant its reinclusion into the sphere of state interests. In 2005, the government released the Federal Strategic Program for the Development of Education for the Period 2006–2010, whose main goal was ensuring Russia's global competitiveness through the creation of new mechanisms for regulation of the education sector. The paradox of the Program was in aiming to achieve that competitiveness by administrative measures (Decree No. 803, 2005).

Beginning in 2004, a number of measures the government applied to the system of higher education as a whole greatly influenced the internationalization process as well.

The Consolidation of Universities

Since 2006, the state has carried out consolidation of universities, highlighting the group of the best that could become a driving force for the entire higher education sector. New types of institutions were created, such as large federal universities that absorbed some regional institutes and universities, and national research universities that were designed to concentrate on education and science, which had traditionally taken place in separate institutions. Accepting new statuses assured institutions of additional funds provided through the various federal programs, but also meant an unprecedented enhancement of bureaucratic control. For example, the first universities to accept the status of "national research universities" were required to provide weekly reports on their activity (Decree No. 2293, 2009).

In 2008, a new law determined the status and terms of operation of autonomous institutions. Formally, universities that selected autonomous status obtained autonomy in organizational and personnel policy, forming the student body and performing educational, scientific, financial and economic activities independently. In fact, the autonomous universities became independent in the implementation of organizational and economic activity (Melikhov, 2009). For example, such institutions can raise wages through budget savings, energy savings and reallocation of the budget of educational institutions, expanding the range of market services (Sorokova, 2012). However, by realizing its authority the institution must be guided by a set of target figures and quotas stipulated by a license for educational activities.

In addition, the autonomous educational institutions lost their "autonomy" in electing the rector. The universities' academic councils were deprived of this right. Rectors are appointed by the Ministry of Science and Education and their authority in solving economic and other issues related to the daily activities of the HEI was significantly limited. The rights of academic councils in addressing the most important issues of educational and scientific work of the educational institution were restricted as well.

As a result of these measures, rectors became managers of the state-owned property of the university and are strictly controlled and regulated by the Ministry of Science and Education. The actual removal of academics from managing the economic and academic development of the university led to the predominance of short-term interests of effective management over the long-term goals and strategies for university development.

Increasing Control and Limitations on International Connections

The end of the 2000s was characterized by the state restricting activities relating to the international connections of HEIs. The export control that applied to engineering and technology sciences was extended to social and humanitarian sciences. In 2012 the Ministry of Science and Education released an order for HEIs and scientific institutions to "expertize" all articles, conference proceedings and other materials before presenting them at events with international participants or publishing in international journals. The increasing number of criminal trials against academics' violation of this order demonstrates the seriousness of this measure (Popova, 2015). In April 2013, Government Decree No. 367 implemented additional procedures for receiving international funds for HEIs and scientific institutions in Russia. According to this decree international grant-makers have to get permission from the Ministry of Science and Education before beginning any projects with Russian educational and scientific institutions. The decree made international cooperation extremely complicated with regard to getting grants and funding from abroad. At the same time universities experienced informal pressure from public prosecution offices to liquidate all scientific units that had grants from international foundations and organizations. This is evident from the innumerable tax inspections and prosecutor investigations of HEIs, which stop after the institution liquidates the undesirable units. This pressure was supported by the Law on Unadvisable Organizations (2015), according to which any Russian or international organization can be placed on the list of prohibited organizations and cooperation with them carries punishment. For instance, in November 2015, the Open Society Foundations (OSI) and OSI Assistance Foundation were included in this list. Thus, the government expels international funding sources from Russia.

Centralization of University Funding

In 2000, the Russian government launched the GIFO experiment educational vouchers (*gosudarstvennyye imennyye finansovyye obyazatel'stva*) in a number of regions. According to the program, budget funding was provided for secondary school graduates with the highest scores in the graduation examination in order for them to choose which HEI to attend. This created competition among HEIs for these students. In fact, the HEIs were pushed into a market environment, when "money followed the student."

The experiment was abandoned in 2003 and the federal government provided funding for universities by admission quotas for HEIs. In 2010, the principle of state funding was changed (Federal Law No. 83). Since then, state HEIs have received federal money as a subsidy for state assignment on education. The size of the subsidies is based on the amount of funds that are at the disposal of the Ministry of Science and Education, and does not depend on the actual needs of the HEIs. The universities are also limited in spending the subsidies according to their actual demands; they have to follow the normative standards of the state.

The other source of federal budget funding was launched in 2005, when the government commenced a new program of education development (Decree No. 803, 2005) to modernize the education system through budgetary performance and management by objectives. The government outlined 41 state programs within five main blocks: "new quality of life"; innovation development and modernization of the economy; ensuring national security; balanced regional development; and effective governance. Education was included in the most highly funded block, "new quality of life." HEIs received an additional avenue of funding from the state – funding by projects, which in fact meant the institutional model of financing (Forrat, 2015).

These measures resulted in an increasing share of state funding in the total structure of university finances. In 2010 the federal budget provided around 54% of state funding. Non-budgetary funding contributed around 45% with a decreasing trend (Education in Russian Federation, 2012). This reduction of non-budgetary funding has a number of conditions. After 2005 Russia entered the demographic bust, which led to a 40% decline in prospective students in 2013 (Statistical Collection, 2015a). Next, the cost of paid education in state universities is artificially low. The government prohibits raising the cost of education and allows inflation indexation only. The share of endowment funds, which universities were permitted to set in 2006, is extremely low because of the lack of a donation culture. Thus, the only tangible source of financing for universities is the federal budget. The main aim of universities in these conditions is competition for budgetary resources. This is especially true in the case of the internationalization of higher education.

The measures listed above influenced the HEIs and also the environment in which they operated. State absorption of higher education resulted in a loss of autonomy and constriction of funding sources for HEIs. The market environment has been replaced by administrative-resource governance, under which universities must compete for state funding.

Internationalization in a Nonmarket Environment

In 2000, the government brought internationalization to the public policy level. Currently there are two documents defining the strategy and tactics of HEI internationalization in Russia. The first is the Concept of State Policy of the Russian Federation in the area of training of national personnel for foreign countries at Russian educational institutions (2002). Despite the stated definition of internationalization as a part of the international economic activity of Russia, the document reflects the general aspiration of regaining the dominant position of Russia among the countries of the former USSR. A few chapters of the Concept are devoted to measures for empowering Russia as an educational center for CIS countries, and explaining the importance of educating international elites to provide the long-term political and geopolitical interests of Russia in international affairs.

The second document was the Concept of Export of Russian Educational Services for the Period 2011–2020 released in 2010. The document utilized the terminology of GATS, and also contained a new goal of internationalization: fostering a competitive economy of knowledge and advanced technology in Russia. It contained a detailed list of measures aiming to achieve the following results: increasing Russia's share in the global higher education market from 2% to 7% by 2020; inclusion of a minimum ten Russian HEIs in the top 100 in international rankings; and reaching 10% of universities' total profit from export revenues. The source of financing of all the programs was the state budget (Concept, 2010).

These measures were taken as the basis for the state's Program 5–100. The main goal of Program 5–100 was improving the competitiveness of HEIs so that at least five Russian universities would be among the 100 top-ranked universities in the world by 2020. The Program was designed for seven years (from 2013 to 2020), and nearly US$1 billion was allocated for it (Program 5–100, 2012). Fifteen universities were selected for participation in the Program. All of them have a prescribed set of key performance indicators (KPIs), including the share of international students and share of international staff recruited to the university; the number of research articles published in scholarly journals that are indexed by the Scopus and Web of Science citation databases; the modernization of institutional infrastructure; and the university's position in the QS and THE rankings of world universities. Despite the stated freedom of universities to allocate the funds they receive from the government, the HEIs in fact are quite limited by the KPIs and pressed to show fast results. The decision to extend each university's participation in the Program is made yearly by the Ministry of Science and Education. As a result, most of the universities have banked on quickly achieved goals: "buying" international staff with high publication activity, setting up various centers of excellence and manipulating data in order to show better results (Arephiev, 2014). An analysis of university expenditures under the Program showed that most of the government subsidies were spent on hiring

Table 11.2 Indicators' values of Russian universities* in the QS World University Rankings

Universities	Ranking place				Academic peer review				Employer reputation				Faculty/Student ratio				Citations per faculty				International staff ratio				International student ratio			
	2015	2014	2013	2007	2015	2014	2013	2007	2015	2014	2013	2007	2015	2014	2013	2007	2015	2014	2013	2007	2015	2014	2013	2007	2015	2014	2013	2007
NSU	317	328	353	440	35.1	36.7	32.7	35.9	43.6	39.2	24.8	22.4	89	85.8	87.3	8.1	9.9	8.1	5.2	44.5	8.4	7.3	4.9	–	45.6	41.1	35.3	27.6
MIPT	411–420	411–420	441–450	–	–	–	–	–	–	–	–	–	99.1	99.9	99.6	–	5.7	3.3	2.7	–	18.1	11.6	11.2	–	38	36.1	35.9	–
UFU	551–600	551–600	501–550	–	–	–	–	–	–	–	–	–	–	–	98.6	–	–	–	1.6	–	–	2.0	–	–	–	5.1	–	–
HSE	501–550	501–550	501–550	–	–	–	–	–	–	–	–	–	–	–	90.0	–	–	–	–	–	–	–	–	–	–	–	–	–
TSU	481–490	491–500	551–600	466	–	–	–	18.3	–	–	–	12.3	74	66.1	58.2	8.1	3.1	–	2.3	96.3	25	27.6	–	2.4	46.6	31.1	–	10.8
TPU	481–490	501–550	551–600	–	–	–	–	–	–	–	–	–	91.4	–	75.3	–	2	–	–	–	12.8	–	–	–	68.1	41.2	–	–
KFU	651–700	551–600	601–450	528	–	–	–	24.0	–	–	–	15.0	–	–	57.7	18.0	–	–	14.3	30.6	–	–	–	14.3	–	–	–	14.8

*Selected universities with the most complete data including NSU (Novosibirsk State University), MIPT (Moscow Institute of Physics and Technology), TSU (Tomsk State University), UFU (Ural Federal University), HSE (Higher School of Economics),

TPU (Tomsk Polytechnic University), KFU (Kazan Federal University).
Source: aggregated from QS World University Rankings, www.topuniversities.com.

international academics, setting up new units of the university and sponsoring academic mobility (Trostyanskaya & Tolstikov, 2014).

In addition to the pressure of Program 5–100, the universities are required to execute "the May decrees of Putin." In 2012, President Vladimir Putin released a number of decrees, one of which increased the salaries of academic teaching staff, which, by 2018, are to be 200% of average salaries in the region where the institution is located. The main source of funds for the increase is to be institutional budgets. To optimize expenses connected with this, most universities are reducing their personnel and splitting full-time positions; thus for one full-time salary the university is able to retain two to seven persons. Along with the general trend of recruiting outside staff instead of developing in-house employees, this has led to the erosion of the composition of university staff (Arephiev, 2014). From 2010 to 2012, the average reduction in the number of higher education employees was 3% per year. In 2013, the reduction was 6% of the previous year. The number of academic teaching staff dropped from 348,200 in 2011–2012 to 319,300 in 2013–2014. During the same period, the number of international teaching staff increased from 1,300 to 3,000 (Education in Russian Federation, 2014).

How effective is the Program in reaching the declared goal of improving the universities' world rankings? From 2013 to 2015, only three universities of the 15 in the Program made some progress on their positions in the QS university ranking: Novosibirsk State University (from 353 to 317), Tomsk State University and Tomsk Polytechnic University (from 551–600 to 481–490 respectively). The best results were in the faculty/student ratio only (see Table 11.2).

Parameters such as the number of international students and export income are also modest. In 2013–2014, revenue from the export of educational services reached US$1,406.5 million against US$891.8 million export income in 2007–2008. The main "customers" of Russian education are citizens of the CIS: 72.1% of total international students in Russia in 2013–2014 (Statistical Collection, 2015b).

The results of Program 5–100 reflect the growth of indicators that are possible to reach without qualitative transformation by universities, primarily the number of laboratories and other science and educational divisions and the student/faculty ratio. Conditioned by the new environment, universities must focus on providing formal indicators of their activity, concentrating their resources and efforts on this. De facto the state has become the major source of funding for HEIs. Along with lost autonomy, this has placed the universities in a position of insecure dependence on the state's ability to provide needed funds and to increase them, in order for HEIs to compete in the international education market.

Conclusion

The education system of Russia, inherited from the USSR, differed from the system of the Western world. By the 1990s, higher education was free, accessible for all citizens and controlled by the state. Reforms in the 1990s gave the HEIs autonomy and freedom in choosing the means and methods of developing and transforming. Internationalization processes were driven mostly by the necessity for universities to get additional sources of funding, such as revenues from international students and grants and funding for research. Active international activity was also a form of reputational capital for attracting more local students. The responsibility for internationalization was transferred to the individual institutions, and this explains the absence of general strategy for internationalization at the national level at that time. How much this strategy needed to be developed by negotiation and close cooperation between the HEIs and the government can be seen from the situation that appeared in the 2000s, when the state returned to full centralized control over the higher education sector through measures that included consolidating the universities, reducing the range of funding sources for HEIs and implementing top-down management. The market imperatives that drove internationalization in Russia in the first period after the end of the USSR were replaced by administrative pressure on universities to attain prescribed achievements in the international sphere, while paying less attention to quality development of the educational programs and local teaching staff. This is the result of considering internationalization as a national goal but not the process of quality improvement through integration in the international education space. The academic rationale for internationalization is still present, but restriction of academic autonomy and the state's administrative management of the universities result in an "external" reorganization (for example, establishing centers of excellence) without "internal" modernization.

These are some of the specifics of Russia's paradoxical attempt to use administrative and nonmarket methods to attain competitiveness in a worldwide educational market that is based on academic freedom, autonomy and decentralized management.

Chapter 12

Internationalization of Higher Education in Vietnam

Moving towards Interdependence

Christopher Ziguras & Anh Pham

Introduction

The contemporary approach to internationalization of higher education in Vietnam, which has been quite consistent since the early 1990s, is driven by economic development imperatives and the government's desire to strengthen the country's political and economic relationships with a wide range of trading partners. This differs markedly from previous eras in which Vietnam's higher education system was heavily influenced by a series of major powers for most of the country's history, with long-standing Chinese Confucian traditions overlaid in the early 20th century by French colonial dominance, and later by the Soviet Union, which played a huge role in the creation of the national higher education system (Welch, 2010). These bilateral relationships were profoundly unbalanced, with Vietnam dominated politically and culturally by much more powerful states, and the Vietnamese higher education system in each period closely modelled on that of the major power of the time. In contrast, since the collapse of the Soviet bloc Vietnam has proactively cultivated extensive and diversified educational relationships with many countries, both in the region (most notably Japan and ASEAN member states) and further afield, including with the United States, Australia, the United Kingdom, France, Germany and Russia. As a consequence, the direct influence of any one of these states is diminished compared with previous eras, and Vietnam, like its partners, finds itself engaging with the same set of global challenges and policy trends. For Vietnam, internationalization of higher education since the 1990s has been primarily a means of integrating the country more deeply into the global economy and enhancing national competitiveness through the transfer of knowledge and skills from abroad.

The History of Foreign Influence on Vietnamese Higher Education

The earliest institutions of higher learning were established by Vietnamese royalty during a period of two centuries in which Vietnam was not under Chinese rule; previously scholars had been required to travel to cities in China for advanced study. As Tran (1998) notes, these first Vietnamese colleges provided a thoroughly Chinese education, ensuring that Vietnamese elites were well versed in Chinese history, culture and language (which remained the official language in periods of both local and Chinese rule). Over the centuries elite colleges expanded their reach, both in Hanoi, the capital city, and in regional centres, but only ever involved a tiny fraction of the male population. These elite state institutions provided a traditional Confucian humanistic curriculum centred on classical Chinese literary texts.

European colonialism left its mark on Vietnamese higher education with the establishment of a modern higher education system by the country's French rulers in the early 20th century (Tran, 1998; Welch, 2010). Like the earlier feudal rulers, the French also imported a pre-existing education system in its entirety, including institutional models, a foreign language of instruction (French replacing Chinese), lecturers trained in France and a European curriculum. The University of Indochina's five colleges illustrate how radically different the curriculum was from the Confucian tradition it supplanted, comprising the College of Law and Administration, College of Sciences, College of Medicines, College of General Civil, and a College of Literature. Traditional examinations in the Confucian tradition ceased between 1915 and 1918 (Tran, 1998).

Like the imperial colleges, enrolment numbers in the French institutions remained very small. In the early 1940s over 95% of the populace remained illiterate and very few Vietnamese studied at the three upper-secondary French-language schools that provided a pathway into French higher learning (London, 2011). The lasting legacy of the French system was to put an end to centuries of Chinese traditional education based on informal local schools established by individual teachers who tutored groups of students of various ages and levels in the literary classics. By contrast, the modern system separated students by discipline, age and level of study within large bureaucratic rule-governed institutions administered by the state. While much of the content of higher education has changed substantially since, the institutional form of Vietnamese higher education today would be immediately recognizable to a French academic of the 1920s.

As the Communist Party of Vietnam took control of higher education, from 1945 in the North and from 1975 in the South, it restructured the system in line with the Soviet model. Education played an important role in fostering links between socialist Vietnam and its new allies. Russian became an important foreign language, alongside French, and tens of thousands of Vietnamese students and scholars travelled from the North of Vietnam to other socialist states between 1955 and 1975, 55% of these to the USSR (Kelly, 2000; Welch, 2010). By contrast students from South Vietnam travelled to the United States or its allies; between 1950 and 1975 South Vietnam was the third largest source country for Australian government sponsored students, after Indonesia and Malaysia, where Cold War conflicts were also raging (Cleverley & Jones, 1976, pp. 26–29). From both the North and the South, state sponsorship of overseas study was one of the few means for a young person to travel abroad.

The Soviet Union's influence on Vietnamese higher education was profound, with the standard features of socialist centrally planned systems being applied to an expanded range of institutions. Industry-specific universities were created under the management of a wide range of government departments to meet sector-specific workforce requirements as part of planning for national workforce development. National research institutes were created outside of universities. Textbooks, curriculum and teaching methods were imported from the USSR and the study of official political ideology – Marxism, Leninism and Ho Chi Minh thought – was made compulsory for all students (Tibbetts, 2007).

This represents the third time Vietnamese higher education had been completely reorganized by the wholesale adoption of a foreign education model. One key difference, however, was the introduction, for the first time, of Vietnamese as the language of instruction, rather than Chinese or French. National liberation from colonial domination was a key feature of socialist ideology, and adopting the Vietnamese language was a key feature of this process of postcolonial nation building through education. Vietnamese scholars have emphasized independence and nation building through this period, arguing that dependency on Russia, as the hegemonic socialist state, had a very different character to earlier periods of foreign domination. Tran (1998), for example, argues that the adoption of the Soviet system was initiated by the Vietnamese rather than being imposed by colonial rulers.

Internationalization in the Global Era

Since 1986, under the impact of the Vietnamese government's programme of national economic renovation, "doi moi", and the accompanying transition from a centrally planned to a regulated market economy, the landscape of Vietnamese higher education has changed significantly. Vietnam's development strategy nominates workforce skill development as its first priority for modernization and industrialization of the economy, and higher education reform is seen as a key agent in providing this workforce with the skills, competencies and qualities needed (London, 2011; St George, 2010). The Communist Party of Vietnam's view of higher education therefore has been closely aligned with those of international agencies such as the World Bank and the United Nations Development Programme, and these agencies have been influential in advising the government of Vietnam at critical phases of policy development. The World Bank's reports on the challenges confronting higher education in Vietnam have been particularly influential, aligned as they are with the government's focus on skill development, with titles such as *Vietnam: Higher Education Skills for Growth* (World Bank, 2008), *Putting Higher Education to Work: Skills and Research for Growth in East Asia* (World Bank, 2012) and *Skilling up Vietnam: Preparing the Workforce for a Modern Market Economy* (World Bank, 2013). The World Bank's approach for two decades has been to "assist Vietnam's transition to a market economy and alleviating poverty through human resource development by providing advanced skills for the market economy through higher education reformation" (World Bank, 2008, p. 2).

This shared human capital development approach to higher education is focused on developing the skills and knowledge needed to adopt advanced techniques and technologies in ways that allow domestic institutions to compete successfully in a more open economy (Dang, 2011). This typically involves two very distinct processes of change in higher education systems – massification and international standardization. The first process involves significantly increasing participation in higher education, reflecting the value accorded to high-level knowledge and skills in the new economy. The second involves reorienting teaching to align with the types of knowledge and skills that are required by a workforce in a globalized economy. The long-term vision for Vietnamese higher education was reasserted in the government's Higher Education Reformation Agenda 2006–2020 (HERA), involving both massification and internationalization in higher education.

Massification of higher education has become accepted by governments across the globe as an unquestioned goal, and participation rates have increased particularly rapidly in Asia in recent decades, despite very different levels of economic development and diverse ideological frames. The Gross Enrolment Ratio is a measure of the total enrolment in tertiary education expressed as a percentage of the total population within five years of secondary school completion. Between 1999 and 2013, this rose in Vietnam from 10.49 to 24.6, driven by ambitious government targets. The Socio-Economic Development Plan 2006–2010, for example, set a goal of increasing enrolments by 10% annually (World Bank, 2008). However, Vietnam's achievement is by no means exceptional in this region. Across the same 15-year period the Gross Enrolment Ratio also rose dramatically in China from 6.6 to 29.7, in India from 9.5 to 24.7, in Indonesia from 14.9 to 31.5, in Thailand from 32.9 to 51.2, Japan 46.6 to 61.5, and in the Republic of Korea from 74.2 to 98.4 (UNESCO, 2015).

Through this period of expansion the key features of the Vietnamese higher education system remained relatively unchanged, and over time institutions with dated curricula and a legacy of Soviet central planning continued to produce graduates whose knowledge and skills were poorly aligned to the needs of a rapidly changing economy (London, 2011; Tran & Swierczek, 2009; Tran, 2015). While massification aims to rapidly increase the quantity of enrolments towards addressing skills shortages, internationalization has been primarily seen as a means of modernizing the skills of the workforce. The vision for international education integration is described in HERA, which sets out three main objectives to upgrade international quality: a more internationally integrated higher education system; more international commitments and agreements; and the development of conditions favourable to increased foreign investment in the higher education system (Harman et al., 2010). It is clear that internationalization is a core element of a broader higher education restructuring that draws on diverse international models in an effort to make higher education provision more demand-driven and responsive to a market economy, to increase student enrolments with greater diversity and to introduce new curricula and teaching methods with strong links to business and industry.

The most recent iteration of Vietnam's national education strategy is even more oriented to internationalization. Outlining the period 2011–2020, the strategy explains that:

> The country's education in the next decade will develop in the context of the world's fast and complex changes. Globalization and international integration for education have become inevitable. The revolution of science and technology, information technology and communication and a knowledge-based economy will continue to vigorously develop, directly impacting the development of education worldwide.
>
> (Socialist Republic of Vietnam, 2012, p. 6)

On one level this statement is unsurprising, and could appear in any number of policy documents in any number of countries, but this just goes to show the extent of convergence in the way countries interpret global influences on education. The differences in world-view (in a literal sense) between East and West, North and South, liberal democratic and communist in this regard have effectively evaporated. And so, too, are the measures adopted by the Vietnam government to promote international engagement more or less consistent with those adopted by many other states. The 2012 strategy proposes:

> To increase state-funded overseas training quotas for key universities and national research institutes, prioritizing spearhead sciences and technologies. To encourage and support Vietnamese citizens in learning and conducting research overseas at their own expense.
>
> To encourage domestic educational institutions to cooperate with foreign educational institutions to raise their capacity for management, training, scientific research, technology transfer and training and retraining of teachers, lecturers, scientists and educational administrators; to increase overseas scholarships for students.
>
> To encourage foreign organizations and individuals, international organizations and overseas Vietnamese to invest in and finance education and participate in teaching, scientific research and application, and technology transfer, contributing to renovating education in Vietnam. To build a number of modern universities and research centers to attract domestic and foreign scientists to conduct training and scientific research.
>
> (Socialist Republic of Vietnam, 2012, p. 14)

Below we consider Vietnam's approach to each of these three forms of collaboration.

Promoting Overseas Study

Through the 20th century a steady stream of Vietnamese travelled to study destinations according to the dominant political influence of each period. In the colonial era, some graduates of the few elite French institutions, including Ho Chi Minh, travelled to France to further their studies. During the Cold War outbound mobility increased but the destinations of students from the South and North of Vietnam diverged markedly. Students from the South mostly travelled to those Western states allied with the government in the South. From the North, students headed to the Soviet Union and Eastern Europe in large numbers, supported by similar government-to-government programmes designed to build solidarity across the socialist bloc. Between 1951 and 1989, former socialist countries reportedly helped train over 30,000 Vietnamese undergraduates, 13,500 postgraduates, 25,000 technicians and thousands of other scientists (Kelly, 2000). Most of these originated in the North of Vietnam, joined by students from the South also after the end of the war in 1975.

While in the past many students were government-funded, since the 1990s the vast majority of Vietnamese students studying abroad have been funded privately. Nevertheless, the number of outbound degree students has been rising steadily this century. In 1999 just 8,169 Vietnamese students were studying in foreign higher education for a period of a year or more according to UNESCO (2015) data, but by 2013 this number had swelled to 53,546. If students in vocational education, language studies and short-term programmes are included, the actual number is nearly double that, according to Ministry of Education figures based on reports from embassies (Tô, 2012).

One means by which the government has sought to promote self-funded overseas study is by supporting articulation programmes that reduce the cost to students by allowing them to undertake part of a foreign degree in the home country. Vietnamese public universities have developed various types of credit-transfer programmes, providing students with the possibility of receiving credit towards a degree overseas. Hundreds of these agreements have been established between Vietnamese institutions and foreign universities, including the ubiquitous anglophones (US, UK, Australia, New Zealand), the Europeans (France, Netherlands, Germany, Belgium) and the neighbours (Singapore, Malaysia, China, Thailand and Taiwan) (MOET, 2013).

Scholarships have been made available under government agreements and protocols, bilateral cooperation projects and programmes, and scholarships. A national project referred to as the "Project for Training Scientific and Technology Staff Abroad by the Government Budget", or "Project 322" for short, sponsored a large number of elite students in key scientific and technological areas not available in Vietnam but much needed for the industrialization and modernization of the country (Welch, 2010, p. 204). By 2011 the project had funded 7,129 students (PhD 3,838, masters 2,042 and the rest undergraduates) at a total expense of 2,500 billion VND. Also, since the early 2000s bilateral agreements with most of Vietnam's key trading partner countries have helped fund and promote overseas study, including major programmes of the Russian Federation and the United States. It is clear that sponsored students are typically completing masters or doctoral studies, while the vast majority of Vietnamese students abroad are self-funded and studying at degree level.

Internationalization of Local Institutions

As noted earlier, the development of Vietnam's universities has always been closely aligned with the country's international relations, and this continues with the government advocating the internationalization of domestic universities as the second pillar in its current strategy. Thanks to this long history of large-scale overseas study programmes, Vietnam's higher education institutions now have many mid-level and senior leaders who have studied abroad, either for short periods or for whole programmes. Aiming to build on this strength, the most recent national education strategy includes an aspiration that all university lecturers will be proficient in a foreign language by 2020 (Socialist Republic of Vietnam, 2012).

Another key means for the government to foster the internationalization of institutions has been through funding or supporting collaborative programs with overseas universities. One of the longest-running examples is an MA in Development Economics between the Erasmus University in Rotterdam, the Netherlands, the University of Economics in Ho Chi Minh City (HCMC) and the National Economics University in Hanoi. This began in 1994, supported by Dutch government funding, with lecturers from both countries. In the decades since, many discipline-specific advanced programmes have been developed in targeted fields. The model has spread from flagship programmes in elite universities in Hanoi and HCMC to a broader range of institutions and disciplines. For example, the People's Police Academy in Hanoi has established a Joint Master's Degree in Justice Leadership with the University of Maryland in the United States, with some of its lecturers funded to undertake doctoral studies abroad. Nguyen et al. (2016) found that university leaders highly valued the transfer of knowledge and skills from foreign teaching staff, which they believed would assist with the internationalization of Vietnamese curricula and, in turn, help develop the country. Tuyết (2014) points out that Vietnamese universities also have a financial incentive to develop such partnerships as the fees can be much higher.

The French government has also been very active since the early 1990s supporting a range of linkages through initiatives such as Campus France (which provides information on scholarships and opportunities for study in France) and collaborative initiatives like the French Vietnamese Centre for Management Education (CFGV). This was established in 1992 with funding from the French Ministry of Foreign Affairs, operated by the Paris Chamber of Commerce and Industry with the Vietnamese Ministry of Education and Training on the steering committee.

It offers MBA and PhD programmes in French, which France is keen to promote as a language of study. Other programmes promoted for French speakers include the Programme de Formation d'Ingénieurs d'Excellence au Viet Nam (Programme of Excellence in Higher Engineering Education in Vietnam) established in 1997 involving four key Vietnamese universities of science and technology in partnership with eight French universities and the Pôle Universitaire Français de l'Universite Nationalé du Vietnam (PUF), established in 2004, which has seen more than 800 Vietnamese students on 28 French programmes in collaboration with Vietnamese universities.

Other early government-supported programmes shared a similar vision of international collaboration for workforce development. The programmes of Université Libre de Bruxelles (ULB), Centre Franco-Vietnamien de formation à la Gestion, the Swiss–AIT–Vietnam Management Development Program, the Vietnam–Netherlands Programme for MA in Development Economics and the Fulbright Economic Teaching Program were among the first of these types, and have been active in Vietnam for almost 20 years. The ULB partnered with HCMC Open University after the Minister of National Education of Vietnam visited ULB in 1994 (ULB, 2014) and the first MBA programme was implemented in 1995.

While government has focused on fostering partnerships among public universities, there has been a huge expansion in private educational provision since the 1990s and some private not-for-profit universities have from the outset adopted a more international outlook as a distinguishing feature. Hoa Sen University in HCMC, for example, aims to provide an international experience for the majority of its students through exchange opportunities, foreign languages and degree programmes in business and hospitality in collaboration with French universities. It also promotes a student-centred approach to learning and teaching, and the university's stated core values reflect this progressive orientation: eagerness for learning and understanding; independent thinking; responsibility; integrity; respect for difference and diversity; proactivity and creativity; and commitment to quality (Hoa Sen University, 2015). Compared with established state universities, private institutions like Hoa Sen have a greater degree of latitude to develop innovative forms of curriculum and pedagogy, and therefore may be more readily able to integrate foreign and Vietnamese influences to shape student experience.

In contrast with the colonial and Cold War eras, internationalization of Vietnamese universities in the contemporary global era involves a wider range of partners and a focus on technological and scientific collaboration rather than the exercise of political and cultural influence. While still dependent upon foreign assistance to develop relatively young institutions, government and institutions can choose among donors and partners in ways impossible in previous eras and the resulting mix of initiatives appears to have broad public support. Nguyen et al.'s (2016) study of the views of university leaders found that they share the government's faith in internationalization as a key means of enhancing the quality and relevance of the curriculum. Nguyen (2009) and Tuyết (2014), like many Vietnamese scholars writing on internationalization of higher education, are wary of the unequal relationship between Vietnamese universities and Western universities. Knowledge, they observe, flows from West to East, while funds flow from East to West, with little reciprocity involved. Nevertheless, these writers accept the logic of technology transfer, and the inevitable quality improvement through such partnerships. However, while there appears to be a consensus among scholars, university leaders, Vietnamese and foreign governments and international donor agencies about the benefits of internationalization in principle, research evaluating the practical impact of such international experience on curriculum, pedagogy, research or student experience is virtually nonexistent. Even in Nguyen's (2009) very detailed case study of internationalization efforts at Vietnam National University, which is perhaps the most extensive of any Vietnamese public institution, while we see much description of activities, real evidence of impact on students' learning or the quality and relevance of research is absent. This focus on process rather than outcomes, as if international engagement is an end in itself, is of course not confined to Vietnam but is a common feature of contemporary discussions of internationalization in many countries.

Foreign Investment

The third pillar of the government's current internationalization strategy is to encourage foreign investment. Hundreds of projects in public universities have benefited from foreign support but the scale is often rather small, with most international collaborative programmes enrolling tens of students rather than hundreds of thousands. By contrast, a small number of foreign institutions have been operating on a much larger scale for some time, and their number is growing.

Australia-based RMIT University established campuses in HCMC and Hanoi in 2001 with support from the International Finance Corporation, the private finance arm of the World Bank (Beanland, 2011; Wilmoth, 2004). It remains the only fully foreign-owned university in Vietnam and, according to the Observatory on Borderless Higher Education, is the world's largest international branch campus (Lawton & Katsomitros, 2011), with 6,272 students in 2014 (RMIT, 2015). Despite the growth of RMIT, no other foreign branch campuses have been established since, although there are several large-scale foreign-linked private vocational education providers, most of which were established around the same time as RMIT and in most cases affiliated with colleges based in Singapore, Australia and India (Ziguras & Pham, 2014). Several of these were closed in recent years by the Ministry of Education while others provide scant details online about their international affiliations, accreditation status or enrolment numbers, making an assessment of their contribution difficult.

In the time since this short-lived wave of independent foreign providers began around 2000, the Vietnamese government has taken a more hands-on approach to establishing new international universities by brokering deals with foreign governments. The Japanese government and the Asian Development Bank collaborated with the Vietnamese government in the development of HCMC International University, a public university established in 2003, offering credit-transfer pathways to overseas study (ADB, 2008, 2010). More recently the government has sponsored bilateral universities with the governments of Germany, France and Japan. The largest of these is the Vietnamese–German University near HCMC, offering programmes from several German universities and enrolling around 750 students by 2013 with future growth expected. As well as support from both governments, it received a US$180 million loan from the World Bank in 2010 to build a new campus. The language of instruction is English but students can study German and complete part of their programme in Germany. Meanwhile, in the North of Vietnam, the government chose France as its partner in 2009 to design and build a new model university, the University of Science and Technology of Hanoi, also called the Vietnam–France University. Like the Vietnamese–German University, it is built upon collaboration with French universities and local industry linkages. Importantly, both new institutions are public universities in the Vietnamese system offering foreign degrees with low tuition fees thanks to subsidies provided by both governments.

Achieving sustainable growth in transnational education requires either ongoing funding from governments (such as the French and German universities) or regulatory frameworks that encourage quality foreign providers to invest and enable them to operate viably, while preventing substandard programmes from being offered (McNamara, 2013; Ziguras & McBurnie, 2015). The Vietnam government has sought to retain close control over all educational institutions, and is determined to avoid the inequalities in access that private education markets can foster (London, 2010). Since 2000, the government has gradually implemented an increasingly comprehensive array of regulations governing transnational providers and international collaborations, so that foreign providers are now subject to more exacting requirements than locally owned providers. These include: higher wages and protections for employees; foreign lecturers need a Graduate Certificate of Higher Education and five years of professional experience for a work visa; new foreign higher education institutions must invest at least 150 million VND (US$7,000) per student, with a minimum total of 300 billion VND (US$14 million); campus size requirements specifying minimum floor-space per student; and student-to-teacher ratios (AEI, 2012). The intent may be to ensure quality, but by focusing on inputs rather than educational outcomes for students, such measures risk increasing the cost of providing transnational education, resulting in less investment, higher fees and smaller enrolments. After a decade of expansion, there is a danger that decisions made at the national level and interpreted by a wide range of national and provincial government agencies may serve to slow future development while having little impact on students' outcomes. The rationale for such a regulatory approach is unclear but the concentration of access to cross-border higher education within an affluent stratum in Vietnam's large cities poses a challenge for authorities concerned about growing inequalities arising from economic liberalization.

Conclusion

While Vietnam has a long history of international influence, the patterns of influence in the current era are very different from the colonial and Cold War periods. Rather than importing wholesale the system characteristics, politics and cultural tropes of a dominant foreign power, contemporary educational flows have been notably multilateral and quite instrumentally geared towards enhancing the country's ability to compete in the global economy through the transfer of knowledge and skills from abroad. The Vietnamese government, while dependent upon collaboration with states having more resources and more established higher education systems, is able to strategically steer the forms of international collaboration much more actively than in the past.

Nevertheless, the ongoing imbalance in international relationships is a cause for concern. Tuyết speaks for many when she worries that "the tendency of continuing buying, importing, receiving, accepting and following Western Policies and practice ties Vietnam HE to the values and norms which may not be appropriate for the local context and culture" (2014, p. 67). Clearly, Vietnam is a diverse society and there are many different views about exactly what values and norms are appropriate, but all would agree that the borrowing of higher education policy and practice should be carefully considered and thoughtful. The continuing challenge is to develop modes of collaboration that allow for forms of internationalization that are responsive to local needs and values, and which promote forms of reciprocity and exchange. Since the early 1990s, many successful partnerships embodying these characteristics have indeed been developed and have been sustained over time, and these can provide guiding models for the next wave of internationalization. Let us hope also that those experiments that did not suit the Vietnamese context and did not foster mutual respect will be consigned to the footnotes of history.

Chapter 13

Internationalization of Higher Education in China

A National Scenario

Rui Yang

Introduction

Over the past three decades, the international dimension and positioning of higher education in the global arena has been high on the agenda of national governments and higher education institutions (Altbach, Reisberg & Rumbley, 2009). Internationalization is a focal point at all levels from national and regional governments to institutions and individual knowledge workers. The process has been particularly facilitated by supra-national and regional initiatives such as the Bologna Process. While nearly all national governments are keen to promote internationalization to address both regional and global challenges as a comparative perspective (Ayoubi & Massoud, 2007), internationalization takes various forms and shapes. The actual experiences of various nations differ markedly, often with strikingly different costs and benefits.

For China, internationalization has long been a survival tool since its earlier encounters with the West in the 19th century. China's modernization started from establishing higher institutions to learn Western languages and knowledge. From the late 1970s, the internationalization of higher education in China has been motivated by a desire for realizing "the four modernizations" (of industry, agriculture, defense and science and technology, through implementation of economic reform). Under such policy reform, the internationalization of higher education takes various forms including studying overseas and dispatching Chinese students and academic staff members abroad for advanced studies and research; attracting foreign students; integrating an international dimension into university teaching and learning including introducing foreign textbooks, references and the development of both English programs and bilingual programs; and providing transnational programs in cooperation with foreign/overseas partner institutions in Chinese universities.

For historical and cultural reasons, China's experience of higher education internationalization contrasts sharply with those of Western societies. For nearly two centuries, external values and knowledge have been imposed on Chinese people and society. Therefore, ever since the 19th century, rather than introducing such values and knowledge, China's priority has been to digest and integrate them with indigenous Chinese traditions. For the Chinese, internationalization has rarely been peaceful and pleasant; in fact the process has been shot through with intense ideological and cultural conflicts. Theoretical frameworks developed in the West thus do not apply well in the Chinese context. Although China faces a number of fundamental issues, its recent internationalization strategies, together with other policies, have drastically transformed its higher education in both quantitative and qualitative terms. China's experience has been highly strategic and, within a much altered context, internationalization of higher education has begun to take different orientations to meet new demands. Built upon some previous work that remains largely valid (e.g., Yang, 2002; Huang, 2003), this chapter reports and assesses some of the latest developments.

China's Higher Education Internationalization in Historical and Cultural Perspective

Although often found on the lips of people in higher education, the concept of internationalization has been elusive. People use this same term with very different meanings (Knight, 1997; Callan, 1998). While higher education institutions worldwide promote internationalization, achieving a common definition has not proved simple. There has even been "an increasing fuzziness of the subject characterized by unclear demarcation of concepts" (Kehm & Teichler, 2007, p. 262). As Bennett and Kane have pointed out (2011), there is allegedly much confusion at the institutional level regarding what internationalization is. According to Elkin, Farnsworth and Templer (2008), while most business schools and departments in the United Kingdom offer numerous courses that incorporate the word "international," the contents, purposes and directions of these courses vary enormously. In some cases, internationalization is interpreted to mean little more than a requirement to improve facilities for foreign students; in others it is associated with root and branch reform of syllabuses and teaching methods.

Different perspectives have been adopted to examine university internationalization, and therefore various understandings of the term abound, with diverse emphases and various approaches. De Wit, Hunter, Howard and Egron-Polak (2015) have revised Knight's definition (Knight, 2003, p. 2) to better serve societal and systemic analyses. They view internationalization as:

> The intentional process of integrating an international, intercultural or global dimension into the purpose, functions and delivery of postsecondary education, in order to enhance the quality of education and research for all students and staff, and to make a meaningful contribution to society.
>
> (De Wit et al., 2015, p. 29)

Treating internationalization as always positive, definitions of this kind are usually based mainly on the experiences of developed Western societies, which have had few external cultural values and knowledge imposed on them in recent centuries.

Unlike most Western higher education systems that badly need to incorporate cultural values other than their own into institutional establishments, internationalization has often been a painful experience for many non-Western societies resulting from historical facts of political colonization and cultural imperialism. Westerners often forget this fact, while non-Westerners never do. Instead of importing further external values, the highest priority for non-Western societies is to package Western and traditional values nicely together. In this sense, internationalization in non-Western societies has been poorly understood. Concepts and theories based only on Western experiences do not always serve non-Western societies well.

Uniquely European in origin and characteristics, modern universities are an imported concept to most non-Western societies. Starting from the establishment of colonies by European states since the late 15th century, the West has come to the non-Western world with immense prestige. Due to colonialism, the Western university model spread worldwide from the mid 19th century to the present time. Even countries that escaped colonial domination adopted Western models (Altbach, 2001). Definitive features of the Western university model include intellectual freedom in research and teaching, university autonomy, the growth of independent disciplines with their own standards and priorities, and internationalism (Anderson, 2009). Such a model has never been tolerant toward alternatives, leading to inefficacy of universities in non-Western societies, for whom a so-called "international" perspective was imposed on them from the outset.

With the diffusion of the European model into universities throughout the world, the colonial heritage and the fact that contemporary universities are Western institutions without much linkage to indigenous intellectual traditions, there has been a failure of non-Western societies to effectively establish modern higher education systems. Non-Western universities have accepted the cultural values underlying the Western model, which may not accurately reflect their own culture and traditions (Altbach, 2001). In China, the integration between Chinese and Western ideas of a university remains unfinished despite many efforts to indigenize the Western concept since the 19th century. The markedly different cultural heritages have caused continuous conflicts between the traditional Chinese and the imported Western ideas of a university. The more developed a Chinese university is, the further away it is from its cultural traditions. China's unique higher learning tradition has been a problem rather than an asset in the modernization of Chinese universities.

Right from the outset, these two value systems have never been on an equal footing. Although China has its centuries-old rich traditions in higher learning, its oldest modern university was only founded in 1893 as a "Self-Strengthening Institute" with European advice (Kirby, 2014). While Chinese higher education has fundamentally operated within the traditional mode of thinking, the Western concept of the modern university has been adopted by the Chinese for its usefulness (Yang, 2011). Since the 1860s, internationalization of higher education has been part of China's salvation movement. Its fundamental meaning is to learn

Western knowledge and technology to make China strong, to "learn from the barbarians to ward off the barbarians," in the words of the then Chinese best thinkers. Such a fundamental understanding of internationalization had remained largely unchanged until China's most recent rise. During the past one-and-a-half centuries, priorities and measures of China's internationalization have changed in accordance with the changing international political economy and China's positioning within it. China imitated major Western countries, leaned toward the former Soviet Union, and has now turned back to Western nations for standards.

Even with recent developments, Western models influence the direction of change in China's higher education institutions. With this fully institutionalized, the coexistence of both value systems proves extremely challenging. The difficulty lies in the fact that Chinese and Western traditions do not tolerate each other. Their clash has become the most fundamental cultural condition for the development of higher education in China. Indeed, it is a specter that has been lingering and haunting China for more than a century. The "pain" caused is felt constantly by individuals, and tensions exist at both institutional and systemic levels. Such cultural experience has not been accurately captured and fully analyzed in the literature, which is more technical than thoughtful, and has overwhelmingly portrayed the powerful influence of economic and political realities. What is lacking is an appropriate combination of the "international" and the local. Within the contemporary context of Western dominance, the internationalization of higher education in China necessarily touches on the long-standing knotty issues of and tensions between Westernization and indigenization. As demonstrated above, although China escaped colonial domination, it has still widely adopted Western models. Elements of China's long historical traditions directly affect its global engagement in higher education. This chapter thus argues for the significance of historical and cultural perspectives on the internationalization of Chinese higher education.

Dilemmas and Paradoxes in China's Internationalization of Higher Education

Ever since China's survival was under serious threat in the 19th century, the crucial significance of internationalization has been widely accepted by Chinese educators and administrators, especially in higher education. Such a fact is not always well understood by international observers, partly because there has been a lack of specific policy on internationalization despite its vital role in China's higher education reform. Instead, internationalization has been scattered throughout various policy documents and speeches by higher education leaders at different levels. This lack of policy could be overestimated. Internationalization strategies and approaches take a variety of forms in China's regions and even between different institutions within the same region, although a general understanding of the internationalization of higher education is largely shared throughout the country. This is of note considering the tight government control over higher education.

Internationalization of Chinese higher education thus faces various dilemmas and even paradoxes since China's priority has long been to catch up with the West, focusing overwhelmingly on practicality with little attention paid to cultural and ideological issues. Once China's material development reaches a certain level, it suddenly realizes its shortage of well-thought-out design for future directions. This is displayed at national and institutional levels in both policy and practice and has led to lack of coordination and integration in policies and practice between government and higher education, causing contradictory decisions and inefficacy.

For instance, in Sino-foreign joint ventures, while central government aims to import the world's most advanced educational resources to boost capacity, individual institutions hope to capitalize on demand for foreign qualifications as they often fail alone to attract students. This mismatch contributes to China's overall failure to upgrade higher education and attract foreign capital through Sino-foreign joint programs. Without a clearly defined legal identity, China fails to govern this new activity within its regulatory frameworks. Central government may approve or charter the establishment of joint education programs in line with existing legal frameworks, but lack of consistent intervention after approval leaves responsibility for quality entirely in the hands of teaching staff and program coordinators. Concerned over quality and reputation, China's Ministry of Education has recently tightened legislation on Sino-foreign programs and revoked approval of existing programs and institutions in a bid to better regulate joint ventures.

The first dilemma is between China's proactive strategies and its anxiety for educational sovereignty. The most striking feature of its strategies for internationalization has been vigorous engagement with the outside world, especially with Western societies. This attitude is not only unprecedented in its modern history, but also differs from many other developing countries' interactions with the developed Western world. China's embrace of the English language is a telling example. At both national policy and individual career development levels, English language education has been a subject of paramount importance since China reopened to the outside world. English proficiency is regarded as a national as well as a personal asset (Hu, 2005). English-language education has been viewed by the leadership and populace as having a vital role in national modernization and development (Pan, 2011). China has initiated various policies to adapt to the dominant status of English, instead of resisting it. Learning English is no longer just important, it is the bare minimum for any serious student and now China is home to more speakers of English than any other country in the world. Examinations in Chinese schools at all levels include English proficiency tests and it is widely required in professional promotion for academics, including many whose work requires little use of English.

This emphasis on the strategic role of English in the modernization process and the high priority given to English on the national agenda of educational development has proven to be beneficial (Hu, 2005). China's efforts are already paying off. The communicative and instrumental function of English as a lingua franca and its global reach has accelerated China's foreign trade and helped China's economic growth in the past decades. It has also promoted China's exchanges with the outside world (Chang, 2006). Chinese scholars and students in major universities have little difficulty in communicating with international scholars. From 1980 to 2010, the number of peer-reviewed papers published by Chinese researchers rose 64-fold (Yang, 2012a). Such experience contrasts markedly with those of many other non-English speaking countries, including China's neighbors.

At the same time, China is concerned about its possible loss of educational sovereignty (Wang & Xue, 2004). With increasingly intensified globalization, unprecedented linkage with the outside world makes even China's top education policy-makers cautious about their "education information security," meaning protection from external influences through foreign media and the Internet. Such a concern, however, is not China-specific. A report commissioned by European university heads warned that as a result of the development of transnational education, national autonomy and sovereignty in higher education have never been challenged on such a scale (Adam, 2001).

Although the issue is increasingly international, China's concern has been particularly due to its tightly centralized higher education system and its, often nominal, emphasis on socialist ideology. One expression of this concern is that no fewer than half the governing body of foreign/Chinese partner institutions must be Chinese citizens, and the president or equivalent must be Chinese and residing in China. This has led to ambiguity regarding the legal status of foreign higher education activity in China. Rather than being integrated into China's higher education system, it is regarded as supplementary during certain stages of higher education development.

The second dilemma is disciplinary disparities between natural, social and human sciences. Previous international studies have shown that internationalization, the means to implement it and the extent of internationalization policies all depend on specific subject matter. Thus, "hard" sciences, like engineering, usually attain higher levels of internationalization than "soft" (Knight & de Wit, 1997; Yang, 2002) and are emphasized over humanities and social sciences in international programs (Cannon & Djajanegara, 1997; de Wit & Callan, 1995). Until now, disciplinary situations have changed very little, especially in non-Western societies. This is due to the varied ideologies, paradigms and discourses inherent in humanities and social sciences and the high dependency on language to convey meaning. In these fields, domestic considerations are given more weight than in natural sciences, technology and medical sciences (Altbach, 1998).

However, in an era characterized by conflicts and contradictions, the social and human sciences have never been more significant, owing to a relentless blend of the state, political parties, social movements and civil society actors (Wagner, 1999). Meanwhile, social sciences and the humanities worldwide face unprecedented complexities. Contemporary globalization challenges all the social sciences both by offering great opportunities and undermining entrenched traditions, putting the fundamental paradigms of each social science discipline into jeopardy. A newly conceptualized global social science is entailed, primarily for non-Western societies as the disciplines evolved in the West, almost completely ignoring the situation in countries formerly under their domination during the age of imperialism, preferring to think of them as *backward* and unworthy of serious attention, to be exploited but not admired (Riggs, 2001). They are foreign imports in the organization of knowledge (Dirlik, 2012, p. 1).

Chinese humanities and social sciences scholars have not achieved the international visibility of their natural science and engineering peers. As noted above, China's overall representation in the international scientific community has grown rapidly since reopening itself to the world. Chinese scholars appearing in prestigious natural and social science journals numbered 1,293 in 1981, climbing to 11,435 by 1995. They were cited 8,517 times in 1981–1985, then 77,841 times by 1993–1997 (World Bank, 2000). In contrast, few publications produced by Chinese social scientists have appeared in international citation indices, an increasingly important tool in evaluation of research at institutional, departmental and individual levels, but not popularly employed in China because academics in the field rarely publish internationally. In 1985, Mainland Chinese social scientists produced 80 international publications, increasing to 202 in 1996 (Fan, 2000). In 2010, China had 121,500 scientific publications listed by the Science Citation Index, of which 5,287 (2.41%) were in social sciences (Zhang & Yuan, 2011).

Such disparities aggravate the tensions between social sciences researchers and those in natural and engineering sciences. It becomes an even more severe problem because an overwhelming majority of institutional and ministerial leaders in China are from natural sciences and engineering, and have traditionally shown scant concern for humanities and social sciences (Deng, 1995). This has also been confirmed repeatedly by my fieldwork interviews at Chinese universities. The humanities and social sciences in China are, however, being confronted with an unprecedented global context in which the international knowledge network has divided nations into center, semi-center and periphery (Altbach, 1998). This has been substantially strengthened by the exponential growth of the Internet (Farquhar, 1999) and by the use of English as a global language (Crystal, 1997; Yang, 2001; Curry & Lillis, 2015). Meanwhile, many signs indicate that China's Open Door policy will continue, so one urgent task for China is to increase internationalization in its humanities and social sciences research, indicating China's intent to integrate with the international scholarly community.

The third dilemma is regional gaps. As reported by Gu (2010), international student numbers in Beijing were 199 times more than those in Guizhou in 2007. The gap between the highest five and the lowest five provinces was 45 times. Similarly, the proportion of international teachers reached 2.5%, 1.1% and 1.0% respectively in institutions in eastern, central and western regions, while the proportion of international students were 2.6%, 0.6% and 1.1%. Most recently, the China Education Association for International Exchange (CEAIE, 2015) was commissioned by the Ministry of Education to conduct a national survey on internationalization of higher education in China. Covering 1,205 national major and provincial institutions located in various regions, it employed 9 first-tier and 22 second-tier indicators and 57 observing points. First-tier indicators include strategy, organization/management, teachers, students, curriculum/teaching, research, joint-running programs/schools, Confucius Institutes and international cooperation and exchanges. The findings show considerable regional differences in the internationalization of higher education.

Fourth, there are uniformities and disparities in China's purposes of and strategies for internationalization. Higher education institutions of varying status within the system act in very similar ways, from national flagships such as Peking and Tsinghua universities to regional specialized institutions like the Ocean University at Qingdao in Shandong Province or Xinjiang University, which neighbors Central Asian Islamic countries. Meanwhile, internal differentiation among higher education institutions is increasing. While China's best institutions have integrated internationalization well into their daily work and life, it is hardly visible in regional institutions. Academics at major institutions are pushed to publish and collaborate with peers in English-speaking countries; such pressure is nonexistent in regional institutions, with some exceptions such as institutions in Guangxi Autonomous Region and Yunnan Province, which have substantial collaboration and exchange with counterparts in the much-neglected Southeast Asian countries (Yang, 2012b).

There have been evident disparities of other types (Gu, 2010), such as gender imbalances among returnees; of those who returned in 2014, 59.16% were female (Lu, 2016). There are also other kinds of dissymmetry. For example, while Chinese national research universities have a strong awareness of national identity, roles and duties, the same is not true of their global identity or responsibilities (Liang, 2016). This is despite the fact that China's best universities now benchmark themselves with major international peers and so in the past two decades they have embraced a much larger international sense of themselves (Yang, 2009). The Chinese government has assigned important roles to a number of research universities to improve China's global competiveness and advance tertiary education to a world-class level. During the last two decades their primary focus has been on catching up with the best in the world and competing on the international stage rather than serving global communities and addressing global issues. These dilemmas and paradoxes are important in fully understanding China's higher education. They have also cost the Chinese system dearly. Their solutions concern the lifeblood of the system.

Latest Developments and New Directions

Over the past decades, Chinese higher education has shifted from nearly complete divorce from the international community to close linkage and proactive engagement. China's overall level of internationalization continues to rise. Chinese institutions have clear strategies for (95%) and designated committees (86.5%) on internationalization (CEAIE, 2015). Over 70% of presidents in member institutions of Project 985, 80% of China's academicians and 90% of Cheung Kong and Thousand Talents Plan scholars have studied overseas. A total of 460,000 Chinese students traveled to over 180 countries to study in 2014 (Yu, 2016). By 2014, 1.7 million Chinese had studied overseas, 1.09 million for degrees. More and more Chinese students studying abroad choose to return upon graduation, from 24.5% in 2010 to 46.6% (Zhang, 2013).

Meanwhile China has become a significant study destination, with over three million international students from more than 200 countries by 2014 and 380,000 in 2014 itself. Over 775 higher education institutions and research institutes had hosted international students, with an institutional average of 390 and a maximum of 6,572 at Beijing Languages and Culture University (CEAIE, 2015). On average, each Chinese institution hosts 390 international students with 214 and 987 respectively in member institutions of Projects 985 and 211. Several national leaders have studied in China, including the Ethiopian president, Kazakhstan prime minister, Vietnamese deputy premier and a Thai princess (Yu, 2016).

China's development has reached a new stage with a growing and much more comprehensive demand for higher education, creating fresh expectations of internationalization. There are increasingly coordinated internationalization efforts between governments and higher education institutions. Internationalization approaches and purposes have become more integrated, combining economic, cultural and political dimensions: for example, the "One Belt, One Road" initiative that has infused much rigor into the process of internationalization. Increasing numbers of Chinese studying abroad and foreigners studying and working in China could generate a greater talent and economic reform. That, in turn, will promote the Chinese economy, accelerating its international expansion and boosting its soft power and global competitiveness. Instead of being a passive recipient influenced by the major world powers, China now reaches out globally and invests heavily overseas, actively using international exchange and cooperation in higher education as an exercise of soft power (Yang, 2012c). China has reached a new phase of global engagement and internationalization, shifting from one-way import of foreign (Western) knowledge into China to a much-improved balance between introducing the world into China and bringing China to the world.

Another demonstration of this is the Confucius Institutes program, linked with universities around the world, which exploit the critical role of higher education in the projection of soft power. Through these institutes, China promotes international exchange and collaboration to expand its global influence, seeking to formalize the benefits of its rich heritage. China has used this network to expand its international influence via promoting Chinese language and culture; arguably China's most systematically planned soft power policy, revealing its ability to plan for the long term. The combination of higher education with the appeal of Confucianism offers Beijing a comparative advantage in its soft power approach

(Shambaugh, 2005; Kurlantzick, 2006), and provides Chinese and foreign universities with a platform for collaboration and exchange.

Against this backdrop, overseas study has been integrated into China's central policy and planning, especially since the national conference held in 2014, with full use being made of studying abroad in talent cultivation, including for national leadership of the country. In line with social and economic developments, a number of policies related to internationalization of higher education have been promulgated. The 2010 Study in China Project aims to host Asia's largest body of half-a-million international students by 2020. In 2015, the Ministry of Education issued the Action Plan for Overseas Study 2015–2017 to bring order to affairs in overseas study. The plan aligns itself with national political and economic initiatives by cultivating cutting-edge talent urgently needed by China's nation-building, training personnel to work in and/or with international organizations, grooming a large number of professionals with proficiency in languages of many developing countries and attracting young future leaders from a variety of countries to study in China.

To fulfill such goals, China has to address various problems. First, while the overwhelming majority of Chinese students studying overseas are enrolled in degree programs, only a small proportion of international students are studying for degrees in China. Second, China's education export faces a number of difficulties and challenges in scale and quality to match its rising global influence and economic status. Financially, earnings from education exports were about US$0.31 billion in 2015, yet it contributed US$20 billion to America, US$11.33 billion to Australia and US$7.6 billion to Canada. Third, China badly needs highly advanced personnel in some areas, but very few returnees are in those fields. For instance, although it is the world's second largest aero-market, China has no academicians in aero-dynamics. It has diplomatic relations with 172 nations speaking 95 official languages, of which only 7 are widely used, so China needs professionals in many less widely used languages. Yet, few Chinese students currently study in those countries (Yu, 2016). Fourth, although China sends its most talented students abroad, the quality of international students in China has long been low.

There have been some new changes to China's landscape of internationalization. According to the bluebook report on Chinese students studying abroad (Center for China & Globalization, 2015), Asia's recent development, with its fast pace of regionalization, has exerted an impact on the conventional pattern of international higher education. More and more Chinese students chose to study in neighboring countries along the "One Belt, One Road" route that have close economic and cultural relations with China (Center for China & Globalization, 2015). From 2012 the Chinese government dramatically increased the number of scholarships to facilitate this. Chinese companies, such as Huawei, PetroChina and Qinghua Group, are also investing in the countries along the route. A support system with multiple layers and dimensions is gradually being set up. In 2012, over 28,000 international students were on Chinese government scholarships (Zhang, 2013).

End Remarks

China's current internationalization of higher education is a continuity of its history, with different periods seeing different forms of internationalization. Since China's first modern university was established in the 1890s, learning from the West has been strongly advocated as the only way to make China strong. The past decades of higher education internationalization continued the importing of foreign (Western) knowledge into China. From the early 2000s, China began to pay more attention to exporting Chinese knowledge to the world (Su, 2009), representing a new era in internationalization. China's internationalization is strongly influenced by economic and political realities and characterized by a lack of cultural perspective, although history has repeatedly shown that transferring Western practices conflicts with Chinese traditions. Modern universities are a foreign transplant in China and indigenous higher learning institutions shared only superficial resemblances with medieval universities in Europe. The central purpose of China's internationalization of higher education is to combine Chinese and Western elements.

There have been only two historical cases in which foreign influences had such a great impact on Chinese culture that it was fundamentally changed. One was the introduction of Buddhism, which took over a millennium to reshape Chinese mentalities at both the intellectual and the popular levels. The other, the intrusion of Western culture into China since the 19th century, is still ongoing as a result of large-scale Western expansion. The magnitude of the second, far greater than the first, began at a time when the vitality of Chinese culture was just about exhausted while Western culture was at its zenith (Hsu, 2001). The process is far from completed, and pain is felt on a daily basis. China's contemporary higher education internationalization is part of this much wider process. Therefore, certain definitions of internationalization that work well in Western societies could be unfit for China. Analyses that fail to recognize this do not grasp the real essence of the issues. Reflecting China's position in the world, higher education internationalization plays a significant role in preparation for China's global roles. In the context of growing Chinese power, the global higher education community waits expectantly for what will happen in the years ahead.

Chapter 14

Human Capital or Talent Development?

A Paradigm Shift by Malaysian Higher Education

Jasvir Kaur Nachatar Singh

Introduction

Many anglophone and Western European countries recognize international students as valuable talents and are making significant progress to retain international students on graduation. Meanwhile, the Malaysian higher education system develops international students as talent to better serve their home countries in particular. International students in Malaysia have come mainly from the Asian region and African countries, partly because of the cultural similarities with Malaysia as a Muslim nation, with ready access to halal food etc. They also come because of affordable tuition fees, the relatively low cost of living (Singh, Schapper & Gavin, 2014), economic and political stability, along with the diversity of local cultures and customs (Ministry of Higher Education (MOHE) Malaysia, 2011a).

These regions are still considered as underdeveloped or developing economies, therefore in this regard the Malaysian higher education system seeks to create a positive impact by subtly improving them through the soft power concept (MOHE Malaysia, 2011b). Soft power includes 'the capabilities and intentions of institutions to capture the hearts and minds of local and international stakeholders to collectively accept values, ideologies and cultures of learning that can benefit communities' (MOHE Malaysia, 2011b, p. 18). The manifestation of soft power in the Malaysian higher education system occurs by capturing the hearts and minds of international students via the internationalization agenda, including knowledge- or technology-transfer activities, student and lecturer exchange programs as well as participation of both students and lecturers in field trips and community activities (MOHE Malaysia, 2011b).

Using this exploration of hearts and minds as the analytic focus, this chapter reports on findings from semi-structured qualitative interviews conducted with 33 postgraduate international students, ten academic staff and 12 professional staff members, which indicate the acquisition of soft and research skills, as well as contribution to home countries/societies. From this study, we will see that the research findings do correspond with the objective of developing international students as talent through the soft power agenda. This significant paradigm shift has important implications for the Malaysian government strategy.

Context

International student mobility is not a recent phenomenon as students have been studying in other countries since 600 bc (Altbach et al., 1993). According to Sirat (2009), the majority of international students were enrolled at universities in Organisation for Economic Cooperation and Development (OECD) countries, particularly the United States, United Kingdom, Germany, France and Australia. In the last decade, due to the rapid expansion of international student mobility, Asian countries such as Malaysia, Singapore, China, Hong Kong and Japan are strengthening their internationalization strategies to attract international students to those countries (Bhandari & Blumenthal, 2011; Knight, 2011a). Over the past decade, international student mobility has become a significant part of the Malaysian international higher education landscape.

The majority of scholarly work on international students comes from English-speaking countries as they have received international students for the past 30 to 40 years. These groundbreaking studies have shed light mostly on the decision-making of international students (Maringe & Carter, 2007; Soutar & Turner, 2002) and international student adjustment issues (Andrade, 2006; Campbell & Li, 2008; Li, Chen & Duanmu, 2009). Similarly, the Malaysian literature on international students is mainly based on general adjustment challenges of international students at undergraduate level (Devi & Nair, 2008; Mahmud, Amat, Rahman & Ishak, 2010; Najafi & Lea-Baranovich, 2013; Olutokunbo et al., 2013; Yusoff, 2012; Yusoff & Chelliah, 2010). Although there are studies on postgraduate international students, the scope is still limited to teaching and learning experiences (Kaur & Sidhu, 2009; Trahar, 2014) and social interactions between international postgraduate students and domestic students (Pandian, 2008), as opposed to exploring the educational outcomes of postgraduate international students.

Therefore, this chapter attempts to produce insights into the question: *What are the soft power outcomes in Malaysia?* It is important to address this because international students are paying significant amounts of money to obtain an international education (Ziguras & Law, 2006). A further rationale is how these educational outcomes resonate with the main motivations or intentions of Malaysian higher education's paradigm shift using the soft power approach.

The first section of this chapter draws attention to the historical development of Malaysian higher education with an emphasis on internationalization policy. This is followed by an overview of the soft power concept adopted by Malaysian higher education, which provides an authentic impact on students, societies and industries at local and international levels. Then, a brief discussion of the research methods underpinning the findings is presented. Finally, the key findings are outlined, along with discussion highlighting the soft power outcomes based on the lived experiences of participants.

Historical Development of Malaysian Higher Education

Malaysian higher education has undergone a series of reforms since the nation's independence from British rule in 1957. A typology of the history of higher education has been developed that builds on the first three phases, or three waves of expansion, as described by Lee in her monograph, *Restructuring Higher Education in Malaysia* (Lee, 2004a). Identification of an additional fourth phase was outlined by an emerging researcher in the Malaysian higher education field (Singh, 2009). These phases reflect economic reform from an agricultural to an industrial and now to a knowledge-based economy, to produce an appropriate workforce or human capital to support economic transformation (Sato, 2005). Table 14.1 provides an overview of these four phases.

Phase 1 is referred to as education for the elite. With an economy predominantly based on agriculture, only one university was established to service the entire tertiary education needs of Malaysia, with emphasis given instead to primary and secondary education (Lee, 2004b; Sirat, 2008a). However, Phase 2 saw a growing demand for skilled workers as the economy shifted to a more industrialized base (Yonezawa, 2003). The ethnic quota admission policy began (Lee, 2004a) with the rationale of assisting 'Bumiputras',[1] or people of Malay ethnicity, to gain equality through education with other ethnic groups such as Chinese and Indians (Selvaratnam, 1988). In short, this policy was designed to bridge the ethnic imbalance since colonization by the British between 1832 and 1946 (Sato, 2005). The main outcome was an increase in the number of Bumiputra students enrolled in public higher learning institutions (Muda, 2008). During this phase more universities were established in the fields of technology, sciences, engineering and business.

Phase 3 is considered the peak point, with massive restructuring of Malaysian higher education, and is referred to as 'Education as and for business'. Private institutions were permitted to be established and a corporatization policy was developed to strengthen and sustain the higher education sector (Lee, 2004a; Marimuthu, 2008). Legislation enabled private universities and university colleges to confer their own degrees from pre-university through to postgraduate levels (Karim & Maarof, 2012). As of 2009, the Ministry of Higher Education reported 44 registered private universities and university colleges, five foreign university branch campuses and more than 300 private colleges (MOHE Malaysia, 2010). Through privatization international student mobility blossomed.

The current position (Phase 4) is 'Education for global competition to compete on a global stage' (Singh, 2009), marking the knowledge-based economy era and focusing on producing a knowledgeable and highly skilled workforce (Baba, 2004). The 2013 merger between the Ministry of Higher Education and the Ministry of Education is perceived as an important event (Lee, 2015). Both ministries had established strategic plans and blueprints for the development of the school and higher education sectors, the MOE's Malaysia Education

Table 14.1 Outline of Malaysian higher education: a brief history

Typology	Education for elite	Education for affirmative action	Education as and for business	Education for global competition
Phase	Pre-1970 (Phase 1)	Post 1970–1990 (Phase 2)	Post 1990–2000 (Phase 3)	Post 2000–now (Phase 4)
Description	Only one university – University of Malaya	Establishment of other state-controlled universities	Establishment of other state-controlled universities	Establishment of Ministry of Higher Education (MOHE)
	Emphasis on primary and secondary education	Ethnic quota admission policy	Evidence of market – Introduction of overseas private post-secondary education including universities and corporatization of public higher learning institutions Establish quality mechanisms [further enhanced in the fourth phase with the establishment of the Malaysian Qualifications Agency (MQA)]	Evidence of internationalization Establishment of Research University Establishment of APEX university Merger between the Ministry of Higher Education (MOHE) and the Ministry of Education (MOE)

Sources: Lee (2004b); Singh (2009).

Blueprint 2013–2025, and the MOHE's National Higher Education Strategic Plan (NHESP) 2007–2020 (Lee, 2015). So the merger was initiated by government to ease implementation and oversee education overall.

This phase also witnessed the constitution of research universities in 2006 and the Accelerated Programme for Excellence (APEX) University in 2008 to develop human capital through 'advanced academic culture that focused on research, collaborative work, meritocratic values and top-quality teaching' (Altbach & Postiglione, 2006, p. 25).

Internationalization of Malaysian Higher Education

This section provides an overview of internationalization in Malaysia, which sees international student mobility as the main indicator (MOHE Malaysia, 2011a). As shown in Table 14.2 and clearly demonstrated by the line graphs

Table 14.2 International student enrolment in Malaysian public and private higher learning institutions

	2001	2002	2003	2004	2005	2006	2007	2008	2009	2010	2011	2012	2013
Public	N/A	5,045	5,239	5,735	6,622	7,941	14,324	18,485	22,456	24,214	25,855	26,232	28,826
Private		22,827	25,158	25,939	33,903	36,449	33,604	50,679	58,294	62,705	45,246	57,306	52,971
Total	**18,242**	**27,872**	**30,397**	**31,674**	**40,525**	**44,390**	**47,928**	**69,164**	**80,750**	**86,919**	**71,101**	**83,538**	**81,797**

Figure 14.1 International student enrolment in Malaysian public and private higher learning institutions.

(Source: Ministry of Education Malaysia, 2011; Ministry of Higher Education Malaysia, 2007, 2010, 2013).

In Figure 14.1, there has been a steady growth in the number of international students in Malaysian public and private higher learning institutions. In 2011, in private higher education institutions alone, 18,242 international students were reported as studying in Malaysia (Ministry Asia etc. 2007, and in just over ten years this grew to 81,797 international students in 2013 (Ministry of Education Malaysia 2014). In addition, students have mainly come from China, Indonesia, Iran and Pakistan in recent years (MOHE Malaysia 2013, 2012). As noted earlier, a key strength is the sense of comfort that Malaysia, as a Muslim majority, with ready ... Islam ... students feel (ibid). On the other hand, students from neighbouring countries such as Indonesia benefit the ease in terms of strong ... families, the ease to adapt to culture, and similar education systems ... ... while Iranian students are known to select their home countries and affected by living costs (Sato 2005).

Most international students enroll in public universities, yet IT post-graduates are in all the research universities, the three social sciences in the case of Malaysia, University Kebangsaan and others and Universiti Teknologi Malaysia. The justification for this... with expansion of the graduate students is to send the world class researchers and services at international research collaborations (Ministry of Education Malaysia, 2007). Fortunately, one

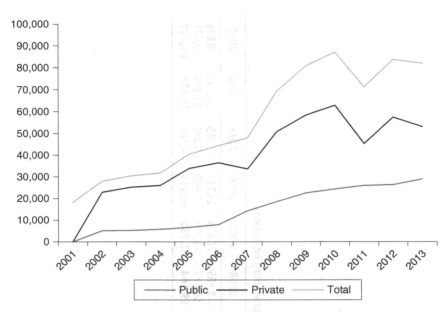

Figure 14.1. International student enrolment in Malaysian public and private higher learning institutions.
(Source: Ministry of Education Malaysia, n.d., 2014; Ministry of Higher Education Malaysia, 2007, 2010, 2012).

in Figure 14.1, there has been a steady growth in the number of international students in Malaysian public universities but there was a dip, starting in 2011, in private higher education institutions. In 2001, 18,242 international students were reported as studying in Malaysia (MOHE Malaysia, 2007) and in just over ten years this grew to 81,797 international students in 2013 (Ministry of Education Malaysia, 2014). International students have mainly come from Iran, China, Indonesia, Yemen and Nigeria in recent years (MOHE Malaysia, 2010, 2012). As noted earlier, a key attraction is the sense of similarity in Malaysia as a Muslim nation, with ready access to halal food (Singh et al., 2014). On the other hand, students from neighbouring countries such as China and Indonesia choose Malaysia due to strong historical links, the sharing of common languages and similar education systems following the British system, as well as proximity to their home countries and affordable living costs (Sirat, 2008b).

Most international students enrolled at public universities, especially postgraduate, are in all five research universities, Universiti Malaya, Universiti Sains Malaysia, Universiti Kebangsaan Malaysia, Universiti Putra Malaysia and Universiti Teknologi Malaysia. The justification for this growth, especially of postgraduate students, is to generate world-class research outputs and strengthen international research collaboration (Ministry of Education Malaysia, 2004). Intriguingly, one criteria for being selected as a research university is that it must have at least 10% international postgraduate students (Ministry of Education Malaysia, 2004).

Based on this growth, Knight (2014) has profiled Malaysia as a student hub. The notion of a student hub focuses on widening access to higher education, modernizing and internationalizing local higher learning institutions, generating revenue from international students and raising the country's higher education ranking (Knight & Lee, 2014). The ministry has set specific targets on attracting international students. For example, in 2010 a target of 100,000 international students was set, accelerating to 150,000 in 2015, and 200,000 for 2020, according to the Internationalisation Policy document (MOHE Malaysia, 2011a).

Malaysian Higher Education: Soft Power Agenda

Globally, higher education institutions are faced with enormous pressure to re-evaluate conventional practices to deliver outcomes in line with the changing political, educational and economic environment (MOHE Malaysia, 2011b). Malaysia, too, has to respond to these challenges and create a more positive impact both for local stakeholders and international communities (MOHE Malaysia, 2011b). There is thus a need for a paradigm shift in higher education to devise new ideas for teaching and learning, research activities and community engagement to better serve underdeveloped economies (MOHE Malaysia, 2011b). Soft power is the focus of this paradigm shift and is a diplomatic tool to propel Malaysia's current status as a student hub to a hub of skills, knowledge and innovation, vital in this competitive global environment (Aziz & Abdullah, 2014).

The Malaysian approach to soft power has two components. First, the process of capturing the hearts and minds of international students is facilitated through the internationalization agenda – knowledge- or technology-transfer activities, student and lecturer exchange programs, participation of students and lecturers in field trips and community activities (MOHE Malaysia, 2011b). In the following sections, this component is explored based on the lived experiences of postgraduate international students, academics and professional staff in one of the Malaysian research universities. Second, to structure the soft power concept, institutions are required to provide physical infrastructure by setting up branches abroad for the realization of the planned project and organizing Malaysian-themed education exhibitions regionally or internationally (MOHE Malaysia, 2011b).

According to Gribble (2008, p. 25), international students are little ambassadors of their country of origin in 'maintaining close political, diplomatic and trade links with the countries where they studied'. Therefore, Grayson (2005) notes that international students are able to develop networks and partnerships that can accelerate the eventual development of economic and trade links between the host country and their countries of origin. This partnership could be further supported and cultivated through the soft power approach. Malaysian higher education institutions are able to win over the hearts and minds of international students via internationalization events, research initiatives, community engagement and teaching activities with a long-term aim of creating significant international trade development and collaborative relations (MOHE Malaysia, 2011b).

In short, the soft power approach broadens the outcomes of Malaysian higher education internationalization to strengthen diplomatic ties between countries, undertake collaborative research initiatives and develop human capital. The outcomes of this agenda will now be explored from the perspectives of international postgraduate students, academics and professional staff members in a Malaysian research university through semi-structured interviews.

Research Approach

Empirical data in this chapter originates from a qualitative doctoral study on academic success and postgraduate international students in Malaysia, in which 55 semi-structured, face-to-face interviews were conducted in English for between 16 and 74 minutes; 33 students were interviewed, representing Iran, Yemen, India, Iraq, Indonesia and China. Most were studying for a PhD (23 students) with only 10 pursuing masters degrees. Interviews were also conducted with 12 professional staff from the Postgraduate Students Office, language support services, library, housing administration and faculties. Ten academics from various faculties such as languages, social sciences, education, management and architecture also participated.

Thematic analysis was adopted to analyse the interview transcripts. The analysis included a coding process involving assignment of keywords, grouping of codes, highlighting of quotes supporting the codes and establishing themes from the codes (Ezzy, 2002). In reporting the findings, for reasons of anonymity and confidentiality participant groups are indicated by the following abbreviations: AS (academic staff), PS (professional staff) and IS (postgraduate international student).

Findings and Discussion

While the study has yielded rich data, for this chapter two vital soft power outcomes are considered: contribution to home countries/societies; and development of research as well as soft skills. These are the outcomes of the soft power agenda that occurred via teaching and learning, research and community engagement activities.

Contribution to Home Countries/Societies

Contribution to home country or community was indicated by all participant groups as the outcome of soft power through the process of knowledge-transfer activities and involvement in research activities. This theme suggests that educational outcomes are not only personal achievements of international students but a social concept. It advocates the application of knowledge learned in Malaysia to their home countries. One senior professor strongly believed that 'Education is all about not just training a person in his discipline, but also able to teach, so that they can do something with it and help the community' (AS 1). Likewise, one professional staff member mentioned that

> when international students complete their studies in [the research university], they receive a holistic education in [the research university], that means in terms of their academic, in terms of their professional and personal skill, when they go back to their home country, they can do something for their home country.
>
> (PS 3)

Holistic education includes developing not only academic but also social skills of international students through academic and non-academic workshops. At this research university, many academic writing and research-related workshops are offered to international students. For example,

> Professional Development Unit provide workshops to all students. Their workshops mostly focus on professional development and management, how to publish, how to be good publisher, how to be a good researcher, and this is open to all and students have benefited from this.
>
> (PS 6)

> A lot of courses: data analysis, how to write your thesis, how to manage your supervisor, time management, many other workshops.
>
> (AS 5)

> The workshop ... can upgrade my knowledge ... mostly, research method and academic writing and statistics.
>
> (IS 15)

Workshops on communication skills, stress-management skills, work-related values, leadership skills and other personal development skills are offered to help students cope with non-academic issues. For instance,

> Conduct workshops for all postgraduate students ... our range of topics ranges from academic skills and also their personal skills ... academic skills, you know, like research skills, management skills, thesis writing, academic writing, and their personal skills are, like, communication skills, stress management, work values, leadership.
>
> (PS 12)

Despite understanding the importance of these programmes, none of the international students in Kingston and Forland's (2008) study used the university's educational development activities/programmes to facilitate their academic and social learning in the new academic environment. One common reason offered was that they lacked time due to being busy studying (Kingston & Forland, 2008). However, in this study, international students highlighted that these skills are then applicable in their home country when they return after studying. Indeed, Montgomery and McDowell's (2009) study acknowledged that the social learning experiences of international students could be considered an aspect of 'global citizenship', as they develop soft skills that are important in preparing them to live and work in a global community.

Specifically, academic staff (who are experienced researchers) and professional staff members perceived that international students could contribute to their home country and society through the application of their knowledge and the discovery of new inventions based on their research findings. The following quotations highlight this view:

> The impact of that PhD to your life … to your current position in your work … like your wisdom, you can tell everybody, you can teach somebody about what you are doing, what the knowledge area in the discipline on what you are doing.
>
> (AS 2)

> Of course to gain knowledge that not only pictures how successful your research is but to be able to spread the knowledge to other people, especially the bottom billion, because most of our students are from those countries where need is in terms of knowledge. So if they are able to spread it to their country and also to us, that is success.
>
> (PS 12)

According to one participant, the 'bottom billion' refers to 'under-developed countries [such as] Laos, Cambodia, Vietnam, Africa [sic], Zimbabwe' (PS 10). These academics and professional staff members believed that, through research projects and the acquisition of research knowledge, international postgraduate students are able to help and contribute to the economic and social development of their home country and society.

Postgraduate international students also confirmed this understanding of academic success. They are capable of helping their community back home through the application of knowledge developed through their international education experience. In particular, two students from Indonesia and Pakistan mentioned that they are able to share and transfer their knowledge as university lecturers in their home countries, articulating their aspiration as follows:

Academic success from my point of view is that, once I return to my society, this knowledge is meaningful for them. So I can use this knowledge to share maybe with the students or with my society, so that encourages them to change. The knowledge is not only for me but, most important, the knowledge is valuable and important for others also.

(IS 2)

I hope when I go back to my home I will re-join my job, I have to transfer this knowledge to my students, and when using these facilities I can enhance my knowledge, I can broaden my vision.

(IS 25)

Further, a Chinese student intends to apply his knowledge in Tourism Planning to develop rural Chinese regions as tourist destinations and raise up the poor in society. His noble thoughts are captured thus:

Before I came here, I worked in a planning company in China, you know, in the tourism field: if you are a tourism planner, you often go to the rural areas to plan tourism destinations, so when I am there, when I saw the poor people, it is my obligation to help them. I want to use my knowledge to help them. I will go back to China and I will continue my career.

(IS 9)

This particular outcome relates to the students' jobs in their home country, as a university lecturer or tourism planner, and their aspirations to share and contribute knowledge learned in Malaysia is considered a success. They are willing to impart valuable knowledge and research to help others and be a useful agent of change in their respective countries and societies. In particular, this outcome accords with the aim of higher education in Malaysia, to 'produce graduates who are knowledgeable and competent in their fields, as well as to be able to put into practice knowledge gained' (MOHE Malaysia, 2007, p. 12), to improve the well-being of the society, nation and the global community.

In short, this finding is in line with the aim of Malaysia's soft power agenda for higher education in terms of developing and empowering human capital globally through teaching, learning, community engagement and research activities.

Research and Soft Skills

As a research university, there are funding systems in place, with supportive management structures, to enhance research activities in developing human capital (Abiddin & Ismail, 2009). Therefore, the development of research and soft skills were also indicated as one of the soft power outcomes at this research university to produce highly skilled people who are able to create, innovate and apply new knowledge and technology to their home countries/societies (MOHE Malaysia, 2011a). These skills are particularly acquired via research activities and cultural engagement initiatives.

For an international student who is a lecturer in Palestine, the ability to conduct research and to develop himself as a good researcher is considered a successful educational outcome:

> Academic success is to know the correct way of doing research. A research problem, for example, or design problem, there is something you should solve. You should find the suitable answer for that thing. So being able to follow the correct procedures to reach the correct answer for this problem is the success.
>
> (IS 8)

The sense of knowledge growth is explained in terms of conducting research in accordance with correct procedures, so that acceptable and accurate findings address specific issues in assisting the bottom billions as well as promoting research/technology-transfer activities (MOHE Malaysia, 2011b).

By developing research skills, one Iraqi student said she wanted to apply her findings to help and inform other research. Her inspiration is captured as follows: 'if you are a researcher, you are doing research, you find something from your research ... what is going to help other researchers or other people, human or animals' (IS 23). Relating to assisting the bottom billions, it is important to develop soft skills such as communication. One professional staff member highlights that, as future academic staff, international students must be good communicators to impart research knowledge:

> I think their communication skills, it's very important, because the life of other people is in their hands, they are going to teach, they are going to coach students to do research, so communication skill is really important.
>
> You might be very good in your research, but you are bad at your interaction with people. They are not socially engaged. How would they transfer their knowledge and share their knowledge if they are not able to reach out to others to share?
>
> (PS 6)

This skill is essential for international students who decide to work in academia, because they can guide future students in research projects and share their knowledge through effective communication skills. These skills are harnessed through participation in cultural activities such as culture nights, culture talks, culture exhibitions and cultural food festivals organized by this particular university.

Williams (2005) supports the notion that international education provides students with skills such as communication skills through attendance at cultural and diversity events. For example, an Indonesian student illustrated her experiences: 'As international students, we experience international life ... get together with others and then share the cultures. I get involved a lot in international activities regarding cultural exchange, cultural shows' (IS 2). In short, the development of research and soft skills is crucial in assisting particular issues in home countries or societies. These skills are obtained through the teaching and learning process as well as involvement in research activities at this university.

Conclusion

It is crucial for Malaysian higher education institutions to attract international students in keeping with the vision of transforming Malaysia into an international hub of higher education excellence (MOHE Malaysia, 2011b). The Malaysian Ministry of Higher Education has a strategic plan to achieve this status through a paradigm shift, i.e. the soft power concept (MOHE Malaysia, 2011b).

Two vital soft power outcomes manifested themselves through the higher education process at this research university. First, a contribution to home countries or societies via research knowledge transfer was obtained through the teaching and learning process and research activities. Second, the development of research and soft skills were also indicated as soft power outcomes. These outcomes firmly indicate that the top-down paradigm shift using the soft power agenda in Malaysian higher education is translated and facilitated by one of the higher learning institutions in Malaysia.

Note

1 The definition of 'Malay' is constituted under Article 160(2) of the Constitution of Malaysia, which stipulates that a Malay is 'a person who professed the Muslim religion, habitually speaks the Malay language and conforms to the Malay customs' (Saw, 2006, p. 13).

Conclusion

Note

Part V

Institutional Internationalization in Emerging and Developing Contexts

Chapter 15

Innovative Approaches to Internationalization in Rural South Africa

The Case of the University of Venda

Cornelius Hagenmeier

Introduction

This chapter explores a novel approach to internationalization implemented at a rural-based South African university, which may be suitable for other rural institutions of higher education in developing contexts. It uses the University of Venda in South Africa (Univen) to demonstrate how an innovatively structured internationalization process can contribute to transforming a tertiary institution, previously labelled as 'historically disadvantaged', into a locally relevant, but globally competitive university. It provides an in-depth case study of the internationalization process at this rural-based South African university and explains how internationalization can be entrenched in the core business of a university that had, in its earlier history, only limited exposure to the mainstream process of internationalization.[1]

Special attention is devoted to demonstrating that internationalization in a postcolonial context must affirm awareness of identity, culture and language. In this regard, the conceptual link between Africanization and internationalization entrenched in this institution's internationalization policy contributes to a model of internationalization that affirms, rather than jeopardizes, its unique identity as an African university embedded in indigenous communities.

Context

In general, rural-based South African universities are committed to internationalization, albeit their processes are commonly still in the developing stage and much remains to be done. Welch et al. (2004) examine this at the University of Zululand, and conclude that 'although the level of internationalisation is not as low as could be suggested by its geographical location and history of marginalisation, it still has a long way to go'. This chapter shows agreement with Jooste's view that comprehensive internationalization is 'the only strategy that will assist the University of the 21st century to be fully integrated in the global knowledge society' (Jooste, 2006, p. 158). According to Hudzik, the American Council of Education views comprehensive internationalization as 'pervasive throughout the institution, affecting a broad spectrum of people, policies, and programs, and which leads to deeper and potentially more challenging change' (Hudzik, 2011, p. 10, with reference to Olsen et al., 2005). In order to ensure this, a high level of institutional coordination is required. Hudzik (2011, p. 24) poignantly states that an 'institutional culture supporting international engagement and campus internationalisation is an essential prerequisite for success'.

To understand the reasons for the relatively slow development of internationalization at rural-based South African universities, it is important to appreciate their context and history. Most are located in areas that in the apartheid period were considered to be 'homelands' for black South Africans, such as the universities of Fort Hare, Limpopo, Venda, the Zululand, Walter Sisulu and North-West (Mafikeng Campus). Nkomo and Sehoole (2007) observe that 'rural-based universities are the progeny of the so-called apartheid policy of "separate development"'. However, they are an important aspect of the current South African higher education (HE) landscape, a fact recognized by the government, with significant resources now being made available to revitalize, support and develop them. Univen belongs to this group, founded in 1982 in the so-called 'Republic of Venda', one of the semi-independent apartheid constructs, not recognized as states by any but South Africa and reintegrated into the country when freedom was attained in 1994.

While this chapter argues from the perspective of Univen, one of the ethnically based black universities conceived during the apartheid era, many aspects are equally relevant to the three other South African rural-based universities, which are unique in character, and may have relevance for universities in similar contexts in other countries.

The Rationale for Internationalizing South African Rural-Based Universities

While the South African government is committing massive financial resources to developing the country's HE sector in general and historically disadvantaged universities in particular, there is a perceived tension between priorities. In the public discourse, it is sometimes advanced that South Africa must prioritize local-capacity development and transformation of higher education over internationalizing it. At times, there even appears to be a perception that a focus on internationalization could jeopardize capacity building in South African higher education because it diverts attention away from national priorities. In the context of rural-based universities, those arguments are brought to the fore, with some advocating a focus on undergraduate teaching, with research and internationalization the preserve of a select few. This negates the fact that an international orientation lies at the heart of the idea of a university. The purpose of HE institutions includes producing globally employable graduates, generating universally valid knowledge and connecting local communities and nations to the world of knowledge. Not only do rural-based universities need to internationalize like other universities, but the process is of specific relevance to them for a number of reasons.

1   Consequent upon their perceived local orientation and their history, the risk
    of parochialism may be higher compared to urban institutions. The process
    of infusing international and intercultural elements into such institutions
    assists in countering these sentiments and fosters an appreciation of diversity
    of thought and a deeper understanding of the complexity of matters.

2   All university alumni face a national and international employment market
    and need to effectively collaborate with peers from anywhere in the world.
    Rural-based universities have to compensate for any lack of prior exposure
    in traditional student catchment areas, including deep-rural areas with lim-
    ited international and intercultural opportunity. This intensifies the urgency
    to provide relevant exposure at tertiary level. It is imperative for graduate
    employability and empowerment for intellectual citizenship that by the time
    students exit tertiary education, they have acquired competencies at least
    equal to their urban compatriots and in line with international peers.

3   It is important to affirm the identity, culture and language of university com-
    munity members and instil in them the value of engaging with a sense of
    pride and self-worth with other cultures. Africanization is a vital intellectual
    current and refers to the idea that the HE system should be informed by the
    shared knowledge, values, experiences, aspirations and economic objectives
    of Africans (Makgopa & Seepe, 2004; Lansink, 2004). Internationalization
    and Africanization are at times wrongly considered as incompatible; Botha
    (2010, p. 200) encapsulates this view by stating 'the more you Africanise
    the less you can internationalise, and vice versa'. However, this view is not
    generally accepted, and this chapter agrees that both are complementary
    processes for South African rural-based universities. Botha notes, 'the point
    of departure for internationalisation activities at South African universities
    needs to take cognizance of the imperative to also be African universities –
    thus promoting compatibility between internationalisation and localization
    of higher education' (Botha, 2010, p. 201).

4   Part of their mandate is to develop new knowledge of local relevance, but
    with universal validity. Consequent to being embedded in rural African com-
    munities, they also carry a special responsibility for unlocking indigenous
    knowledge for the benefit of humanity. Development of successful research
    and innovation is impossible in national or regional isolation. Therefore,
    rural-based universities must take part in the global knowledge society to
    successfully fulfil local mandates in research and innovation.

5   South African rural-based universities also play important roles as catalysts
    connecting rural communities to the global world of knowledge. Engaging
    relevant communities in a mutually beneficial manner and utilizing best
    international practices is an essential function of rural-based universities. The
    nature of development in the world today makes it imperative that rural
    communities become part of the globalized world while preserving their
    unique identities. Universities based in rural communities are ideally posi-
    tioned to take forward this agenda, as long as their internal stakeholders

possess relevant international and intercultural competencies as well as networking and engagement skills (Netshandama et al., 2011).

6   Internationalization is an essential aspect of transformation at South African rural-based universities. Transformation of higher education in South Africa has been prioritized as an ongoing effort for the past two decades. Much has been achieved, according to the 'Durban Statement on Transformation in Higher Education' (DHET, 2015); expansion of access and participation, particularly for black students, and increased research outputs are among the core gains. However, transformation remains an ongoing challenge, exacerbated by pressure from current student movements such as '#FeesMustFall', which emerged in 2015, successfully demanding a moratorium on fee increases at all South African universities. Ultimately, it falls on universities to define their respective transformation agendas, and clear goals are core to this. In the case of Univen, transformation means that the university must become a 'locally relevant, but globally competitive University' (Univen, 2015c).

7   Univen's geographic position of being very close to the colonial boundary between Zimbabwe, Mozambique and South Africa provides an additional motivation for internationalization, Africanization and regionalization. The borders were drawn up in the colonial period, and have little to do with the origin of the people residing in the region. For the VhaVenda people, the Limpopo river boundary artificially divides the settlement area. Regionalization can help overcome artificial boundaries, and contribute to uniting a region and its people.

Thus, internationalization is of paramount importance for South African rural-based universities, including Univen. They will need to establish themselves as an integral part of the global knowledge society and become comprehensively internationalized. At the very least, these institutions should constitute the international knowledge production avant-garde in their areas of strength, while at the same time implementing best international practices across their core business.

Univen's Strategic Approach to Internationalization

To fully appreciate the University of Venda's strategic approach to internationalization, it is important to consider the internationalization policy framework in South Africa. The influence of South African higher education on institutional internationalization has been succinctly described as 'minimalist' (Jooste, 2006), and this is especially correct for rural-based universities. HE internationalization is entrenched in the 2014 White Paper for Post-Secondary Education, which argues that it 'is necessary to develop a suitable policy framework for international cooperation in post-school education' (DHET, 2014). However, the country has yet to complete the process of developing and adopting a comprehensive HE internationalization policy. The 1997 Southern African Development

Community Protocol on Education and Training (SADC, 1997, Article 7) promotes student and staff mobility in the Southern African region, development of jointly taught programmes, academic programme design and other forms of academic collaboration. Its influence, however, on internationalization processes has been limited, with many South African universities following minimalist practices or being at the early implementation stage. (Jooste, 2006, p. 157). In this regulatory environment, a sound strategic approach to internationalization is vital for any South African university.

The inclusion of internationalization in strategic plans is prerequisite to successful implementation. Ideally, vision and mission statements should reflect and define the tenets of internationalization, responding to and capitalizing on specific strengths of the university. Internationalization policies should embed fundamental matters and important procedures should be transparently set out (Jooste, 2006, p. 160). Equally important is monitoring and evaluation of the relevant policy, procedures and guidelines and their seamless integration in the universities' system of policies.

Univen's vision and mission statement incorporates a direct reference to internationalization. While the vision of the university is 'to be at the centre of tertiary education for rural and regional development in Southern Africa' (Univen, 2016, p. 2), its newly adopted mission states: 'The University of Venda, anchored on the pillars of excellence in teaching, learning, research and community engagement, produces graduates imbued with knowledge, skills and qualifications which are locally relevant and globally competitive' (Univen, 2016, p. 2). A clear understanding of internationalization at the institutional level as the 'the process of integrating international and intercultural dimensions into the teaching, research, community engagement and service functions of an institution of higher learning' has been entrenched in its strategic plan (Univen, 2016, p. 43). This strategy differentiates this institution from other universities and takes cognizance of its focus on community engagement in its internationalization activities.

Internationalization has been incorporated into Univen's strategic plans since 2009; the most recent 2016–2020 strategic plan sets out the basic tenets of the university's internationalization process and provides select specific targets relating to internationalization. Notably, it recognizes that 'the process of internationalisation can and should be entrenched in various ways, in its different programmes, academic fields and Schools' (Univen, 2016, p. 43). It also emphasizes the need to consider the context of its students and the importance of affirming student identity:

> However, the University is cognisant of the fact that the large majority of its students have had limited international exposure. It is important therefore that they should be affirmed in developing competencies to engage outside their home contexts. In doing so, the University is sensitive to the need to emphasise that an understanding of, and taking pride in, one's own cultural identity and respecting those of others, is essential to the

successful acquisition of inter-cultural and international competencies. To put it another way, the intention is not to assimilate to a perceived 'global identity', but to nurture students to recognise that pride in and asserting one's own cultural identity ... does not preclude interacting and working with members of other cultures and persons of other nationalities in a respectful manner. This approach will contribute to facilitating social cohesion, which Univen believes is a central piece of higher education.

(Univen, 2016, p. 29)

Another novelty entrenched in the blueprint for advancing internationalization at Univen is the link between transformation and internationalization, with the latter being considered an integral part of the institution's transformation process, aiming to establish Univen as a 'locally relevant, but globally competitive institution of higher learning in which all people, irrespective of race, gender or nationality would feel welcome to contribute' (Univen, 2015c, p. 2).

An internationalization policy has been adopted (Univen, 2013), which stresses the nexus between Africanization and internationalization. Notably, the policy entrenches comprehensive internationalization, prioritizes engagement with BRICS countries and wider Africa and stresses the importance of promoting diversity through internationalization. The policy establishes a conceptual link between internationalization and Africanization. It stipulates that 'Univen is committed to Africanization as an important aspect of internationalisation. It supports the promotion of African languages at the international level. Where appropriate, African languages will be used for internationalisation activities and African culture will be promoted' (Univen, 2013).

Building on the Inherent Strength of the University

Strategically, the university utilizes its competitive advantages to advance internationalization. The unintended positive outcome of the region's sad history as a 'homeland' is that the classification has, to a certain extent, spared the area from mass evictions and ethnic cleansing that were commonplace in other parts of South Africa. It has also resulted in the indigenous fabric of society remaining largely intact. Indigenous knowledge systems have been retained; indigenous culture celebrated and practised; indigenous law is alive and being actively developed and adapted to the needs of modern times; and African languages flourish. The region's rural setting provides direct access to areas with unique biodiversity. Rural poverty generally lacks the same biting dimension that characterizes urban poverty; the richness of the soil and the social fabric alleviate its impact.

This rural setting is in stark contrast to the developing state-of-the-art facilities on the university's campus, currently undergoing an immense infrastructure redevelopment guided by an infrastructural masterplan. This is matched by comprehensive academic transformation towards a culture of excellence and exponentially growing research output (Univen, 2015a). The university is developing into a node for engagement with the surrounding communities. Indigenous knowledge systems and culture are subjects of community-engaged research while the university assumes its rightful role as catalyst for rural development and promotion of African languages.

In close proximity to the campus, the modern urban centre of Thohoyandou is rapidly developing modern facilities while collaborating with Univen on a university-town concept. Multiple public transport hubs, contemporary shopping and conference facilities are available or being developed. It offers an ideal context and setting in which to pursue African studies, languages, indigenous culture, knowledge systems or law. The university is an appropriate destination for international students interested in studying in an 'authentic' African context without compromising on modern facilities.

The university is leveraging its strategic advantage, for example, by attracting a research chair in 'Biodiversity Value and Change in the Vhembe Biodiversity Reservate' under the South African National Research Foundation Research Chairs Initiative. This is indicative of the value of building on the inherent academic strength of rural-based universities.

Important Aspects of Internationalization at Univen

Appropriate Institutional Structures for the Steering of Internationalization

To achieve comprehensive internationalization, it is not necessary or desirable for international activities to be centralized; rather individual initiatives should be supported, strengthened and synergized and best practices in internationalization adopted in all spheres of institutional activities. A central support structure is beneficial to coordinate individual activities, ensure compliance with policy and relevant legislation and create synergies across various undertakings. Furthermore, accountability requires central oversight structures, such as an internationalization committee (Jooste, 2006, p. 160).

In the wake of Univen's 2009 Strategic Plan, an international office was established and coordination of internationalization through a new Directorate of International Relations commenced. Shortly thereafter, Senate Committees on Linkages, Partnerships and Internationalisation and Academic Liaison became active. This framework has created impetus for and institutional awareness of internationalization processes, with a policy on comprehensive internationalization adopted. The combined effect of these measures offers an institutional framework for internationalization.

Partnerships

Sutton, Egginton and Favela (2012) correctly observe that international affiliations have been repositioned 'as both key strategy and core philosophy for internationalisation', hence the process is becoming more collaborative. Ethical and equal mutual partnerships, which permeate the entire core business of a university and in which both sides are able to contribute unique strengths, are an ideal way to advance internationalization. Taking this approach and entrenching the concept of substantive equality in its internationalization policy (Univen, 2013), Univen was able to develop viable partnerships with universities globally. For example, its flagship partnership with the University of Virginia permeates all aspects of teaching and learning, research and community engagement with high levels of bidirectional student and staff mobility, including at doctoral level.

While theoretical consensus prevails that HE partnerships should be equal or at least equitable, rural-based universities like Univen have to regularly affirm themselves in relationships with 'stronger' partners, a process that can be complicated by recourse to a formal understanding of equality (Hagenmeier, 2015). The adoption of a substantive conception of equality – 'that every partner to a relationship should make contributions which are equally meaningful taking the specific context of the partner into consideration' – is entrenched in Univen's internationalization policy and has assisted in affirming the university when developing partnerships.

Internationalization at Home

While it is possible to implement outgoing student exchange programmes at rural-based South African universities, it is unrealistic to hope that a significant percentage or even the majority of students can take advantage of such opportunities. International and intercultural skills can be acquired through internationalization at home by focusing on internationalization of the curriculum and other activities to internationalize teaching and learning processes (De Wit, 2013b). Many activities, such as Independence Day celebrations, Africa Day celebrations and an international student buddy programme (Univen, 2014), are implemented by the university in partnership with the Student Representative Council (SRC) and the Union of International Students (UNISU). The close collaboration between management, SRC and UNISU ensures that student views are considered and any students involved in organizing activities get added international exposure. In addition, it provides an opportunity to implement such activities in a cost-efficient way and to involve a maximum number of local students. For example, in 2015 a year-end 'internationalization evening', with more than 300 students participating, took place in collaboration with SRC and UNISU, using minimum financial resources (Univen, 2015b).

Internationalization of the curriculum is entrenched in the internationalization policy and under constructive internal debate. The university first considered using a model developed by Australian scholar Betty Leask (2012). However, it soon became apparent that there could be no consensus based on an imported model, perceived by academics as counter-productive and not acceptable to Univen's context, and it would be necessary to develop its own approach. The university is now embarking on a process of curriculum transformation simultaneously aiming at Africanizing, contextualizing, localizing and internationalizing the curriculum. Thereby, it will reflect the strategic approach embedded in the university's internationalization policy to pursue internationalization and Africanization as complementary processes.

It is submitted that the lack of an appropriate approach to internationalization of the curriculum embedded in the broader curriculum transformation process may be a core reason why internationalization of the curriculum is generally lagging behind in South African higher education. The new approach being explored at Univen carries a promise to possibly provide a sound basis for successful curriculum transformation and internationalization in the South African context.

Regional Focus and Responsiveness to the Process of Africanization

We have already considered regional integration and overcoming arbitrary colonial boundaries as one of the rationales for advancing internationalization at South African universities. Regional integration in Southern Africa can also be used strategically to advance internationalization. For example, exchange programmes with universities in neighbouring countries can be implemented cost-efficiently. The SADC Protocol on Higher Education is a reflection of the political will for regional HE integration, and rural-based universities can take advantage of this goodwill to support such collaborations. Univen has developed mutually beneficial partnerships with regional universities. Together with Botho University, Botswana, an undergraduate regional student and staff exchange programme was established in 2015. Geographic proximity allows for broader participation of students and provides, in a resource-constrained environment, opportunities for students from rural backgrounds to gain international experience.

Developmental Activities

Globally, there is great interest in the implementation of service learning, voluntary and developmental programmes in rural areas in Southern Africa. Universities in the developed world, such as North America, Europe and Australia, aim to offer education that transcends traditional parochial boundaries. They also implement developmental activities as a means of image-building and marketing. It should be in the interest of rural-based universities to act as catalysts for these developmental activities. Their core business includes reciprocal, mutually beneficial community engagement activities, so universities are ideally situated to ensure that the community's interest is safeguarded in developmental and research engagements. Additionally, they have the expertise to ensure smooth and appropriate entry into communities and to assist in academically contextualizing the experience. In the case of Univen, this is already a reality through international community engagement projects such as 'Water and Health in Limpopo' and 'Warwick in Africa', implemented in collaboration with international partners (Netshandama et al., 2011).

Appropriate Services for International Students

International full-degree students are an important feature of internationalization, and traditionally rural-based South African universities have hosted students from neighbouring countries, often sponsored by national scholarship schemes. The recent demise of many such programmes has resulted in an urgent need to diversify the international student body but appropriate services are a prerequisite for attracting them. For many years this was the preserve of major universities with established and effective international offices. Univen recognized this gap and, in 2015, established an international student helpdesk to assist with immigration, accommodation and other matters.

Generating Awareness of the Benefits of Internationalization among all Members of the University Community

Traditionally, internationalization has not taken centre stage at South African rural-based universities. Often, as is the situation at Univen, a relatively high degree of internationalization has been achieved through satisfactory international student and staff contingents and an array of often uncoordinated institutional international activities. However, these did not always develop the university community's awareness of internationalization processes and the relevance of internationalization sometimes comes into question at rural-based universities. Internal marketing strategies for internationalization can help promote the concept, raise awareness for what has already been achieved and encourage an acceleration of the process. Disseminating information on internationalization through email communiqués and university newsletters have helped, and lately the university radio station, 'Radio Univen', has become more involved.

Ethical Income-Generation

In times of limited budgets and continuing threats of adverse economic development, it is imperative to focus on ethical income-generation from internationalization activities to sustain the process. This is a two-edged sword: while it has the potential to guarantee relative independence from budgetary decisions at central level, it carries the risk of undue commercialization of internationalization. In the worst-case scenario, such activities can be evaluated primarily against the financial contribution they make rather than as a genuine contribution to the process of internationalization. Ethical best practice demands that income generated from internationalization activities be ring-fenced.

Ethical income-generation for internationalization in rural-based universities requires appropriate marketing strategies. Traditionally, income for internationalization is produced through administrative fees and international student fees, which are significantly higher than fees paid by local students. In the case of rural-based universities, this method of income-generation is problematic in the long term. The SADC Protocol on Education (SADC, 1997) does not permit the charging of international fees for students from SADC member states; administrative levies are needed to finance specific services required by this student group. At Univen, the majority of international students hail from SADC countries, so diversification beyond this group is needed to generate the income required to drive internationalization, for example by developing internationally marketable academic degree programmes attractive to international students from beyond the SADC region. Another possibility is the development of study abroad programmes for fee-paying international short-term visiting students. At Univen, ethical income-generation will be one of the future priorities to further strengthen the sustainability of its internationalization process.

Challenges to Internationalization at Rural-Based Universities

While significant progress has been made in internationalizing Univen and other South African rural-based universities, risk factors need to be identified and countered.

1   One of the most significant risks lies in stakeholders construing internationalization as a competing priority to Africanization, a tendency that can best be avoided by emphasizing the conceptual link between the two processes and advancing both simultaneously.

2   Internationalization and the development of the core business can be perceived by stakeholders as competing priorities. This can best be countered through deeply embedding internationalization in the university's core business, advancing the process through academic staff members and university structures at all levels, avoiding a scenario where internationalization is mostly based in an international office. Any office tasked with creating synergies for internationalization at a rural-based South African university must position itself as coordinating, supporting and advancing a process that is driven by academics for the benefit of the academic core project.

3   Discrimination, xenophobia, tribal tensions and lack of transformation jeopardize the international attractiveness and competiveness of rural-based universities, including Univen. Discrimination on the basis of nationality is generally embedded in a matrix of complex layers of prejudice. It is indeed the mindset of disliking the unknown, which especially thrives in an environment in which parochialism may still be a reality. Rural-based universities, like all educational institutions, have to take any kind of discrimination seriously. If xenophobia were to manifest itself significantly on any campus, this would not only threaten internationalization for the university concerned, but could also have a domino effect on similar universities and even on the whole South African HE system. This chapter argues that pre-emptive steps should be taken to counter any xenophobic tendencies. Univen has successfully implemented an anti-xenophobia campaign and adopted a

Transformation Charter that includes a focus on diversity. Furthermore, it strategically uses its internationalization process to advance transformation more broadly.

4   The lack of diversity in the international student body, largely from Southern Africa, jeopardizes the success of internationalization. First, international students from neighbouring countries do not contribute to diversity as students from other world regions would. Second, if events in a source country sharply reduce international student numbers, this can have a serious effect on international student numbers. Historically, reliance on neighbouring countries for international students may be attributed to dependency on scholarship providers, such as governmental scholarship offices.

5   Lack of funding challenges internationalization efforts. In South Africa, the student movement #FeesMustFall resulted in a fees moratorium in public higher education for 2016. In the resulting restrained-resource environment, the sector is debating how to reprioritize funding allocations, and internationalization is at risk. With modest financial reserves, rural-based universities may be particularly affected and, unless a consensus is reached that internationalization is essential, funding to drive the process is in jeopardy. Consequently, ethical income-generation should be prioritized. Furthermore, it is also necessary to consider how internationalization can be cost-effectively advanced. Virtual mobility, regional student exchanges, a focus on internationalization at home are among the strategies that can be pursued to successfully internationalize rural-based universities in a resource-constrained environment.

6   Perceived lack of transformation in the South African HE system endangers the future of the system in general and internationalization in particular. At the time of writing, the South African sector is in turmoil. The #FeesMustFall movement highlighted the urgency of ensuring equity in universities, particularly in access for students from all layers of society. For internationalization to remain relevant and flourish in this environment, it must be seen as a catalyst for transformation of the sector.

Conclusion

The case study of Univen illustrates that a strategic institutional approach to internationalization, building on the inherent strengths of the university, connecting the international and local spheres and adopting a substantive understanding of equality can develop and sustain a successful internationalization process at a South African rural-based university. This approach assists in preventing new dominance by other world regions or international partners while enhancing the quality of teaching and learning, research and community engagement. Critical for success is the strengthening of the university's role as a catalyst connecting indigenous knowledge, language and culture to the wider world for the mutual benefit of local communities, international stakeholders and the university.

However, it has to be noted that distinct risks to the process remain. Internationalization cannot flourish unless they are countered as outlined above and the culture of excellence is further strengthened in all core and support activities of the university. A critical role falls onto academic departments that are most involved in community engagement activities. University core business should take advantage of the opportunities presented by its context, specifically with regard to indigenous knowledge, African linguistics and biodiversity. This will contribute to international profiling of the university and enhance its appeal to potential international partners, researchers and students.

By focusing on academic excellence and utilizing the strategies outlined in this chapter, a high level of internationalization can be achieved and sustained at rural-based universities. Internationalization is seminal for advancing quality and transformation, and the process needs to receive the attention it deserves, as is presently the case at Univen.

Note

1 This chapter is partially based on the article, 'The Future of Internationalisation: Perspectives for South African Rural-based Universities', published by the same author (Hagenmeier, 2015a).

Chapter 16

Internationalizing the Curriculum in Kazakhstan

Perceptions, Rationales and Challenges

Lynne Parmenter, Jason Sparks, Aisi Li, Sulushash Kerimkulova, Adil Ashirbekov & Zakir Jumakulov

The aim of this chapter is to explore ways in which higher education institutions (HEIs) in Kazakhstan are responding to the imperative to internationalize their curricula. While there are strong drivers for HEIs to internationalize in Kazakhstan, rationales for and opinions about doing this vary from one institution to another. The chapter focuses on three questions: (1) How is internationalization of curriculum interpreted and defined in Kazakhstan's higher education institutions? (2) What are the rationales for internationalization of curriculum? (3) What are the challenges encountered in internationalizing curricula?

After a brief description of the context of internationalization of higher education in Kazakhstan, relevant literature addressing each of these three questions will be discussed. This is followed by a brief explanation of the methodology of the study, then analysis and discussion of findings in relation to the same three questions. The conclusion juxtaposes key ideas from the literature with findings to highlight common themes and distinctive definitions, rationales and challenges.

The Kazakhstan Context

Since gaining independence from the former Soviet Union in 1991, Kazakhstan has worked to transform its higher education system to meet the needs of the "new social and political conditions" (OECD & World Bank, 2007, p. 12) of nationhood in the 21st century. Internationalization has been an explicit part of this higher education reform strategy, through a major government-sponsored outbound student mobility program begun in 1993 (Perna, Orosz, Jumakulov, Kishkentayeva & Ashirbekov, 2015), through joining the Bologna Process from 2010 (Sparks, Ashirbekov, Parmenter, Jumakulov & Sagintayeva, 2015) and, most recently, through greater institutional autonomy and curriculum reform initiatives aimed at increasing the number of Kazakhstani universities internationally ranked and accredited (Ministry of Education and Science of the Republic of Kazakhstan, 2010).

Internationalization of Curriculum: Definitions and Interpretations

The operational definition for internationalization of curriculum (IoC) used in the study is provided by Leask: "the incorporation of an international and intercultural dimension into the content of the curriculum as well as the teaching and learning arrangements and support services of a program of study" (2009, p. 209). This definition extends the conventional understanding of curriculum to include three dimensions: (1) curriculum content (state-required content, individual institutional content and course syllabus content); (2) faculty teaching strategies and activities; and (3) student support services in both academic and non-academic contexts. This extended definition provided the flexibility to explore various perspectives, perceptions and experiences of IoC in a previously under-researched context.

Rationales for Internationalization of Curriculum

As Jones and de Wit (2012) point out, there are differing interpretations and rationales for internationalization of higher education (p. 35). However, there is little doubt that rationales for higher education change are increasingly linked to "internationalization" within the contemporary global higher education space, as Leask stresses:

> Internationalisation of the curriculum is core business for an internationalised university, of relevance to *all* students ... The impact of globalisation makes it imperative that all students are prepared to live and work in a complex, globalised world, as professionals and citizens, ready to rise to the challenge of being human in a supercomplex world.
>
> (Leask, 2015b, p. 2)

Accepting the idea that IoC is necessary for all students, the next question is "What for?" While there is still much more research to be done in this area, a review of current research suggests three main categories of rationales: (1) developing globally competent professionals; (2) developing global citizens; and (3) attracting and accommodating inbound international students. Each of these categories will be discussed briefly below.

Developing Globally Competent Professionals

The first category refers to responses to "growing pressures on universities across the world to equip greater proportions of the population with higher order skills that can be used productively in the knowledge economy" (Naidoo & Jamieson, 2005, p. 38). In this conception, "higher education should equip students with the advanced knowledge, skills and competences" (Bologna Process, 2009, p. 3) required for what de Wit (2015e, p. 17) describes as "the professional aspect (employability)." The dual agendas of internationalization and employability tend to converge around wider discussion of 21st-century skills or core competences at all levels of education (Perkins, 2014), and the confluence of transferable employability skills and intercultural competence (Jones, 2013c). However, the question of whether internationalization leads to greater employability in most of the world has not been empirically evaluated.

Developing Global Citizens

Another rationale for IoC is the development of global citizens. While increasingly commonplace in university mission statements, it is still relatively rare to find concrete details of how this is being translated into strategies, policies and practices in specific contexts. With no consensus definition of global citizenship, and with conceptions of global citizenship education contested (Parmenter, 2013), nonetheless, for the purposes of this chapter, Clifford and Montgomery (2011) provide a starting point: global citizens are aware of the wider world from a variety of dimensions; they respect its inherent diversity; they participate in developing community at local and global levels (p. 17); and they have "an understanding of a common humanity, a shared planet and a shared future" (p. 17). The rationale for HEIs to develop global citizens' links to their social role to both respond to and positively influence social change. Consistent with this role, HEIs have a responsibility to provide learning experiences and a learning environment that facilitates students' awareness and understanding of the reality of an increasingly interconnected and interdependent world, which requires professionals who are aware of and able to deal with worldwide intercultural collaborations (Rizvi, 2009); vastly unequal global distribution of wealth (Killick, 2015, p. 7); global production, distribution and consumption of cultural products (Rizvi, 2009, p. 258); and the unprecedented increase in volume and speed of intercultural exchange (Rizvi, 2009, p. 267).

Attracting and Accommodating Inbound International Students

The third rationale for IoC is attracting international students. This strategy is often closely connected to the marketization of higher education (Molesworth, Scullion & Nixon, 2011), and has been restricted to a minority of countries worldwide. In the context of the United Kingdom and Australia, for example, "successful competition for fee-paying international students is ... the key to survival" (Haigh, 2008, p. 8). Internationalization based in this rationale impacts language of instruction and curriculum content. One dominant feature of IoC is offering curricula in English, a move often limiting participation to English-competent faculty and limiting curriculum content and materials to those found in English, both with significant consequences for reinforcing patterns of power in the global higher education sphere (Pusser & Marginson, 2013).

Taken together, these three rationales are widely recognized and relatively well-documented in academic literature as rationales for IoC, but most of the evidence for them currently comes from a small number of countries and regions.

Challenges in Internationalization of Curriculum

Turning to the third question to be addressed in this chapter, in this section, key challenges in IoC discussions in recent literature will be briefly summarized. The challenges for IoC highlighted here are (1) focus on a few; (2) disconnected initiatives and superficiality; (3) faculty motivation; (4) resources; but this is obviously not an exhaustive list.

Focus on a Few

In many countries, IoC initiatives have tended to focus on mobile students, adapting program structures or curriculum to accommodate inbound and outbound mobility. Here, the challenge is twofold: compartmentalization of curriculum (e.g., courses specifically for international students) and equity (resources that should be available to all students are focused on a few). The response to this challenge has been "internationalization at home," defined by Beelen and Jones as "the purposeful integration of international and intercultural dimensions into the formal and informal curriculum for all students within domestic learning environments" (2015a, p. 69).

Disconnected Initiatives and Superficiality

A second challenge for IoC is that it often results in a set of disconnected and superficial institutional initiatives rather than a clear and coherent institutional strategy. For example, while inbound student mobility is often a strategic institutional priority, "it is not always clear what the expected impact would be" (Beelen, 2014, p. 293) beyond the financial. Addressing these issues of disconnection and superficiality, de Wit et al. argue that an internationalized curriculum should have specific learning outcomes, course content, and learning and assessment tasks "internationalised through a planned and systematic process," with the larger goal of developing "international, intercultural and global perspectives" (de Wit, Hunter, Howard & Egron-Polak, 2015, p. 50) in all students.

Faculty Motivation

The third challenge for IoC is faculty and staff motivation. In order to develop and implement an internationalized curriculum, the commitment of faculty is essential, as Postiglione and Altbach emphasize: "without the full, active and enthusiastic participation of the academics, internationalization efforts are doomed to fail" (2013, p. 11). This assertion is further supported by an OECD report, which suggests that HEIs should develop clear incentive policies to help faculty engage in IoC, including access to international networks and necessary linguistic skills (Hénard, Diamond & Roseveare, 2012, p. 22).

Resources

In terms of this final challenge, resources, one issue facing those who are not in English-dominant environments is language-related. Many faculty members face requirements to use books or articles written in English, or even to teach in English, as part of IoC initiatives (Yang, 2003). Alternatively, the challenge may be access to resources (e.g., library, Internet) for teaching and learning, access to international contacts and networks (student and faculty mobility, conference participation, etc.), or access to financial resources or expertise to internationalize the curriculum. Barker, Hibbins and Farrelly highlight another potential resource challenge for any institution seeking to foster global citizenship in students: institutional professional development support that will "enable academic staff themselves to develop the attributes of global citizens" (2011, p. 47).

Methodology

For this study, a "collective case study" (Stake, 1995) approach was used in order to explore the research questions in the context of the unique experiences of four university schools or departments selected because of their ability to provide multiple perspectives on the same research questions, highlighting "both their uniqueness and commonality" (p. 1). A total of 91 participants shared their thoughts and experiences in 31 individual interviews and 10 focus group interviews across the four cases, between March and July 2015. The four cases were as follows:

1 Internationalization of an International Studies curriculum;
2 Internationalization of a "bridge" first-year foundation curriculum;
3 Internationalization of a teacher education curriculum;
4 Impact of international accreditation on internationalization of a science curriculum.

The "case" here is conceptualized as those leaders and faculty working in a specific institution or school, engaged in initiatives to incorporate "an international and intercultural dimension into the content of the curriculum as well as the teaching and learning arrangements and support services of a program of study" (Leask, 2009, p. 209).

Case Studies: Analysis and Discussion

In this section, some of the main findings are presented and discussed. The section is divided into three parts, with each addressing one focus question of the chapter: (1) How is internationalization of curriculum interpreted and defined in

Kazakhstan's HEIs? (2) What are the rationales for internationalization of curriculum? (3) What are the challenges encountered in internationalizing curricula?

How Is Internationalization of Curriculum Interpreted and Defined in Kazakhstan's Higher Education Institutions?

Participants generally referred to internationalization in terms of response to globalization or engagement with the process of globalization. This is closely in line with Leask's (2015b) assertion that IoC is "a dynamic, intellectually demanding process often associated with globalization" (p. 2). An interesting point is that internationalization is often described as responding to the imperatives of an external force, such as the Bologna Process or a government policy. For example: "we have the task to make transition ... So, transition to new platform, new requirements ... If we want to satisfy the European standards, we need to have the European structure" (Case 4). The implications are that internationalization initiatives within the university are more about regulatory compliance than the "core business" of the university associated with comprehensive internationalization. This suggests IoC is detached from the mission of the university and its community.

Interestingly, while many respondents link IoC to globalization in the current era, some emphasized that certain aspects of internationalization have a long regional history based in past Soviet experience:

> academic mobility is not a new process. When I studied, we had mobility within Komsomol organizations framework. That is youth trip exchanges. We always had this. In other words, we were not a closed country. Trips to socialist countries always took place. If we didn't go to capitalist countries, we visited socialist ones.
>
> (Case 3)

The references to past experiences of internationalization as part of the Soviet Union were frequent, and were the basis for many of the participants' current stances on IoC. As one participant clearly stated, internationalization is the "symbiosis of classical old Soviet and international systems" (Case 4), or evolutionary rather than revolutionary change.

What Are the Rationales for Internationalization of Curriculum in HEIs?

Three main rationales for IoC were identified in this study, namely, (1) integration into the global educational sphere; (2) competitiveness, benchmarking and employability; and (3) natural extension of multicultural Kazakhstan.

For the vast majority of participants, the dominant rationale for IoC was integration into the global educational sphere. For some participants, this was simply a case of responding to the inevitable, or to policies dictated externally: "We do not choose whether we want it or not. This is a trend. If we want to build a good university – good in the Western sense" (Case 4). The connotation here is the view that there is a drive to fit universities to an external model, even if what is "good" in the Western sense may not be "good" in other senses. Other participants analyzed the situation in relation to Kazakhstan's trajectory from a post-Soviet system to being a Bologna signatory from 2010:

> after joining the Bologna Process, Kazakhstan's main directions in education are certainly guided to get closer to that. Even our educational program on the base of the Bologna Process is a way to pull together with foreign colleagues, so educational program of each subject aims to develop modernization of processes between countries.
>
> (Case 3)

This was an opinion repeated across all cases, although the gap between rationale and reality was also raised: "Bologna Process is a good model on the whole ... [but] its introduction is complicated in realization" (Case 1). The comments of the participants reflect the rationales discussed in the literature, specifically relating to Rizvi's (2009) statement about "recognition that our world is increasingly interconnected and interdependent globally" (p. 253). Participants in this study recognized the need to engage with this interconnected world through IoC, whether as compliance with international standards or for their own and their students' benefit.

A second rationale for IoC was competitiveness, benchmarking and employability in a global world. An employability example appears here, in relation to the emphasis on languages in the new curriculum: "there's lack of specialists in labor market ... who can write official letters in Kazakh and Russian, and a huge lack of specialists in English" (Case 2). The IoC rationale for global competitiveness and benchmarking was particularly strong in the discussion of curriculum reform for international accreditation:

> This [creation of world class research university] is possible only when our educational services are comparable and competitive with those services provided by other research universities. First of all, we should compare, conduct benchmarking of our educational services. This can be done only if we conduct international accreditation of our educational programs.
>
> (Case 4)

Here, accreditation provides the external criteria for competition:

> We need international accreditation to be competitive. We need it as a must ... for ourselves, because it can help us to see what we do right and what wrong ... we need it necessarily to be on the same level as other countries.
>
> (Case 4)

Again, this quotation makes reference to the idea that there is some external "right and wrong" way to do things, like the earlier quotation about being "good" in a Western sense. While participants were implicitly critical about whether their universities should be chasing this external standard, they did not directly question its existence, and therefore did not go so far as discussing "whose standard?", "whose good?" or "whose right and wrong?". Again, while the rationale of confirming that the university is on the right path may be valid as a means to a bigger purpose, it shows a great deal of trust in the existence of an external standard that is implicitly assumed to be somehow "better" than current practice.

The final major rationale emerging in this study was IoC as a natural expansion of Kazakhstan as a multiethnic, multicultural society. The history and demographic flux of Kazakhstan over the past 100 years, together with the more recent large-scale inward migration of ethnic Kazakhs from other countries, make Kazakhstan an unusual model for internationalization, and it is significant that participants emphasized this as part of the natural process of IoC. For some participants, this was linked to the "inevitability" of internationalization, as stated here:

> Internationalization is a natural process, and it will be always – well probably it won't be in more closed countries – but in Kazakhstan where we have a multinational state, where there are so many nationalities and ethnic groups and so many students, and we have more open, democratic country, therefore this process [of internationalization] will go on anyway.
>
> (Case 1)

A similar argument is made by a senior leader in another university:

> You know, it is ... We do not really put so much emphasis on internationalization, because actually it is already the basis here since the Soviet Union era, because Kazakhstan is a multinational country, multinational republic, right? This issue was always existing in our minds subconsciously, latently ... the friendship between cultures, between the many ethnic groups that live in Kazakhstan have always been considered in study processes and education.
>
> (Case 3)

This rationale provides a very strong basis for internationalization at home, and is certainly an important aspect of internationalization in Kazakhstan, as in some other Asia-Pacific countries (Knight & de Wit, 1997, p. 175), which may partly explain why the "focus on the few" issue is not evident in IoC discourse or practices in HEIs in Kazakhstan.

What Are the Challenges Encountered in Internationalizing Curricula?

A number of key challenges arose from the data collected through interviews and focus groups in this study. The four challenges briefly discussed in this section are (1) national vs global; (2) resistance to change; (3) quality; and (4) language issues.

First, the issue of balancing the national with the global/international is a challenge that is certainly not unique to Kazakhstan. However, it may be even more acute in Kazakhstan than in other countries, due to the nation-building process that is occurring concurrently with the internationalization process. Across cases, the dilemma of how to balance national interests and national identity with IoC was a topic of discussion: "Unfortunately, often, the introduction of this internationalization … often follows a method of blind copying of foreign experience, not taking into account the specific character of Kazakh originality, of Kazakhstan on the whole" (Case 1). While there is genuine enthusiasm to engage internationally, it is mitigated by caution and a clear awareness that a simple "cut and paste" of internationalization is unlikely to work. Participants recognized the need to find a way of internationalizing appropriate to their own institutional, regional and national contexts, but finding the balance was still a challenge, as this senior leader explains:

> these are all globalization issues, … but we still want all our national things including language, culture of Kazakhs, history never to be forgotten, we want to save it and save our language. It is also in the first place for us. It is on the same level as internationalization politics, internationalization. At the same time we do not want to forget our roots, in the education system we also consider it … we try to keep balance.
>
> (Case 3)

There are no easy answers to this issue, of course, and the optimum balance may be different at different times and in different circumstances. The conceptual framework of Leask and Bridge (2013) clearly shows that these are interconnected layers of context (institutional, local, national and regional, global), not a dichotomy, and it is important to recognize that IoC can take on different forms and present different challenges in contexts where a concurrent process of nation-building is occurring, like Kazakhstan, or in transitional or fragile contexts.

Connected to this, the second challenge emerging was resistance to change, framed as Soviet versus Bologna, or old versus new. Respondents in some cases expressed concerns that the positive aspects of Soviet teaching and learning practices were being devalued and abandoned because of the new wave of internationalization:

> We have a common proverb: "Don't throw out the baby with the bathwater." I was brought up in Soviet traditions established in Soviet times. I suppose that we had good moments [of education] we should not reject. On the contrary, they should be applied. I mean it is necessary somehow to harmonize everything together. There should be harmonization [of new and old education] for sure.
>
> (Case 1)

With all the reforms occurring in Kazakhstan, and the danger of reform fatigue, this is an important concern, and it is certainly related to the challenge of faculty motivation discussed above. This is especially true when IoC (in the form of Bologna-compliance reforms) threatens faculty job security and salaries, as in this case:

> I face some difficulties with old teachers, Soviet-thinking teachers, and I [had] to save some courses just in terms of saving their hours, their wages, and the problem is to save workplace ... we focus not on students, we focus on how to save their workplace hours ... when we remove subjects, it of course affects teaching hours, affects people, affects their financial situation, it is very difficult.
>
> (Case 3)

While this is a deeply rooted challenge requiring substantial structural change of salary systems as well as faculty motivation, Postiglione and Altbach's observation that "without the full, active and enthusiastic participation of the academics, internationalization efforts are doomed to fail" (2013, p. 11) is highly relevant here.

Connected to this is the third challenge of ensuring quality of IoC. Kazakhstan invests heavily in international consultancy/experts in processes of education reform, and universities can spend significant sums of money inviting international experts to teach students or conduct professional development. Expectations are high that these international experts will contribute to high-quality IoC, but these are not always met. There was a clear recognition among participants that not all international experts are more expert than they themselves are. Respondents did not reject learning from international trends in teaching and learning, but they were able to critically analyze and evaluate the usefulness of what they saw and experienced and, in so doing, identify the strengths and good points of their own teaching and learning. This quotation from a faculty member was representative of a number of similar comments:

> Often foreign specialists are invited to conduct training. While listening to them I am surprised by the low level of their information presented. It is the same level as our students' level! We would not even give such material to our students. I do not know why this happens. Thus, it is difficult to describe this training as "professional development."
>
> (Case 1)

This adds an extra dimension to the discussion on resources, insofar as the "international experts" often have a mono-perspective view of issues they are consulting or training on, whereas the academics being "trained" often already have multi-perspective views, are already aware of theories and trends in the expert's country/region as well as their own, and are able to integrate different perspectives.

192 L. Parmenter et al.

The fourth challenge is language. The pressure to use English as a medium of instruction is apparent across the four cases, as are the challenges of doing so. This is closely linked to the dominant rationale for IoC discussed above, namely, integration into the global educational sphere. The assumption is that this integration requires mastery (to some extent) of the global lingua franca – English. One key aspect that came up in most of the cases was the issue of teaching programs and courses in English. While the barriers to doing this are fully recognized, from lack of capacity among teachers to lack of textbooks and materials, there is still a drive to move in this direction, and commitment to doing so:

> According to the Kazakhstan policy, the policy of our President, every young person has to know three languages. The trilingual policy is going on, but why? Because as Kazakhstan is supposed to enter the group of 30 developed countries, all these people of Kazakhstan that are young, they should know 3 languages ... What I want to underline is that each person has to know English as an international language, because the language of science, the language of co-operation, the language of friendship is English.
>
> (Case 3)

While this imperative to operate in English, or at least make a move in that direction, is shared by many other countries, Kazakhstan, with its trilingual policy, has the added complication of concurrently attempting to raise national levels of proficiency in the state language, leading to a complex language education system that HEIs in many other countries do not have to deal with.

Conclusion

This chapter aimed to examine definitions, rationales and challenges of higher education internationalization in Kazakhstan, focusing on three specific questions. Data from case studies show that IoC in Kazakhstan faces similar challenges to others going through the process, but its unique context also offers fresh insights into internationalizing the higher education curriculum.

In response to the first question on definitions and interpretations of internationalization in general and IoC in particular, findings from the case studies aligned closely in many respects with international literature, especially in terms of internationalization and IoC as a dynamic response to processes of globalization. On the other hand, for a number of respondents, internationalization and IoC were seen as a natural continuation of Soviet times and principles, a concept that has started to be explored in the Russian context (Kuraev, 2014), and warrants further study in Kazakhstan.

Turning to the second question of rationales for IoC, the responses given by participants in this study showed some overlap with the dominant literature, but also raised several other issues. The rationales related to competitiveness, employability and benchmarking in the case studies all connect closely to the rationale of developing global competence and competitiveness in the mainstream academic literature. The most frequently cited rationale in this study, "integration into the global education sphere," does not feature prominently in the literature, although elements of it are apparent in the rationale of developing global citizens and, to a lesser extent, attracting and accommodating international students. This rationale, and the way it is framed, are based on an assumption, which was not explicitly stated by participants, that Kazakhstan until now has somehow been "outside" the global education sphere, in spite of over 20 years of large-scale study abroad scholarship programs and high levels of global awareness and knowledge among academics. It would be interesting to explore internationally how far and in what ways this "insider–outsider" concept of internationalization of higher education is evident in other countries and regions. The other rationale given for IoC, that it is just a natural extension of multicultural Kazakhstan, is connected to the above idea of internationalization as a natural continuation of previous times, but this is also an alternative perspective on IoC, particularly in terms of internationalization at home as something that has already been happening for the past 80 years or more.

Finally, on the third question of challenges, it is clear from the juxtaposition of challenges discussed in recent literature and challenges raised by participants in Kazakhstan HEIs that their concerns are different at this point in time. Challenges for IoC in the literature are mainly focused on the institutional level (achieving inclusive, connected, coherent, deep, well-resourced IoC, with motivated faculty on board), while the discussion in Kazakhstan is focused more on national and conceptual levels (negotiating change and mediating reform, while trying to access and achieve quality of IoC). Participants in this study provide insights into the challenges of IoC in a rapidly reforming higher education sector at many different levels, offering alternative perspectives on issues such as commitment and resistance to change, faculty motivation and power issues in the form of languages and people.

In conclusion, this chapter has presented insights and perspectives from higher education leaders and faculty members in Kazakhstan, with the aim of contributing to the discussion of the "globalization of internationalization" in different contexts around the world.

Chapter 17

Higher Education Stakeholder Perceptions on Internationalization of the Curriculum

Evidence from an Institutional Study in Cambodia

Tapas R. Dash

Introduction

The diverse nature of today's environment requires highly knowledgeable and skilled people to meet global challenges and there is demand for higher education relevant to a globally mobile workforce by an increasing number of students. In response to the compelling requirements of globalization as well as to demands by a growing population in search of better knowledge and skills or internationally accredited qualifications, institutions of higher learning are under pressure to internationalize their curricula. Furthermore, the increased interconnectedness of the world has resulted in the growing significance of relations among nations, which in turn requires universities to infuse the curriculum with international content. Curriculum internationalization is thus 'a response to the need to prepare graduates for work in the new reality of a globally interconnected world' (Jones, 2013d, p. 1).

Internationalization of the Curriculum: Meaning

Internationalizing the curriculum is proposed as a strategy for the internationalization of higher education, and Knight (1994, p. 6) describes curriculum as 'the backbone of the internationalisation process'. Bremer and van der Wende (1995) point out that internationalization of the curriculum can refer to such varied internationalization activities as study abroad programmes, foreign language courses, interdisciplinary or area programmes, or the provision of programmes or courses with an international, intercultural or comparative focus. Leask defines it as follows: 'internationalisation of the curriculum is the incorporation of international, intercultural and/or global dimensions into the content of the curriculum as well as the learning outcomes, assessment tasks, teaching methods and support services of a program of study' (Leask, 2015a, p. 9). Therefore, internationalization should not only be integrated into the curriculum but also measured in the outcomes. Leask (2005) argues that the internationalization of curriculum is not an 'end to a means', developed simply to be able to claim that the curriculum is internationalized. Instead, it should be 'a strategy which will assist learners to become more aware of their own and others' cultures'. Haigh (2009) holds that real internationalization of the curriculum requires that courses may be constructed on multicultural foundations.

Jones states that

helping students to challenge their own identity, values, assumptions and stereotypes requires us to adopt an inclusive approach to curriculum and pedagogy, and to recognise and value the cultural insights that our students (and staff) can offer and that might otherwise be overlooked.

(Jones, 2013d, p. 1)

In a more recent work, Beelen and Jones (2015b) point out that internationalization at home is a convenient term to designate internationalization activity aimed at the whole student body; however,

internationalisation of the curriculum refers to dimensions of the curriculum regardless of where it is delivered – it may include mobility for the students that choose that option, or it can refer to curriculum for transnational or other forms of cross-border education.

(Beelen & Jones, 2015b, p. 12)

In the Cambodian context, however, curriculum internationalization is very new and it may simply be referred to as study abroad programmes, foreign language courses, provision of programmes or courses with an international and intercultural focus and incorporation of international, intercultural and/or global dimensions into the content of the curriculum.

Rationale for Internationalizing the Curriculum in Cambodia

Developing an internationalized curriculum has been rooted to many factors. Jones and Killick (2007, p. 110) suggest that

Interest in an internationalised curriculum seems to come relatively late in the development of the notion of an international university; generally being articulated following a focus on international student recruitment, student exchanges, study-abroad, off-shore delivery, and, perhaps, related staff development.

In the Cambodian context, it would be justified to say that the rationale for curriculum internationalization is typically pragmatically based. Cambodia's integration into the ASEAN community strongly requires Cambodian students to build necessary skills and understanding to work not only in the Southeast Asian region but also globally. Larger numbers coming into the Cambodian labour market every year is a more likely scenario than outflow of the Cambodian labour force to regional as well as global labour markets.

With a negligible presence of international students in Cambodian universities, the focus on an internationalized curriculum is linked to the recognition that Cambodian students are much less well-prepared to face the complexities of a culturally diverse world than those in neighbouring countries in Asia and beyond. Thus, Cambodian universities are paying greater attention to producing a successful workforce to seize the opportunities of regional and global integration as well as to develop and maintain the country's international competitiveness.

Although we justify the rationale as pragmatically based, we cannot overlook the values-based rationale altogether. Ultimately, the focus is to imbue a range of values among Cambodian students that include openness, tolerance and, in particular, sensitivity to other cultures. 'Values-based rationales will typically align themselves to notions of global citizenship, responsibility, ethics, and justice, and are likely to include references to global issues such as poverty reduction, human rights, and sustainable futures' (Jones & Killick, 2007, p. 111). Jones argues that students should be seen as 'the main beneficiaries of internationalisation efforts in spite of an increasing trend to view internationalisation as a marker of institutional reputation or as a proxy for quality' (2013d, p. 1).

The Cambodian Context

Cambodia has had a turbulent past, with many dramatic transitions. Several of these have had serious implications for education. However, education activities were revived during the 1980s and have taken a new direction since the early 1990s. Over the last decade, higher education in Cambodia has witnessed phenomenal expansion due to increasing attention by both the government and the private sector. As the integration of Cambodia into the ASEAN as well as the global community strongly requires a knowledgeable and skilled labour force to meet regional and global needs, one means of achieving this is through the gradual internationalization of higher education. So far this has been mainly via the development of online courses, student mobility, the establishment of branch campuses of foreign universities, international partnerships, research collaboration and the presence of foreign teaching staff (Dash, 2016). Apart from these, international orientation of the curriculum is considered an effective way to meet the requirements of regional as well as global labour markets. For Cambodia, this study on internationalization of the higher education curriculum is new, and seeks to fill a gap in knowledge from an institutional perspective.

Outline of the Study

The main objective was to understand the perception of higher education stakeholders (Cambodian learners, teachers and academic leaders) regarding internationalization of the curriculum. The largest private university in Cambodia, Build

Bright University (BBU), was used as the focus for the study. The university has eight campuses located in different parts of the country and around 25,000 students on associate, bachelor, masters and doctoral programmes.

The study focused on a number of masters and doctoral programmes offered in English at the central campus. The sample involved 155 students and 60 academic staff. In addition, six academic leaders, such as vice presidents and deans, were included using proportionate stratified random sampling. Primary data were gathered through direct personal interview with the help of a questionnaire, on the perception of students, teachers and academic leaders on selected indictors of curriculum internationalization. The questionnaire was prepared by reviewing literature and through informal discussions with target respondents on their understanding of curriculum internationalization.

Stakeholders were asked to consider a range of indicators (see Tables 17.1–6) and to specify the extent to which they perceive these as present in the current curriculum (actual) or desirable to be included (desired).

Results

Student Perceptions on Internationalization of the Curriculum

Table 17.1 shows that as far as the current curriculum is concerned, results indicate that among the 15 selected areas of curriculum internationalization, on a scale from 1 to 5, only three areas had a mean higher than 3 in terms of student perceptions of the existing curriculum: (i) inclusion of materials from international and intergovernmental organizations (including international research) to broaden the learning experience and knowledge base of students; (ii) encouragement to learn a second language by students as a basis for appreciating the challenges of self-experience in a language other than one's mother tongue; and (iii) openness to own local and indigenous cultures and cultures of other communities. The areas with mean values less than 2 were (i) provision to reflect cultural diversities of organizations; and (ii) inclusion of lectures/presentations from guest lecturers using their international experience.

In terms of student perceptions on the *desired* level of curriculum internationalization, Table 17.2 shows that all 15 selected areas had a high rating, with the highest-rated areas being (i) provision of continuous review, improvement and self-evaluation of curriculum; followed by (ii) inclusion of materials from international and intergovernmental organizations (including international research) to broaden the learning experience and knowledge base of students; and (iii) inclusion of innovative international content in the curriculum, such as international as well as national case studies. Respondents considered the discussion of studies on professional practices in other nations/cultures as the lowest in terms of desired internationalization practice.

To compare the ratings of actual with desired perceptions on internationalization of curriculum, as revealed by students, a paired-sample 't' test was

Table 17.1 Rank ordering of students' actual perception on internationalization of curriculum

Areas on students' perception	1 N (%)	2 N (%)	3 N (%)	4 N (%)	5 N (%)	M (SD)
Inclusion of materials from international and intergovernmental organizations (including international research) to broaden the learning experience and knowledge base of students	5 (3.2)	28 (18.1)	60 (38.7)	52 (33.5)	10 (6.5)	3.22 (0.928)
Encouragement of learning second language by students as a basis for appreciating the challenges of self-experience in language other than one's mother tongue	12 (7.7)	7 (4.5)	84 (54.2)	41 (26.5)	11 (7.1)	3.21 (0.931)
Openness to own local and indigenous cultures and cultures of other communities	15 (9.7)	17 (11.0)	85 (54.8)	27 (17.4)	11 (7.1)	3.01 (0.980)
Inclusion of ethical issues in globalization such as social justice, equity, human rights and related social, economic and environmental issues	8 (5.2)	28 (18.1)	112 (72.3)	5 (3.2)	2 (1.3)	2.77 (0.650)
Use of diverse range of assessment to meet the learning needs of students	9 (5.8)	69 (44.5)	59 (38.1)	10 (6.5)	8 (5.2)	2.61 (0.894)
Engagement of nationality mix of instructors to facilitate discussion and exchange of ideas	5 (3.2)	69 (44.5)	75 (48.4)	4 (2.6)	2 (1.3)	2.54 (0.667)
Discussion of studies on professional practices in other nations/cultures	14 (9.0)	68 (43.9)	58 (37.4)	10 (6.5)	5 (3.2)	2.51 (0.871)
Provision to broaden learners' global knowledge, skills and understanding	33 (21.3)	54 (34.8)	40 (25.8)	24 (15.5)	4 (2.6)	2.43 (1.069)
Provision of continuous review, improvement and self-evaluation of curriculum	9 (5.8)	95 (61.3)	38 (24.5)	5 (3.2)	8 (5.2)	2.41 (0.858)
Inclusion of innovative international contents in the curriculum (international as well as national case studies)	40 (25.8)	58 (37.4)	25 (16.1)	20 (12.9)	12 (7.7)	2.39 (1.219)
Requirement for the students to discuss, arrange, evaluate information from a range of international sources	14 (9.0)	94 (60.6)	33 (21.3)	9 (5.8)	5 (3.2)	2.34 (0.847)
Provision of flexibilities in the curriculum to meet the global need	48 (31.0)	65 (41.9)	24 (15.5)	9 (5.8)	9 (5.8)	2.14 (1.099)
Provision of study abroad/exchange programmes in overseas institutions as a fully credited option in the programmes	56 (36.1)	47 (30.3)	34 (21.9)	14 (9.0)	4 (2.6)	2.12 (0.081)
Provision to reflect cultural diversities of organizations	60 (38.7)	63 (40.6)	19 (12.3)	6 (3.9)	7 (4.5)	1.95 (1.037)
Inclusion or lectures/presentations from guest lecturers using their international experience	80 (51.6)	33 (21.3)	28 (18.1)	9 (5.8)	5 (3.2)	1.88 (1.101)

Note: (i) Likert scale: never = 1, rarely = 2, occasionally = 3, frequently = 4, very frequently = 5.

Table 17.2 Rank ordering of students' desired perception on internationalization of curriculum

Areas on students' perception	1 N (%)	2 N (%)	3 N (%)	4 N (%)	5 N (%)	M (SD)
Provision of continuous review, improvement and self-evaluation of curriculum	—	4 (2.6)	3 (1.9)	35 (22.6)	113 (72.9)	4.66 (0.649)
Inclusion of materials from international and intergovernmental organizations (including international research) to broaden the learning experience and knowledge base of students	—	—	3 (1.9)	62 (40.0)	90 (58.1)	4.56 (0.536)
Inclusion of innovative international contents in the curriculum (international as well as national case studies)	—	—	5 (3.2)	69 (49.5)	81 (52.3)	4.49 (0.563)
Provision to broaden learners' global knowledge, skills and understanding	—	—	11 (7.1)	62 (40.0)	82 (52.9)	4.46 (0.627)
Provision of flexibilities in the curriculum to meet the global need	3 (1.9)	6 (3.9)	6 (3.9)	47 (30.3)	93 (60.0)	4.43 (0.890)
Engagement of nationality mix of instructors to facilitate discussion and exchange of ideas	—	3 (1.9)	3 (1.9)	84 (59.2)	65 (41.9)	4.36 (0.623)
Use of diverse range of assessment to meet the learning needs of students	1 (0.6)	14 (9.0)	8 (5.2)	53 (34.2)	79 (51.0)	4.26 (0.959)
Encouragement of learning second language by students as a basis for appreciating the challenges of self-experience in language other than one's mother tongue	—	8 (5.2)	4 (2.6)	94 (60.6)	49 (31.6)	4.19 (0.719)
Inclusion of ethical issues in globalization such as social justice, equity, human rights and related social, economic and environmental issues	—	4 (2.6)	5 (3.2)	108 (69.7)	38 (24.5)	4.16 (0.597)
Provision of study abroad/exchange programmes in overseas institutions as a fully credited option in the programmes	2 (1.3)	6 (3.9)	21 (13.5)	64 (41.3)	62 (40.0)	4.15 (0.889)
Requirement for the students to discuss, arrange, evaluate information from a range of international sources	3 (1.9)	10 (6.5)	3 (1.9)	90 (58.1)	49 (31.6)	4.11 (0.872)
Provision to reflect cultural diversities of organizations	4 (2.6)	12 (7.7)	17 (11.0)	64 (41.3)	58 (37.4)	4.03 (1.016)
Inclusion or lectures/presentations from guest lecturers using their international experience	8 (5.2)	15 (9.7)	10 (6.5)	63 (40.6)	59 (38.1)	3.97 (1.142)
Openness to own local and indigenous cultures and cultures of other communities	4 (2.6)	18 (11.6)	19 (12.3)	52 (33.5)	62 (40.0)	3.97 (1.107)
Discussion of studies on professional practices in other nations/cultures	—	—	53 (34.2)	85 (54.8)	17 (11.0)	3.77 (0.633)

Note: (i) Likert scale: never = 1, rarely = 2, occasionally = 3, frequently = 4, very frequently = 5. (ii) M = Mean, SD = Standard Deviation.

Table 17.3 Desired and actual perception of students on internationalization of curriculum

Areas on students' perception	Desired mean	Actual mean	Mean diff.	't' value
Inclusion of innovative international contents in the curriculum (international as well as national case studies)	4.49	2.39	-2.097	-20.844**
Discussion of studies on professional practices in other nations/cultures	3.77	2.51	-1.258	-17.767**
Inclusion of materials from international and intergovernmental organizations (including international research) to broaden the learning experience and knowledge base of students	4.56	3.22	-1.342	-20.441**
Inclusion of ethical issues in globalization such as social justice, equity, human rights and related social, economic and environmental issues	4.16	2.77	-1.387	-23.555**
Engagement of nationality mix of instructors to facilitate discussion and exchange of ideas	4.36	2.54	-1.819	-25.147**
Encouragement of learning second language by students as a basis for appreciating the challenges of self-experience in language other than one's mother tongue	4.19	3.21	-0.981	-24.279**
Provision of continuous review, improvement and self-evaluation of curriculum	4.66	2.41	-2.252	-31.343**
Openness to own local and indigenous cultures and cultures of other communities	3.97	3.01	-0.955	-16.224**
Requirement for the students to discuss, arrange, evaluate information from a range of international sources	4.11	2.34	-1.774	-29.372**
Provision of study abroad/exchange programmes in overseas institutions as a fully credited option in the programme	4.15	2.12	-2.032	-19.904**
Inclusion or lectures/presentations from guest lecturers using their international experience	3.97	1.88	-2.090	-20.902**
Provision of flexibilities in the curriculum to meet the global need	4.43	2.14	-2.290	-22.844**
Provision to broaden learners' global knowledge, skills and understanding	4.46	2.43	-2.026	-22.477**
Provision to reflect cultural diversities of organizations	4.03	1.95	-2.084	-20.048**
Use of diverse range of assessment to meet the learning needs of students	4.26	2.61	-1.652	-20.225**

Note: ** Difference is significant at $p < 0.1$.

performed. As Table 17.3 shows, for all 15 areas, all the means in the 'desired' category were higher than those in the 'actual' perception. In all 15 selected areas, the mean differences were found to be significant at the 1% level. A higher difference was found in (i) the provision of flexibilities in the curriculum to meet the global need; followed by (ii) provision of continuous review, improvement and self-evaluation of curriculum; and (iii) provision to broaden learners' global knowledge, skills and understanding. This simply means that in the changing environment (ASEAN integration and globalization), the university should put more effort into all the selected areas of curriculum internationalization to meet the level students are looking for. In addition, through open-ended questions, the majority of students (69%) suggested that to successfully carry out curriculum internationalization, an active leadership and wide participation from students, faculty and administration, among others, are required.

Perceptions of Teachers and Academic Leaders on Internationalization of Curriculum

With regard to the perception of teachers and academic leaders on the current degree of internationalization of the curriculum, the results as seen in Table 17.4 indicate that among the 20 selected areas, on a scale from 1 to 5, only five areas had means higher than 3. These were:

i   openness to own local and indigenous cultures and cultures of other communities;
ii   inclusion of materials from international and intergovernmental organizations (including international research) to broaden the learning experience and knowledge base of students;
iii development of strong institutional linkages with partner institutions abroad to complement faculty expertise;
iv   inclusion of different teaching strategies to engage students from diverse cultural backgrounds;
v   encouragement of learning a second language by students as a basis for appreciating the challenges of self-experience in a language other than one's mother tongue.

The areas with mean values less than 2 were:

i   provision to reflect cultural diversities of organizations; and
ii   inclusion of lectures/presentations from guest lecturers using their international experience.

As for the perception of teachers and academic leaders on the desirability of different aspects of internationalization of the curriculum, seen in Table 17.5, all 20 selected areas had a high rating, with the highest-rated area provision of

Table 17.4 Rank ordering of teachers' and academic leaders' actual perception on internationalization of curriculum

Areas on teachers' and academic leaders' perception	1	2	3	4	5	M (SD)
	N (%)	N (%)	N (%)	N (%)	N (%)	
Openness to own local and indigenous cultures and cultures of other communities	2 (3.0)	3 (4.5)	41 (62.1)	15 (22.7)	5 (7.6)	3.27 (0.795)
Inclusion of materials from international and intergovernmental organizations (including international research) to broaden the learning experience and knowledge base of students	1 (1.5)	13 (19.7)	26 (39.4)	20 (30.3)	6 (9.1)	3.26 (0.933)
Development of strong institutional linkages with partner institutions abroad to complement faculty expertise	1 (1.5)	13 (19.7)	26 (39.4)	20 (30.3)	6 (9.1)	3.26 (0.933)
Inclusion of different teaching strategies to engage students from diverse cultural backgrounds	1 (1.5)	13 (19.7)	26 (39.4)	20 (30.3)	6 (9.1)	3.26 (0.933)
Encouragement of learning second language by students as a basis for appreciating the challenges of self-experience in language other than one's mother tongue	3 (4.5)	1 (1.5)	45 (68.2)	16 (24.2)	1 (1.5)	3.17 (0.692)
Inclusion of ethical issues in globalization such as social justice, equity, human rights and related social, economic and environmental issues	4 (6.1)	12 (18.2)	46 (69.7)	3 (4.5)	1 (1.5)	2.77 (0.697)
Provision of participation in seminars/conferences/workshops/training programmes abroad to faculty members in order to enhance their understanding in new areas of study	4 (6.1)	12 (18.2)	46 (69.7)	3 (4.5)	1 (1.5)	2.77 (0.697)
Inclusion of international/intercultural learning goals, aims and outcomes in a course as well as programme	4 (6.1)	12 (18.2)	46 (69.7)	3 (4.5)	1 (1.5)	2.77 (0.697)
Provision to broaden learners' global knowledge, skills and understanding	9 (13.6)	25 (37.9)	21 (31.8)	11 (16.7)	–	2.52 (0.932)
Provision of teaching and learning activities and modes of instruction supportive of the development of students' interpersonal and relational understandings and skills	9 (13.6)	25 (37.9)	21 (31.8)	11 (16.7)	–	2.52 (0.932)
Engagement of nationality mix of instructors to facilitate discussion and exchange of ideas	2 (3.0)	31 (47.0)	31 (47.0)	2 (3.0)	–	2.50 (0.614)
Use of diverse range of assessment to meet the learning needs of students	2 (3.0)	36 (54.5)	28 (42.4)	–	–	2.39 (0.551)

						M (SD)
Requirement for the students to discuss, arrange, evaluate information from a range of international sources	9 (13.6)	36 (54.5)	15 (22.7)	5 (7.6)	1 (1.5)	2.29 (0.855)
Discussion of studies on professional practices in other nations/cultures	9 (13.6)	32 (48.5)	24 (36.4)	–	1 (1.5)	2.27 (0.755)
Inclusion of innovative international contents in the curriculum (international as well as national case studies)	18 (27.3)	26 (39.4)	12 (18.2)	7 (10.6)	3 (4.5)	2.26 (1.114)
Provision of flexibilities in the curriculum to meet the global need	20 (30.3)	26 (39.4)	10 (15.2)	4 (6.1)	6 (9.1)	2.24 (1.216)
Provision of continuous review, improvement and self-evaluation of curriculum	2 (3.0)	48 (72.7)	16 (24.2)	–	–	2.21 (0.481)
Provision of study abroad/exchange programmes in overseas institutions as a fully credited option in the programme	27 (40.9)	17 (25.8)	17 (25.8)	3 (4.5)	2 (3.0)	2.03 (1.067)
Provision to reflect cultural diversities of organizations	25 (37.9)	27 (40.9)	8 (12.1)	3 (4.5)	3 (4.5)	1.97 (1.052)
Inclusion of lectures/presentations from guest lecturers using their international experience	38 (57.6)	14 (21.2)	10 (15.2)	3 (4.5)	1 (1.5)	1.71 (0.989)

Note: (i) Likert scale: never = 1, rarely = 2, occasionally = 3, frequently = 4, very frequently = 5. (ii) M = Mean, SD = Standard Deviation.

Table 17.5 Rank ordering of teachers' and academic leaders' desired perception on internationalization of curriculum

Areas on teachers' and academic leaders' perception	1 N (%)	2 N (%)	3 N (%)	4 N (%)	5 N (%)	M (SD)
Provision of continuous review, improvement and self-evaluation of curriculum	–	–	2 (3.0)	14 (21.2)	50 (75.8)	4.73 (0.513)
Inclusion of materials from international and intergovernmental organizations (including international research) to broaden the learning experience and knowledge base of students	–	–	1 (1.5)	26 (39.4)	39 (59.1)	4.58 (0.528)
Development of strong institutional linkages with partner institutions abroad to complement faculty expertise	–	–	1 (1.5)	26 (39.4)	39 (59.1)	4.58 (0.528)
Inclusion of different teaching strategies to engage students from diverse cultural backgrounds	–	–	1 (1.5)	26 (39.4)	39 (59.1)	4.58 (0.528)
Provision to broaden learners' global knowledge, skills and understanding	–	–	3 (4.5)	24 (36.4)	39 (59.1)	4.55 (0.587)
Provision of teaching and learning activities and modes of instruction supportive of the development of students' interpersonal and relational understandings and skills	–	–	3 (4.5)	24 (36.4)	39 (59.1)	4.55 (0.587)
Inclusion of innovative international contents in the curriculum (international as well as national case studies)	–	–	1 (1.5)	33 (50.0)	32 (48.5)	4.47 (0.533)
Engagement of nationality mix of instructors to facilitate discussion and exchange of ideas	–	1 (1.5)	1 (1.5)	35 (53.0)	29 (43.9)	4.39 (0.605)
Use of diverse range of assessment to meet the learning needs of students	–	6 (9.1)	2 (3.0)	22 (33.3)	36 (54.5)	4.33 (0.917)
Provision of flexibilities in the curriculum to meet the global need	2 (3.0)	3 (4.5)	4 (6.1)	21 (31.8)	36 (54.5)	4.30 (0.992)

Item	1	2	3	4	5	M (SD)
Provision of study abroad/exchange programmes in overseas institutions as a fully credited option in the programme	–	2 (3.0)	9 (13.6)	26 (39.4)	29 (43.9)	4.24 (0.805)
Openness to own local and indigenous cultures and cultures of other communities	–	4 (6.1)	9 (13.6)	24 (36.4)	29 (43.9)	4.18 (0.893)
Inclusion of ethical issues in globalization such as social justice, equity, human rights and related social, economic and environmental issues	–	2 (3.0)	1 (1.5)	46 (69.7)	17 (25.8)	4.18 (0.605)
Provision of participation in seminars/conferences/ workshops/training programmes abroad to faculty members in order to enhance their understanding in new areas of study	–	2 (3.0)	1 (1.5)	46 (69.7)	17 (25.8)	4.18 (0.605)
Inclusion of international/intercultural learning goals, aims and outcomes in a course as well as programme	–	2 (3.0)	1 (1.5)	46 (69.7)	17 (25.8)	4.18 (0.605)
Encouragement of learning second language by students as a basis for appreciating the challenges of self-experience in language other than one's mother tongue	–	2 (3.0)	–	48 (72.7)	16 (24.2)	4.18 (0.579)
Provision to reflect cultural diversities of organizations	–	4 (6.1)	8 (12.1)	29 (43.9)	25 (37.9)	4.14 (0.857)
Requirement for the students to discuss, arrange, evaluate information from a range of international sources	2 (3.0)	5 (7.6)	2 (3.0)	36 (54.5)	21 (31.8)	4.05 (0.968)
Inclusion of lectures/presentations from guest lecturers using their international experience	6 (9.1)	7 (10.6)	4 (6.1)	24 (36.4)	25 (37.9)	3.83 (1.296)
Discussion of studies on professional practices in other nations/cultures	–	7 (10.6)	26 (39.4)	33 (50.0)	7 (10.6)	3.71 (0.651)

Note: (i) Likert scale: never = 1, rarely = 2, occasionally = 3, frequently = 4, very frequently = 5. (ii) M = Mean, SD = Standard Deviation.

continuous review, improvement and self-evaluation of curriculum. All areas except two had means greater than 4:

i   inclusion of lectures/presentations from guest lectures using their international experience; and
ii   discussion of studies on professional practices in other nations/cultures.

This indicates the areas that teachers and academic leaders perceive as important for internationalization of curriculum.

Table 17.6 compares the perception ratings of actual with desired internationalization of the curriculum by teachers and academic leaders using a paired-sample 't' test. All means for the 20 areas in the category 'desired' were higher than the means for 'actual'. In all the selected areas, the mean differences were found to be significant at the 1% level. Higher mean difference, i.e. −2.515, was found in:

i   the provision of continuous review, improvement and self-evaluation of curriculum; followed by
ii   provision of study abroad/exchange programmes in overseas institutions as a fully credited option in the programme; and
iii inclusion of innovative international contents in the curriculum (international as well as national case studies).

Thus, this means that in the present environment, the university should put more effort into all the selected areas of curriculum internationalization to meet the perceived level desired by teachers and academic leaders. In addition, just as with the students, through the open-ended questions the majority of teachers and academic leaders (82%) were of the opinion that to successfully carry out internationalization of the curriculum, the following aspects are required, among others:

1   active leadership;
2   adequate provision of funds for internationalization efforts;
3   wide participation from stakeholders such as faculty and administration;
4   clear establishment of a strategic framework to govern these efforts.

Teachers and academic leaders also expressed the view that strengthening international partnerships would facilitate internationalization of the curriculum.

Discussion and Innovativeness of the Study

The study is innovative in the sense that, for the first time in Cambodia, it tries to explore what internationalization of curriculum means from the point of view of higher education stakeholders. It offers possible areas of curriculum internationalization to frame stakeholder perceptions, based on a review of the literature

Table 17.6 Desired and actual perception of teachers' and academic leaders' on internationalization of curriculum

Areas on teachers' and academic leaders' perception	Desired mean	Actual mean	Mean diff.	't' value
Inclusion of innovative international contents in the curriculum (international as well as national case studies)	4.47	2.26	-2.212	-15.356
Discussion of studies on professional practices in other nations/cultures	3.71	2.27	-1.439	-14.171
Inclusion of materials from international and intergovernmental organizations (including international research) to broaden the learning experience and knowledge base of students	4.58	3.26	-1.318	-12.421
Inclusion of ethical issues in globalization such as social justice, equity, human rights and related social, economic and environmental issues	4.18	2.77	-1.409	-14.601
Engagement of nationality mix of instructors to facilitate discussion and exchange of ideas	4.39	2.50	-1.894	-16.252
Encouragement of learning second language by students as a basis for appreciating the challenges of self-experience in language other than one's mother tongue	4.18	3.17	-1.015	-18.452
Provision of continuous review, improvement and self-evaluation of curriculum	4.73	2.21	-2.515	-29.837
Openness to own local and indigenous cultures and cultures of other communities	4.18	3.27	-0.909	-10.000
Requirement for the students to discuss, arrange, evaluate information from a range of international sources	4.05	2.29	-1.758	-18.645
Provision of study abroad/exchange programmes in overseas institutions as a fully credited option in the programme	4.24	2.03	-2.212	-14.560
Inclusion of lectures/presentations from guest lecturers using their international experience	3.83	1.71	-2.121	-13.688
Provision of flexibilities in the curriculum to meet the global need	4.30	2.24	-2.061	-13.124
Provision to broaden learners' global knowledge, skills and understanding	4.55	2.52	-0.030	-15.901
Provision to reflect cultural diversities of organizations	4.14	1.97	-2.167	-14.702
Use of diverse range of assessment to meet the learning needs of students	4.33	2.39	-1.939	-17.325
Development of strong institutional linkages with partner institutions abroad to complement faculty expertise	4.58	3.26	-1.318	-12.421
Provision of participation in seminars/conferences/workshops/training programmes abroad to faculty members in order to enhance their understanding in new areas of study	4.18	2.77	-1.409	-14.601
Inclusion of different teaching strategies to engage students from diverse cultural backgrounds	4.58	3.26	-1.318	-12.421
Inclusion of international/intercultural learning goals, aims and outcomes in a course as well as programme	4.18	2.77	-1.409	-14.601
Provision of teaching and learning activities and modes of instruction supportive of the development of students' interpersonal and relational understandings and skills	4.55	2.52	-2.030	-15.901

Note: (i) ** Difference is significant at p < 0.1.

and an understanding of the Cambodian context. No significant differences were observed in how stakeholders perceive the different areas of curriculum internationalization, meaning that these aspects were seen as important for all stakeholders surveyed. In each case, the perceptions of all stakeholders were that 'desired' characteristics for curriculum internationalization were higher than the 'actual' in all areas studied. This signifies that students, academic staff and academic leaders all perceive the need for curriculum internationalization and have views on the different dimensions of how this can be achieved and their relative importance. The university should therefore put more effort into the selected 'desired' areas to meet the requirements of stakeholders for curriculum internationalization. Although this study was based in a single institution, it may be considered as an example for other institutions in Cambodia as well as for countries with similar characteristics. In the absence of any other study of this kind in Cambodia or other countries, this study can be considered as the base on which future studies may be undertaken. For these five reasons and outcomes, it has been an innovative study in the context of Cambodia and countries at a similar stage of development in curriculum internationalization.

Conclusion

In the globally competitive economy, countries have been facing tremendous challenges to meet the demand for higher education made by a growing population in search of better knowledge and skills. This demands a new approach to curriculum development, responsive to the diverse nature of the global environment. As such, this has caused universities to infuse the curriculum with international content, but not necessarily to consider other dimensions of curriculum internationalization. In the present study an attempt is made to understand the perception of higher education stakeholders (students, teachers and academic leaders) towards internationalization of the curriculum as practised in one Cambodian university. The result reveals that in all the selected areas of curriculum internationalization much improvement is required.

From the perception of students, the areas that require improvement are flexibilities in the curriculum to meet global needs; provision of continuous review, improvement and self-evaluation of curriculum; and inclusion of innovative international content in the curriculum (international as well as national case studies). Similarly, from the point of teachers and academic leaders, a range of areas require improvement, namely: provision of continuous review, improvement and self-evaluation of curriculum; study abroad/exchange programmes in overseas institutions as a fully credited option in the programme; and inclusion of innovative international content in the curriculum (international and national case studies).

Taking into account the perceptions of different groups on 'actual' versus 'desired' levels of curriculum internationalization, it is recommended that the case study university, as well as others in a similar position, put more effort into all the selected areas to meet the expressed desires of stakeholders for enhanced higher education curriculum internationalization.

Chapter 18

Internationalization Strategies in Ghana's Public Universities

Oforiwaa Gifty Gyamera

Introduction

Internationalization has become a revolution influencing many postsecondary educational policies and practices globally (Altbach, Reisburg & Rumbley, 2009). In response to this, higher education institutions worldwide, including those in Ghana, have adopted varied strategies to position themselves in a globalized higher education arena.

Many writers and academics have argued that some university internationalization strategies are underpinned by neoliberal principles, dictated by the market rather than aimed at enhancing international understanding and intercultural exchange, with the result that inequalities continue (Desjardins, 2013; Harris, 2007, 2008, 2011; Torres & Jones, 2013). In the neoliberal world, the rich get richer, and the poor get poorer. Postcolonial theorists have also linked the concepts of internationalization, globalization and neoliberalism to the perpetuation of ideologies and principles of slavery and colonialism (e.g. Fanon, 2004; Hardt & Negri, 2000; Rizvi, Lingard & Lavia, 2006). Thus, many international strategies adopted by ex-colonial countries serve to continue colonial legacies and inequalities.

This chapter uses the findings from an empirical, qualitative study by the author of three public universities in Ghana (Gyamera, 2015), chosen to reflect variables such as age, size, mandate, prestige and location. The study involved senior management, deans, heads of departments, academics and students, using semi-structured interviews with open-ended questions, analysed for content and discourse. Document analysis was used to add to the interview findings. The current chapter draws on the outcomes of that study to consider features of internationalization strategies in Ghanaian public universities.

Internationalization Strategies

The main strategies in Ghanaian universities include mission statements, strategic collaborations, establishment of international centres, benchmarking and foreign experts. I shall consider each one in turn. The names of universities have not been included.

Mission Statements

A major strategy to emphasize internationalization of universities is the development of new mission statements and strategic plans. The main thrust of these is to develop the universities into 'world-class' institutions. One university, for instance, has as its mission statement to develop 'world-class human resources and capabilities to meet national development needs and global challenges through quality teaching, learning, research and knowledge dissemination'. The statement indicates the ambition of the university to turn out graduates who will be recognized as possessing world-class abilities and qualities. The mission of another is to be:

> An equal opportunity University uniquely placed to provide quality education through the provision of comprehensive, liberal and professional programmes that challenge learners to be creative, innovative and morally responsible citizens ... The University constantly seeks alternative ways to respond to changing needs; to expand its existing highly qualified faculty and administrative staff; offer a conducive environment that motivates them to position the University to respond effectively to the developmental needs of a changing world.
>
> (Website of institution)

Though this university does not explicitly state in its mission that it wants to become a first-class university, its vision is to be a 'world class university'. The emphasis of 'world class' in these statements indicates how universities in Ghana are focused on positioning themselves in the international arena.

Strategic Collaborations

In addition to developing mission statements and strategic plans, a major university strategy is to develop collaborations with universities both within and outside the African region. The level of interest and the number varies by institution. One university has over 400 memoranda of understanding (MOUs) with various universities both inside and outside the African region. Most collaborations are with institutions in the United States, followed by institutions in Europe, Canada, Asia and Africa, in that order.

At the other end of the scale, another university has, according to its website, about 35 MOUs, while others may have even fewer. Agreements may be at the departmental and/or institutional levels, centred on areas of mutual interest such as staff and student exchange programmes, joint graduate programmes, research collaborations and joint conferences and seminars.

Establishment of International Centres

To enhance their collaborations, marketing and international student recruitment, universities have established centres that run international programmes

(Gyamera, 2015). To emphasize the importance attached to internationalization, all the centres are directed by professors who are assisted by assistant registrars and other supporting staff. The centres also have mission and vision statements, which are concerned with helping to project the universities as centres of excellence and enhance exchange of resources and knowledge.

The centres coordinate many of the international programmes, activities and relations with other universities. In addition to handling international collaborations and other international affairs, they run student and staff exchange programmes. All centre activities require the approval of the universities' vice-chancellors.

Benchmarking

Altbach and Salmi (2011) define benchmarking as the process of comparing one's business processes and performance metrics to industry bests and/or best practice from other industries to improve one's performance. They have indicated that a major challenge of universities in what is perceived as the 'less developed world' is 'how to participate effectively in the global knowledge network'. According to them, in order to do this and to attain world-class status, universities need to benchmark most of their policies, strategies and practices to leading universities abroad. There appears to be a guiding maxim that, as one vice-chancellor explained, 'if Harvard is coming, then we have to be like Harvard' (participant cited in Gyamera, 2015). Though this could be described as a cliché, it appears to be guiding the other universities; it also signifies the universities' aspirations to benchmark against leading universities abroad.

It is assumed that 'following international standards' will increase the competitiveness of universities and their prestige. It is also thought of as a valuable way to develop Ghanaian universities. Such views, however, are deeply steeped in colonial legacies where everything about the West is perceived as 'excellent'. This approach confirms much of the literature, particularly on postcolonialism, which suggests that many Africans were not emancipated from the psychological domination of the West beyond political independence (Fanon, 2004; Rizvi et al., 2006). There is the need for institutions to have a historical understanding that much contemporary discourse on strategies for enhanced relationships among world universities and nations cannot be dissociated from its roots in the European projects of imperialism. Following international 'blueprints' will continue to submerge African/Ghanaian cultures and values, and the gradual gain in psychological emancipation achieved over the years will gradually but completely be lost.

Benchmarking is pursued in two main ways: the use of foreign experts and benchmarking the curriculum to that of universities abroad. In this chapter, I will limit myself to the use of foreign experts.

Foreign Experts

Examples of ways in which foreign experts have been utilized include relying on a 'Visitation Team' to advise the university on its efforts to satisfy local and external demands. Terms of reference include examining the university curriculum to determine its currency, quality and relevance in relation to world-class universities; investigating and advising on infrastructural needs; and advising on governance and structure. Members of the Visitation Team typically make visits of several days. Much of the information has to be provided by local academics.

In one case the university made a series of changes based on the report and recommendations of the Visitation Team. The team recommended, for instance, changes and improvement in infrastructure, financial management and the curriculum. Upon the recommendations of the Visitation Team, a Western expert was brought in to look at the university's curriculum development. Such practices equally confirm the notion that 'the West is always right'. In the Ghanaian setting, it could be argued that many of the assumptions underlying knowledge contestations and the universities' efforts to strategize, and the strategies adopted in the curriculum, are underpinned by these colonial influences. One wonders how many times institutions in the West invite academics from the South to help them design their curriculum in the context of internationalization.

Another university brought in Western experts to examine the curriculum and examinations of the institution to determine whether they are compatible with international standards, which invariably means Western standards.

Though the strategies adopted are similar, the rate of involvement differs among institutions. It could be argued that various factors including location, size, age and infrastructural strength influence the particular perceptions and rationales that each of the institutions attach to internationalization and also their level of interest in internationalization strategies. The next topic presents these factors.

Demographic Influence and Nuances

It is clear that universities in Ghana are at different stages of development in terms of internationalization. Just as in some other countries, internationalization strategies are more highly developed in older and larger universities. A greater number of collaborations, more emphasis on benchmarking and offices for international programmes are all examples of higher infrastructural development. Unsurprisingly, this kind of university attracts the highest number of international students, and internationalization is mainly seen as an 'all good thing'. In one case, internationalization is a 'do or die affair', and the vice-chancellor said, 'either you internationalise or you are left behind in the face of globalisation. If we at … do not internationalise, we will not be existing' (participant cited in Gyamera, 2015).

With such a student-recruitment approach, universities appear to be missing out on an essential aspect of internationalization that involves the emphasis on intercultural exchange and international understanding. There is the need for universities to embrace internationalization with the objective of championing global understanding and the development of global citizens who will not only understand, tolerate and respect the 'other', but also have confidence in himself/ herself. The focus should not be on the 'international student' only, but also on the local student. This is especially true in the context of Ghana where, due to various factors including socialization both at home and in the school, students appear to have an inherent sense of inferiority in the face of Western superiority. There is the need for students to be educated to have confidence in themselves as Ghanaians and as Africans.

Other universities are less engaged in internationalization strategies, and these tend to be comparatively younger institutions, smaller and located far from the capital. They have fewer collaborations and relatively fewer international students. Distance from the capital and other demographic factors including age, size and infrastructural availability do not provide the incentives to attract international students. On the other hand, such universities appear to attach the meaning of internationalization more to intercultural exchange, with less involvement in utilizing foreign experts and benchmarking. There is a sense that the goal is to let others benchmark what they are doing locally.

Yet while the benefits of internationalization may be recognized, there is also scepticism about it and concern about the dominance of the West. One response exemplifies this anxiety: 'I don't necessarily disagree with internationalisation, I disagree with the way internationalisation has meant that we westernise our system' (Professor of African Studies cited in Gyamera, 2015). Despite these variations across the sector in terms of internationalization, all the changes in the universities, I argue, exhibit the influences of neoliberal and colonial legacies. The next sub-topic focuses on these neoliberal underpinnings.

Neoliberal Influences

On the taking office of the New Patriotic Party (NPP) government in 2001, President Kuffour, as part of his Presidential Special Initiatives, declared a year of 'the Golden Age of Business' (Asante, 2012, p. 9). This was to encourage wealth creation in almost all organizations and institutions including higher education institutions. It was also part of the NPP government's agenda 'to move Ghana's economy beyond highly indebted poor countries status and reduce the country's over-dependence on aid and donor support and a few commodity exports by finding new pillars of growth' (Asante, 2012). With this declaration, the concept of the superiority of the market was embraced by many organizations, including universities. Most of the strategies adopted by universities, therefore, have been influenced primarily by neoliberal economic thinking, which sees higher education as a quasi marketplace where knowledge is bought and sold.

The 'world class' emphasized in the mission and vision statements of universities, I argue, is an attempt to enhance their marketing strategies and positions in a world of higher education steeped deeply in competition. As Altbach (2004) indicates, though almost all universities wish to be world class, nobody knows what world class is or how to be world class. He indicates that a world-class university presently 'might take more than $500 million along with clever leadership and much good luck' to succeed (Altbach, 2004, para. 2). In many cases, the emphasis on world class has become a maxim for marketing universities. There is an imperative to build a brand that will attract students: the underlying focus being the market and profit. As one vice-chancellor indicated:

> I have been in this office for just over one and a half years, and in this period, I have set as my broad objective to raise the University ... to a world-class status. What this means for us is that in addition to our Ghanaian students, we will attract more students from outside Ghana. We are anxious to attract students, not only from Africa, but also from Europe and America.
>
> (Vice-chancellor cited in Gyamera, 2015)

In relation to such marketing logic, public universities in Ghana have developed 'corporate' strategic plans, which were hitherto unknown in universities. With these plans, universities appeared set to adopt and implement business-related plans, principles and procedures in achieving their goals. At a glance, the captions and use of words are revealing: universities have 'operating environments', 'competitors', 'markets', 'customers', 'clients' and 'products'. A dean in one university, in expressing his misgivings about the business nature of the strategic plans, said:

> We are masquerading as something we are not. We are not a corporate world. Of course we can borrow some but I don't think that we should have a whole sale of universities as corporate bodies. Sometimes it even sounds ridiculous and trivial that suddenly something that used to be called personnel office is now called human resource something, I mean all of it looks like painting an old house and pretending that it is new ... So I don't personally agree that that is the way we should go. I think that we could remain a university and yet you know, borrow what we have to from other sections.
>
> (Dean cited in Gyamera, 2015)

The major goal of universities, presently, is to 'sell' themselves to 'stakeholders', 'customers' and 'clients', which includes not only students, but the various government ministries, industries, alumni and parents. In some universities, adverts targeting international students have been taken beyond the borders of Ghana and are done explicitly through the media in neighbouring countries. There has also been intensive usage of emails and fax to market and provide extensive information about the universities. Again, there is intensive usage of social media, including Facebook, to attract students.

In furtherance of their marketing strategies, all universities have adopted fee-paying programmes and increased student user and tuition fees. With the approval of the government in 2002, the universities give 5% admission slots for international students and 5% for local fee-paying students. The fee-paying programme is for local students who qualify to gain admission to university, but who otherwise would not have been admitted because of limited facilities. These students pay fees similar to international students.

As part of these marketing strategies, universities also organize fairs and open days, amidst other programmes to showcase themselves, their activities and programmes to people both locally and externally. It is hoped that such programmes would generate more confidence in the universities and through that attract both local and international students.

This market emphasis reflects a broader trend worldwide. Presently, how universities showcase themselves is marked by market-centric principles and logic (e.g. Torres & Jones, 2013), which has become the 'neoliberal commonsense' (Torres, 2011). Market principles are also based on dwindling government subventions to universities. With the exception of personal emoluments, monies for other purposes, including administration and services, keep reducing. The main challenge acknowledged by all is limited funding. With these conditions in Ghana, it is difficult for universities to think beyond the neoliberal agenda.

This market logic is not limited to mission statements and strategic plans. Some perceive relationships with foreign universities in economic terms. Others recognize that different benefits can result, including scholarships and resources for teaching, learning and research that universities could accrue from such collaborations. International offices, it could be argued, have been used to emphasize and boost the market-centric logic of universities.

The assumption underlying university benchmarking, I argue, is also a source of economic gain. When they are perceived as benchmarking with 'big universities' abroad, it enhances their prestige and thus collaboration and marketization endeavours. Almost all these strategies could equally be situated in colonial discourses and legacies. I will now discuss the colonial implications.

Colonial Legacies

These collaborations, benchmarking and the use of foreign experts, among other strategies, could also reflect colonial tendencies and unequal power relations. The relatively few collaborations with African universities is a case in point, and it is interesting since the mission of the Association of African Universities emphasizes the need for universities to collaborate at the African regional level. Writers, for example, Crossman (2004), have emphasized the importance of South–South collaboration. Such collaborations, according to him, will foster greater understanding between institutions and enhance their ability to mutually address local and regional problems. Many of the problems and needs confronting institutions and countries are across borders in the region. Again according to Crossman (2004), South–South collaborations would help to reduce Western hegemony in the international domain.

There are well-recognized challenges of North–South collaborations, including a seemingly unequal relationship between the North and the South, differences in expectations and at times what is perceived as exploitation of universities in the South by some universities in the North. Examples include an institution in the North receiving funding for so-called collaborative research, but with the project being undertaken in their country, the partners in Ghana felt they did not gain anything from the project. Another involved joint research between Ghana and the West but, in the end, the Ghanaian collaborators were not cited as contributors to the research. Since the collaborative partners in the North have more financial resources, they are able to influence and control the collaborations.

However, others perceive collaborations in a more positive light. Here is one example:

> And me I don't see any negative aspect of it. So people who say this give room for exploitation. I don't understand it at all, I don't understand it. If you are linking up with another university you sit down and prepare the MOU; if you are not satisfied with it you don't agree to it but once you have prepared an MOU with your own signature, where is the exploitation? Why will you allow yourself to be exploited [laughs]. So internationalisation, me I don't see any negative aspect, it's all positive.
>
> (Professor cited in Gyamera, 2015)

Yet while some respondents may not be pressurized, they may enter into certain collaborations expecting some benefits, such as financial or as contributing partners in research. As indicated above, in some cases, the anticipated benefits do not materialize and it leaves a feeling of exploitation.

Dependence on Western societies and using foreign experts in some cases creates tensions in institutions, as we can see from the following quotations from two professors:

> Well let's say the changes to some extent were imposed on us. The university got someone to come and value our programmes and so on and so forth. It was out of the ... report that we moved in this direction ... I understand they came here and talked to people. The university asked them to come and look at the courses and advise us, you know these days we are all trying to become a world-class university.
>
> (Gyamera, 2015)

Another professor said: 'And I think most of the suggestions that they made are things that we know must be done. You know, we know them already but unfortunately we hadn't been able to implement them. For what reason I don't know' (Gyamera, 2015). These two statements indicate the subtle discomfort of these professors with importing foreign experts to guide the university in its plans. The first shows a level of uninterest in what actually happened and is happening. The second shows that the visit was seen as unnecessary. They believe the recommendations were things they should have already implemented.

Ways to Challenge Dominant Views of Internationalization

It is important, as universities in Ghana embark on internationalization strategies, that they should avoid uncritical acceptance of everything Western. This section looks at ways in which universities could challenge the hegemony of particular views on internationalization.

Deemphasizing the Economic Lens

In agreement with critics of the dominance of neoliberal influences in educational institutions (e.g. Harris, 2011; Sandel, 2012; Torres, 2011), universities should avoid viewing internationalization policies through a primarily economic lens. Sandel, in his remarkable book, *What Money Can't Buy: The Moral Limits of the Market*, has argued that not everything can be perceived and valued in economic terms. According to him, 'some of the good things in life are corrupted or degraded if turned into commodities' (2012, p. 86). One of these good things that, I argue, should not be perceived in monetary terms is internationalization. Internationalization has the important feature of enhancing intercultural experiences. These intercultural experiences should rather be encouraged and underlined. Intercultural experiences can enhance understanding, peace, mutual respect and trust among different cultures, which are essential in a globalized world (e.g. UNESCO, 2014–2017).

It is significant to say that money could buy good teaching and experiences in intercultural recognition and acknowledgement, but whether people would learn from these is another matter. Thus, though money is essential to emphasize activities that will encourage intercultural learning, this economic aspect should not be the main goal. Attention should be given to enhancing intercultural dimensions. However, not only should intercultural knowledge be emphasized, but also appreciation of differences should be recognized and valued, rather than demeaned and shrouded in an economic cloak (Harris, 2008, 2011).

Identifying Institutional Strengths: Indigenous Knowledge Systems

In addition to intercultural exchange, an important aspect of internationalization, I would argue, is for institutions to identify their strengths and create a niche to penetrate the international arena; an important strength of the universities is indigenous knowledge systems (IKS). I argue that if ever there was a time for African IKS to be promoted, then it is now. In addition to the emerging interest in intercultural exchange as explained above, there is presently a heightened interest in the generation and application of knowledge (Sawyerr, 2004). These knowledge systems involve indigenous epistemology, including African thoughts, concepts, literature, beliefs and perceptions. They also involve the experiences of Africans and their natural and human-built environments (see, for example, Dei, 2002).

The IKS differ from universal science in various ways. They are rooted in concepts and theories generated from African sociohistorical experiences and sociocultural practices, unlike universal science, which is mainly ingrained in the philosophy of ancient Greece, the Renaissance and Western traditional systems (Le Grange, 2008). The different knowledge systems also involve different methodology and have different strategies for transmitting knowledge. For instance, while Western science adopts a mainly positivist and materialist approach, traditional knowledge is mainly spiritual.

However, these knowledge systems are not mutually exclusive. IKS complements Western science. In effect, indigenous knowledges do not 'sit in pristine fashion' outside the effects of other knowledges (Dei, 2002). For example, in teaching history, there is a need to explore the history of Africa, how Africans have contributed to world history and how African history is related to world history (Le Grange, 2008).

Again, in addition to what is perceived, for instance, as global medicine, psychiatry or botany, there could be ethno-medicine, ethno-psychiatry and ethno-botany (Le Grange, 2008). These ethnographic programmes move beyond conventional scientific inquiry and involve utilizing qualitative research methods including interviews with community experts and observation of indigenous practices (Smith, 2005, p. 94).

Sustainability studies could also explore indigenous belief systems, and how these beliefs could help address many environmental challenges. Apusiga (2011) has emphasized how belief systems, including myths and taboos in Ghana, helped to sustain the environment from unwarranted exploitation. In former times, under the guise of offending deities, people were prevented from entering preserved forests, from fishing on certain days and killing certain animals. These prevented the depletion of the forests and the extinction of species of animals and fish. Under Christianity, modernity and Western education, the environment is being depleted with careless abandon. Universities could incorporate some of these beliefs and practices into the curriculum.

It should be explained that emphasizing African knowledge systems is not to reduce the continent to a homogeneous entity (Horsthemke, 2004). However, some beliefs, practices and philosophies are common among the people of sub-Saharan Africa, and more dominant in sub-Saharan Africa than in Anglo-American and continental philosophies (Metz, 2007). Again, with the historical experiences and effects of colonization, many African countries tend to share similar social, economic, political and cultural contexts.

An emphasis on African IKS would also help to attract increased interest from foreign students and institutions by offering unique perspectives not available elsewhere. As already indicated, with the emerging interest in intercultural learning, there is renewed interest in African studies and IKS. One vice-chancellor reminisced how the university, at its inception and when it was emphasizing African studies, was able to attract a lot of students from all over the world (Gyamera, 2015). This is not to say that universities in Ghana should not learn from other universities worldwide. However, in creating their own niche, there could be reciprocity where other universities will benchmark against Ghanaian universities. Creating this kind of niche would also ensure that universities do not become overly dependent on Western policies.

Embracing IKS will also enhance the internationalization experiences of local students. As Seepe maintains, 'starting with IKS would encourage learners to draw on their cultural practices and daily experiences as they negotiate and grapple with new situations and unfamiliar terrain' (2004, p. 139).

In relation to promoting IKS, I would argue for an emphasis on Africanization. I would define the Africanization of higher education as a process of education and research that is grounded in African culture, knowledge systems and practices. There is a saying that it is only when you know where you are from that you will know where you are going. In the context of the present emphasis on international relations and globalization, there is a need for the concept of Africanization to be explored and further developed to provide socioeconomic and ethical directions, not only in Africa but in Western societies as well. It is also important for the concept to be emphasized to mitigate some of the psychological and economic effects of colonization, and to enhance the confidence of Africans as Africans. According to Louw (2009), Africanization is important for the whole African community; not only does it give each individual a sense of belonging on this continent, but it also unifies a very diverse community with diverse cultures and values. The national, local and global, I argue, are mutually dependent, like a three-legged table. One cannot stand without the other and each enhances and develops the other.

Use of the Community–University Approach

Some universities practise university–community engagement where students spend between two and eight weeks in rural communities staying with community members and families. The programmes offer students the opportunity to blend the academic world with that of the community to provide constructive interaction between the two for the total development of the communities. This programme could be very helpful in the internationalization process of universities. It plays an important role in developing an individual who understands and can engage in his/her local community and in understanding the global context. Such programmes have already attracted students from other African countries to participate in the programme and could be exported to other countries, especially in the African region, in the form of technical assistance (i.e. giving expert advice).

Research into Internationalization

De Wit, as indicated by MacGregor (2012), has called for internationalization of higher education to be taken out of international offices and 'brought back to where it belongs – in academia'. He argues that since 'research is not part of administration, internationalisation is not part of administration'. Concurring with de Wit, I argue that not perceiving internationalization as part of the administration will enhance research into internationalization. In arguing further, I will say, it is important for institutions to promote research into how internationalization will, on the one hand, avoid the hegemony of Western ideologies and, on the other, promote IKS.

Conclusion

In spite of the strategies adopted by universities over the years to position themselves internationally, universities in Ghana continue to be at the periphery of the international arena. It has been argued in this chapter that the global influences of capitalism pervade many university strategies. The strategies are also influenced by legacies of colonialism, including the perception of Western superiority. I have argued that universities need to adopt strategies that are proactive and promote alternative notions of internationalization. These include emphasizing intercultural exchange and the recognition and appreciation of difference. There is also the need to accentuate the concepts of IKS and Africanization. It was argued for university–community engagements to be emphasized. Most importantly, universities need to identify their strengths in order to penetrate the international arena. It has also been argued that there is a need for research into internationalization within an African context, and how IKS could be enhanced. In this way, notions of the supremacy of Western ideologies can be broken down.

What Ashby (1967) said 50 years ago is still relevant. He indicated that Africa would continue to be at the periphery of the global terrain until its universities became sources of world knowledge, and not simply recipients. If universities in Ghana, instead of benchmarking universities in the North, are able to create their own niche, then universities in the North may also be prepared to benchmark Ghanaian universities in those niche areas.

Chapter 19

Voices and Perspectives on Internationalization from the Emerging and Developing World
Where Are We Heading?

Hans de Wit, Jocelyne Gacel-Ávila & Elspeth Jones

Attention to the international dimension of higher education is increasingly visible as national and institutional agendas rise to the challenge of globalization and seize its opportunities. Yet, in the current global knowledge society, the concept of internationalization of higher education has itself become globalized, demanding further consideration of its impact on policy and practice as more countries and types of institution around the world engage in the process.

Internationalization should no longer be considered in terms of a Westernized, largely Anglo-Saxon and predominantly English-speaking paradigm. Notions of importing and exporting countries are being turned upside down as students choose study destinations in countries that were once seen as merely sending students to the "West" to study. Global mobility flows are increasingly complex, offering new opportunities for those able and willing to access them. At the same time, other countries are emerging as key players and beginning to challenge the dominance of Western discourse on internationalization. Alongside rising student demand for study overseas, the globalization of working practices and environments are reflected in increasing expectations of employers for cross-culturally capable graduates, ideally with international experience, to meet these demands (Jones & de Wit, 2014).

The chapters in this book address voices and perspectives on internationalization of higher education, in particular from regions, countries and institutions that normally do not have a strong presence in the discourse on this important theme. As stated in our Introduction, our intention was to give voice to some of those perspectives as an increasing range of countries engage in the process of internationalization, as an alternative to the dominant paradigms in the conception of internationalization that have traditionally come from the English-speaking world and Western Europe. The book does not attempt to provide a framework for a globalized internationalization of higher education; that would be premature. We are seeking to explore what internationalization means in countries and regions whose perspectives have received little attention to date.

While some argue that "in higher education and knowledge we can detect a continuing long-term trend to global convergence and integration" (Marginson,

2013, p. 49), we must remember that "the notion of 'internationalization' is not only a question of the relations between nations but even more to the relations between cultures and between the global and the local" (de Wit, 2012). Indeed, "under the impact of accelerating globalization ... a new paradigm of international education might emerge that is both more threatening and more helpful" (Scott, 2013, p. 55). Just as the emphasis on global perspectives for students should be a key theme, so the globalization of internationalization itself requires us to consider the responsibilities of Western universities if we are not to see internationalization as exploitative or as a "slave trade in education" (Jegede, 2012). In addition to the benefits, there is increasing awareness of the risks internationalization may bring (Egron-Polak, 2012). And one of the main risks is that internationalization is perceived as strengthening the dominance of the existing powers in international higher education: regions, nations and institutions. Will new regional alliances such as BRICS (Brazil, Russia, India, China, South Africa) become an alternative for the European Union and the United States, and will the creation of new post-Cold War political and economic influence blocs provide a new focus to higher education institutions and national higher education systems? Will institutions from Asia, Latin America and Africa be able to compete as world-class universities in ranking and branding? Will successful forms of South–South cooperation emerge as an alternative to current unequal North–South partnerships? Important questions, and although the chapters in this book do not provide final answers to them, they provide an interesting but complex picture of both imitation and innovation.

As countries in parts of the developing world open up to internationalization and enter into partnerships with institutions in the so-called developed world, their reflections on discourse, practice and outcomes of internationalization offer significant learning opportunities for those with longer histories in the field. At the same time, it is interesting to see that, although they may have quite different starting points, in the end they all are faced with the need to focus on the teaching and learning process and learning outcomes in order to support their aims (Jones & de Wit, 2014).

This concluding chapter sets out to see whether we have been able to answer the questions we posed in the Introduction, based on the previous chapters that are the core of this book. We have to admit that it was not an easy task, and the challenges were greater than the opportunities we encountered. Internationalization in higher education certainly has become a broader global concept than its dominant perception in the developed, in particular English-speaking, world. The number of articles, books and reports on internationalization of higher education, and the active role of national governments, higher education organizations and institutions as well as international educator associations in emerging and developing countries, illustrate this increasing importance, also reflected in the Global Surveys on Internationalization by the International Association of Universities (IAU). Two recent studies on national policies and strategies for internationalization for the European Parliament (de Wit et al., 2015) and for the

British Council (Ilieva & Peak, 2016) provide interesting findings and analyses of such policies in the developed and the developing world.

But at the same time we see a trend towards homogenization of activities, approaches, policies and strategies, similar to those in the traditional industrialized world. This is, to a great extent, driven by economic rationales and increased competitiveness, and dominance of the Western university model, as well as the role of rankings and the indicators they use to measure internationalization: number of international students, number of international scholars, number of mobile students and staff and number of internationally co-authored publications. These indicators tend to drive governments and institutional leaders in higher education to focus on increasing these quantitative targets, and related policies to realize them, such as teaching in English, tuition-fee policies, exclusive focus on research and marketing strategies, etc. Little space is left for new and innovative ideas for internationalization, embedded in the local and institutional context.

This pessimistic view would not do justice, though, to the number of contributions in this book that provide a different approach to internationalization and that embed internationalization in its specific regional, national and/or institutional context. Eva Egron-Polak and Francisco Marmolejo state that

> the concept of "emerging voices" in the new higher education landscape should be comprehensive and inclusive in scope. It is not only one single, unified voice, nor does it always come from the same cluster of countries or from the same type of institutions.

That is ambitious and valuable as an objective. For the moment, though, the diversity of new voices that this book collects are only the first steps in the direction of a comprehensive, inclusive and innovative perspective on internationalization in the emerging and developing world. Here we identify some thematic trends in them.

Internationalization in School Education

Fazal Rizvi, in his contribution, points to an approach towards internationalization, important for developing and developed countries:

> while issues internal to higher education are well-researched, seldom examined are the questions of the ways in which the schools sector prepares students for international higher education, as well as the implications for universities of the attempts by schools to internationalize their policies, programs and practices.

Something that sounds so obvious has indeed been rather neglected in the discourse on internationalization. Notwithstanding the fact that internationalization at the level of school education has evolved substantially over the years, it has largely been ignored until recently in the debate on internationalization of higher education. Its considerable impact on the higher education sector has thus been missing from the discourse. Rizvi quotes de Wit (2015a), who has observed that

> higher education has to realise that internationalisation starts not only at the university but before that and they should support and collaborate with the other levels of education, take advantage of this development and build their own strategy on it.

According to Rizvi this underlines the need for universities to develop closer and more direct links with schools and school systems around the world. Internationalization is not the exclusive domain of higher education; one can even say that internationalization in higher education can only reach its full potential if it is aligned with and built on international primary, secondary and other levels of education.

Internationalization and Social Responsibility

Another dimension of higher education internationalization that has been rather ignored concerns the social role and responsibility of higher education. Eva Egron-Polak and Francisco Marmolejo argue that

> *Transforming Our World: The 2030 Agenda for Sustainable Development,* adopted by the United Nations in September 2015, may offer a new framework within which internationalization of higher education could thrive, reconnecting with a broader set of purposes, rationales and institutional partners.

And they conclude that, although there are examples of such social roles,

> these valuable activities are often somewhat marginal in the overwhelming focus of internationalization strategies on attracting more international students, on finding partner institutions that enjoy a strong international reputation, on building partnerships according to self-interest due to pressure to show impact at home, focusing on research that has the greatest potential to raise both individual and institutional status, and others.

The book provides three thematic examples of such roles: (1) how internationalization can contribute to the role of higher education in the refugee crisis facing the Middle East and Europe as well as provide lessons for similar crises elsewhere; (2) how it can contribute to rebuilding post-conflict countries; and (3) how it can enhance social inclusion.

Immigration Patterns and Refugees

Bernhard Streitwieser, Cynthia Miller-Idriss and Hans de Wit in their chapter argue that

> universities' reception of refugees ought to be understood within broader higher education internationalization frameworks and global engagements, because receiving countries' efforts to help refugees maintain and acquire high-level skills during periods of crisis and displacement will have a significant and ongoing impact on the recovery and reconstruction efforts of sending regions once the conflict ends. While developing countries are usually the primary senders and receivers of refugees, the crisis that began in Europe in 2015 has changed that pattern once again.

And they state that this will not only solve the immediate problems of the individuals concerned but also will help to ensure that these individuals will have the skills and knowledge needed for reconstruction when political stability has returned. They believe that the Syrian refugee crisis has helped to showcase on a grand scale, arguably unprecedented in modern times, how university internationalization can be connected to broader issues of global stability in the short and long term.

International Dimensions of Higher Education in Post-Conflict Settings

Savo Heleta, in his contribution on the role of higher education and its international dimensions in post-conflict settings, argues that,

> despite the enormous challenges facing post-conflict countries, rebuilding and gradual internationalization of higher education need to be considered as priorities by local and international actors. Students in these countries deserve quality and relevant education that prepares them for global engagement and functioning.

And he continues by stating that universities from the developed and emerging world need to play a crucial role in this through collaboration and provision of assistance. This is in line with other authors dealing with the issue of higher education internationalization and post-conflict settings. See, for instance, "Internationalised Higher Education as a Conflict Zone" (Moosavi, 2016), in which Leo Moosavi states that "it is the responsibility of university academics to ensure that we are sufficiently reflecting upon our educational interventions in the era of internationalization" (p. 37).

Internationalization and Social Inclusion

For the Latin American and Caribbean region, there are some interesting examples of how internationalization can be used as a means to enhance social inclusion of traditionally disadvantaged populations, such as women living in rural areas struggling to set up their own business as a means of subsistence. The chapter written by Carlos Ramirez, Cesar Cáceres and Carolina Pinto, on internationalization strategies and social inclusion, showcases the experience of a group of women entrepreneurs who were able to consolidate their marketing strategies and make innovations in their products thanks to the internationalization programme of the Viña del Mar University, Chile. This institution created training opportunities and transfer of experiences from a group of entrepreneurs in Arequipa, Peru, in order to foster production and export to the European market. The international interaction of the women entrepreneurs generated change at the individual level through a better definition of their societal role. On a collective level, the internationalization programme enabled this group of women to access a higher "level" or status by collaborating with international networks. In their own words, this international experience now differentiates them from their local peers in the Valparaiso region, and has provided them with ideas on areas for improvement. The study provides concrete examples of how universities can use their international networks to further development at the local level. It also shows the importance of taking forward the design of national policies on the internationalization of universities, incorporating the social inclusion aspect that can be applied to local communities and disadvantaged groups.

Social responsibility and global citizenship development are increasingly more present in the discourse on internationalization of higher education and, in particular for developing countries, this is a theme that affects them directly. Higher education in the developing world acknowledges the social mission of universities more than universities in the developed world, where the notion of "society" has become more market-focused, and terms such as workforce development and employability dominate the agenda of higher education and its internationalization. The three chapters in the section of the book on politics, conflict and social issues illustrate alternative socially responsible internationalization models.

Besides the thematic points presented above, the book chapters also provide a rich overview of how regions, countries and institutions in the developing and emerging world try to define their own approach to internationalization.

Regional Trends in Internationalization

Regional trends in internationalization take a diversity of forms, of which student mobility is still the main activity focused on, with emerging and developing regions more on the sending than the receiving side of mobility. As far as student mobility is concerned, the chapter written by Jocelyne Gacel-Ávila, Magdalena Bustos-Aguirre and Jose Celso Freire Jr describes some recent trends in Latin America and the Caribbean and analyses some of the region's most innovative programmes in terms of short-term and degree-seeking mobility. The study highlights that degree-seeking mobility has been continuously expanded in the region during the last 40 years through large national public policies on training highly skilled human resources for national development. However, it notes that short-term mobility is a more innovative and recent strategy, which has been gaining importance in the past ten years. The chapter's main conclusion is that, on the positive side, these programmes have expanded international opportunities to students, but the region still needs great improvement in terms of effective planning and implementation capacity. Indeed, the regional, economic and political instability of recent years have begun to undermine the efforts and the progress made. Insufficient financing, lack of long-term planning and continuity are emerging once again as a constant characteristic of the region.

However, mobility is only one dimension of internationalization. The study on the Middle East and North Africa (MENA) written by Kamal Abouchedid and Maria Bou Zeid definitely provides valuable lessons for policy-makers and researchers in the region. The study's main findings are, among others, that (1) internationalization requires important physical and financial resources that many institutions in the region lack. In public universities this is due to inadequate government funding, and in private institutions it results from their financial dependence on students' tuition fees. (2) They argue that internationalization requires a commitment from higher education leaders that should be reflected in policies, mission statements and strategic plans, but in reality only a few universities surveyed mentioned internationalization in their mission statements. (3) Cooperation exists only as piecemeal initiatives taken by some higher education institutions on an individual basis. (4) The region lacks a regional qualification framework that will facilitate transferability of credits and mobility of students across the diverse higher education institutions of the region. Student mobility is also challenged by security problems and political instability in the wider MENA region, and the outbound flow of students is curbed by visa problems to Europe and the United States, due to fear of terrorism and illegal immigration in the Western world. They also argue that privatization policies that allow the establishment of foreign institutions are mainly motivated by political and commercial considerations. This is at the expense of quality in terms of curricula, faculty qualifications and deficient research facilities, which greatly limit the involvement of higher education institutions in the regional internationalization process.

Manja Klemenčič, in her chapter on internationalization of universities in the peripheries, argues that "for universities in peripheral locations, the imperatives for internationalization are magnified by the limited 'organic' intake of talent and the high salience of international networks and graduates with international competences to aid economic development and growth". For institutions in peripheral locations, a deliberate internationalization strategy is indeed a necessary ingredient of their own modernization and institutional capacity building. She observes that, for such institutions, regional cooperation is a particularly desirable option, since it potentially helps strengthen the regional relevance of partner institutions and their collective international status and visibility:

> Regional cooperation refers specifically to cooperation built among universities in neighbouring countries and/or within the same region within a country. Universities in peripheral countries may not be the most desired international partners of institutions in the educational hot spots, but they are often preferred partners to other institutions in the peripheral neighbouring countries.

The reality, though, is that, according to her, for peripheral universities, the internationalization of higher education is often associated with modernization, or catching up with the more internationalized peers in more developed higher education hubs and this sense of catching up is precisely the one that can prompt universities into uncritical imitation.

For the Caribbean, David Rampersad depicts the unique case of the University of the West Indies that illustrates the approach of using internationalization as an engine of national and regional development. Among others, it highlights the use of information and communication technology to facilitate entry to new markets and engender demand for programmes in which the university enjoys a strong reputation and has market appeal. Furthermore, the strategy of expanding research links with traditional partners that are leaders in their field and of aggressively pursuing relationships with counterparts in regions offering new opportunities for growth and development are spelt out, especially where it can leverage historical and cultural links.

In his chapter on collaboration in Latin America and the Caribbean, Carlos Alberto Vigil Taquechel highlights the importance of regional integration as a critical driver of internationalization. The chapter suggests that internationalization strategies of national systems should focus more on the reinforcement of potential at regional level rather than on higher education institutions individually. The necessity of finding new and innovative solutions is stressed in order to engender better participation of the region in internationalization of the higher education sector. To this end, the author describes a model of specialized units designed to provide valuable services to various institutions in order to support internationalization in a collaborative and comprehensive approach.

From these five chapters a picture emerges of a dynamic and broad regional approach to internationalization, in which student mobility is certainly an important activity but other dimensions, in particular regional and sub-regional integration and cooperation, are even more important, and should have more prominence in the analysis of internationalization in higher education.

National Cases of Internationalization

As Christopher Ziguras and Anh Pham observe, for Vietnam, "internationalization of higher education since the 1990s has been primarily a means of integrating the country more deeply into the global economy and enhancing national competitiveness through the transfer of knowledge and skills from abroad". That does not go without challenges and obstacles as they make clear: "the ongoing imbalance in international relationships is a cause for concern." They quote Tuyét (2014), who states that "the tendency of continuing buying, importing, receiving, accepting and following Western Policies and practice ties Vietnam HE to the values and norms which may not be appropriate for the local context and culture" (p. 67). The continuing challenge for Vietnam, they argue, is to develop modes of collaboration that allow for forms of internationalization responsive to local needs and values, and which promote forms of reciprocity and exchange.

In that challenge there is quite some similarity with the case of China, as analysed by Rui Yang. He argues that, for China, internationalization has long been a survival tool since its encounters with the West in the 19th century. But for historical and cultural reasons, China's experience of higher education internationalization contrasts sharply with those of Western societies. According to him,

> For nearly two centuries, external values and knowledge have been imposed on Chinese people and society. Therefore, ever since the 19th century, rather than introducing such values and knowledge, China's priority has been to digest and integrate them with indigenous Chinese traditions. For the Chinese, internationalization has rarely been peaceful and pleasant; in fact the process has been shot through with intense ideological and cultural conflicts. Theoretical frameworks developed in the West thus do not apply well in the Chinese context.

He concludes that the central purpose of China's internationalization of higher education is to combine Chinese and Western elements.

Olga Ustyuzhantseva, in her contribution on internationalization in a non-market environment, argues that traditionally Russia has been a country with a dominating state governing all areas of life. For the Russian higher education system, the state has always been a founder, sponsor and consumer. The attempt to change this model that occurred in the early 1990s, after the collapse of the USSR, failed. The freedom of universities in the development and conduct of international activity that was established in 1992 was progressively narrowed down to local decision-making, without an opportunity to choose a strategic path. The role of universities shifted back to being facilitators of public policy and state interests. She concludes that

> The market imperatives that drove internationalization in Russia in the first period after the end of the USSR were replaced by administrative pressure on universities to attain prescribed achievements in the international sphere, while paying less attention to quality development of the educational programs and local teaching staff. This is the result of considering internationalization as a national goal but not the process of quality improvement through integration in the international educational space.

Vietnam, China and Russia cannot be considered as peripheral countries; they are important economic and political players, in particular the last two, which are also part of the emerging economic group of BRICS countries. These countries are investing in higher education and world-class universities and want to move up in the rankings, and national interests prevail above institutional autonomy and initiative.

The chapter on the paradigm shift by Malaysian higher education, by Jasvir Kaur Nachatar Singh, is an interesting case of how an emerging country is adopting as one of its main internationalization strategies the attraction of international students in order to transform Malaysia into an international hub of higher education excellence. In this respect, the Ministry of Higher Education has designed a strategic plan to achieve hub of excellence status through a paradigm shift, namely the soft power concept. The gist of this concept is to empower and develop human capital (i.e. international students) for the benefit of global development in their home countries through the internationalization agenda, knowledge transfer initiatives, field trips and student and lecturer participation in community activities.

These cases demonstrate that national policies for internationalization in emerging and developing countries are driven by the same political and economic rationales as in the developed world. However, they encounter, at the same time, stronger obstacles and challenges in that process, and the danger of uncritical imitation instead of developing their own strategies and approaches is high. We now consider chapters that look at the institutional level.

Institutional Initiatives for Internationalization

Cornelius Hagenmeier, in his contribution, uses the University of Venda in South Africa (Univen) as an example to demonstrate how an innovatively structured internationalization process can contribute to transforming a tertiary institution previously labelled as "historically disadvantaged" into a locally relevant, but globally competitive, university. Special attention is devoted to demonstrating that internationalization in a postcolonial context must affirm awareness of identity, culture and language. According to him, "the conceptual link between Africanization and internationalization entrenched in this institution's internationalization policy contributes to a model of internationalization which affirms, rather than jeopardizes, its unique identity as an African university embedded in indigenous communities". Critical for success, he argues, is the strengthening of the university's role as a catalyst connecting indigenous knowledge, language and culture embedded in local communities to the wider world, for the mutual benefit of local communities, international stakeholders and the university.

Two other cases, Kazakhstan and Cambodia, provide interesting views on how institutions in developing countries address the need to internationalize their curricula. Dash states in his chapter on the Cambodian context that curriculum internationalization is very new and may simply be referred to as study abroad programs, foreign language courses, provision of programmes or courses with an international and intercultural focus and incorporation of international, intercultural and/or global dimensions into the content of the curriculum. The author concludes from a study among stakeholders in his university that students, academic staff and academic leaders all perceive the need for curriculum internationalization and have views on the different dimensions, and their relative importance, of how this can be achieved. From the perception of students, the areas that require improvement are flexibilities in the curriculum to meet global needs; provision of continuous review, improvement and self-evaluation of curriculum; and inclusion of innovative international content in the curriculum. Similarly, from the point of teachers and academic leaders, a range of areas require improvement: namely, provision of continuous review, improvement and self-evaluation of curriculum; study abroad/exchange programmes in overseas institutions as a fully credited option in the programme; and inclusion of innovative international content in the curriculum. He argues that the university should put more effort into the selected "desired" areas to meet the requirements of stakeholders for curriculum internationalization.

Lynne Parmenter, Jason Sparks, Aisi Li, Sulushash Kerimkulova, Adil Ashirbekov and Zakir Jumakulov, in their chapter on curriculum internationalization in Kazakhstan, explore ways in which higher education institutions in Kazakhstan are responding to the imperative to internationalize their curricula. On definitions and interpretations of internationalization in general and of curriculum (IoC) in particular, findings from the case studies aligned closely in many respects with international literature, especially in terms of internationalization and IoC as a dynamic response to processes of globalization. On the other hand, for a number of respondents, internationalization and IoC were seen as a natural continuation of Soviet times and principles.

On rationales for IoC, the responses given by participants raised several interesting issues. The most frequently cited rationale in this study, "integration into the global education sphere", does not feature prominently in the literature, although elements of it are apparent in the rationale of developing global citizens and, to a lesser extent, attracting and accommodating international students. This rationale, and the way it is framed, are based on an assumption, which was not explicitly stated by participants, that Kazakhstan until now has somehow been "outside" the global education sphere, in spite of over 20 years of large-scale study abroad scholarship programmes and high levels of global awareness and knowledge among academics. As the authors state, it would be interesting to explore internationally how far and in what ways this "insider–outsider" concept of internationalization of higher education is evident in other countries and regions.

The other rationale given for IoC, that it is just a natural extension of multicultural Kazakhstan, is connected to the above idea of internationalization as a natural continuation of previous times. But this is also an alternative perspective on IoC, particularly in terms of internationalization at home being seen as something that has been happening for the past 80 years or more.

Finally, while challenges for IoC in the literature are mainly focused at institutional level (achieving inclusive, connected, coherent, deep, well-resourced IoC, with motivated faculty on board), the discussion in Kazakhstan is focused more on national and conceptual levels (negotiating change and mediating reform, while trying to access and achieve quality in IoC). The study provides insights into the challenges of IoC in a rapidly reforming higher education sector at many different levels, offering alternative perspectives on issues such as commitment and resistance to change, faculty motivation and power issues in the form of languages and people.

Oforiwaa Gifty Gyamera in her chapter on internationalization in Ghana's public universities describes the challenges these universities encounter in developing a rationale based less on economic considerations and more on taking a proactive and innovative approach to internationalization. Various strategies have been adopted and adapted by universities in Ghana to re/position themselves in the international arena. It is argued that these strategies appear to be embedded in postcolonialism, with economic rationales based mainly on neoliberal economic thinking, which sees higher education as a quasi marketplace where knowledge is bought and sold. The chapter argues that universities need to adopt strategies that are proactive and that promote alternative notions of internationalization in ways that challenge the status quo.

The institutional cases provide an interesting overview of how universities in emerging and developing countries are dealing with internationalization. That such a process is not an easy process is clear, but it is interesting to see what internationalization strategy development and internationalization of the curriculum mean in their contexts.

Lessons to Learn

The regional, national and institutional cases from the emerging and developing world illustrate that higher education, in its international dimensions and efforts to become more internationalized, struggles between past colonial influences and current presence and related challenges, its social role and the increasingly competitive environment universities have to operate in. In this complex context, regions, countries and institutions have to make choices that find the right balance between their local, national, regional and global roles. As mentioned before, the inclination is to go for similar pathways as used by higher education in the developed world, but that way is no guarantee for success. Universities have to respond to the questions we posed at the beginning of this concluding chapter, not simply on the basis of how successful they can be in their competition with the developed world, but on how they can operate successfully in their local and regional contexts and make a meaningful and responsible contribution to the society they are part of. Internationalization strategies can go both ways, either in a competitive direction or towards a more socially responsible approach.

The first way is difficult, requires substantive public and private investment and can increase the social divide. As de Wit et al. (2015) and Ilieva and Peak (2016) observe, both in the developed and the developing world, the main point of policy and action in internationalization still focuses on mobility, in particular student mobility, and quality assurance of that process is weak. De Wit et al. (2015) also point to the fact that this focus on mobility is not inclusive but rather elitist, only reaching a small minority of students and academics.

The second way, towards a more socially responsible approach, is also not easy and also requires substantial public and private resources, but it is more socially inclusive and in the long run will result in a higher-quality sector. It implies a stronger attention to Internationalization at Home and of the Curriculum. It should align with other levels of education, and address more the international dimensions of social responsibility. The chapters in this book provide some interesting examples of both the opportunities and the obstacles that such an approach faces.

In their article, "Globalization of Internationalization: Thematic and Regional Reflections on a Traditional Concept", Jones and de Wit (2012) highlight eight priorities as internationalization itself becomes globalized. The first of these is "The need to learn from other non-western national and cultural contexts – to understand the full extent of internationalization as a phenomenon and what we can learn from each other in order to benefit students, employers and nations". It is hoped that the chapters in this book go some way to supporting this priority and that readers in more developed, Anglo-Western countries, as well as in developing and emerging environments, may find food for thought in these alternative views of internationalization in diverse higher education contexts. Fanta Aw correctly remarks in her Foreword to this book that "the work of internationalization is complex, multifaceted and fraught with power relations. The need to examine carefully the role of culture, access, knowledge and relevance in internationalization practices, policies and initiatives cannot be understated". This book is an attempt to further such examination, and through this volume we hope to stimulate further reflection, understanding and actions towards innovative and socially inclusive internationalization policies.

References

Abiddin, N. Z. & Ismail, A. (2009). Identification of resource needs in postgraduate studies. *Research Journal of Social Sciences*, 4, 33–44.

Abouchedid, K. & Abdelnour, G. (2015). Faculty research productivity in six Arab countries. *International Review of Education*, 61(5), 673–690.

Academic Networking, a Gate for Learning Experiences. (n.d.). Retrieved August 2015 from http://angle.up.pt.

Adam, S. (2001). *Transnational education project:* Report *and recommendations.* Brussels: Confederation of European Union Rectors' Conference.

ADB. (2008). *Socialist Republic of Viet Nam: Preparing the Higher Education Sector Development Project (financed by the Japan Special Fund).* Mandaluyong City, Philippines: Asian Development Bank.

ADB. (2010). *Vietnam: Preparing the Higher Education Sector Development Project (HESDP).* Mandaluyong City, Philippines: Asian Development Bank.

AEI. (2012). *Overview of the legal framework affecting the provision of foreign education in Vietnam.* Canberra: Australian Education International.

Agarwal, P., Said, M. E., Sehoole, M., Sirozi, M. & de Wit, H. (eds). (2008). *The dynamics of international student circulation in a global context.* Rotterdam: SensePublishers.

Ali, T. & Matthews, R. (2004a). Introduction. In T. Ali & R. Matthews (eds), *Durable peace: Challenges for peacebuilding in Africa* (pp. 3–15). Toronto: University of Toronto Press.

Ali, T. & Matthews, R. (2004b). Conclusion: The long and difficult road to peace. In T. Ali & R. Matthews (eds), *Durable peace: Challenges for peacebuilding in Africa* (pp. 393–425). Toronto: University of Toronto Press.

Altbach, P. (1998). *Comparative higher education: Knowledge, the university and development.* Hong Kong: Comparative Education Research Centre, University of Hong Kong.

Altbach, P. (2001). The American academic model in comparative perspective. In P. Altbach, P. Gumport & B. Johnstone (eds), *In defense of American higher education* (pp. 11–37). Baltimore, MD: Johns Hopkins University Press.

Altbach, P. (2004). Higher education crosses borders: Can the United States remain the top destination for foreign students? *Change: The Magazine of Higher Learning*, 36, 18–25.

Altbach, P. (2016). *Global perspectives on higher education.* Baltimore, MD: Johns Hopkins University Press.

Altbach, P. & de Wit, H. (2015). Internationalization and global tension: Lessons from history. *Journal of Studies in International Education*, 19(1), 4–10.

Altbach, P. & Knight, J. (2007). The internationalization of higher education: Motivations and realities. *Journal of Studies in International Education*, 11(3/4), 290–305.

Altbach, P. & Salmi, J. (eds). (2011). *The road to academic excellence: The making of world-class research universities.* Washington, DC: World Bank.

Altbach, P. G., Kelly, D. H. & Luyat, Y. G.-M. (1993). *Research on foreign students and international study.* New York: Prager.

Altbach, P. G. & Postiglione, G. (2006). Can Hong Kong keep its lead in the Britain race? *International Higher Education*, 45(Fall), 24–26.

Altbach, P., Reisberg, L. & Rumbley, L. E. (2009). *Trends in global higher education: Tracking an academic revolution.* Report prepared for the UNESCO 2009 World Conference on Higher Education. Retrieved 2 February 2014 from http://uis.unesco.org/Library/Documents/trends-global-higher-education-2009-world-conference-en.pdf.

Altbach, P., Reisberg, L. & Rumbley, L. E. (2010). *Trends in global higher education: Tracking an academic revolution.* Rotterdam: Sense.

Anderson, R. (2009). The idea of a university. In K. Withers (ed.), *First class? Challenges and opportunities for the UK's university sector* (pp. 37–45). London: Institute for Public Policy Research.

Andrade, M. S. (2006). International students in English-speaking universities: Adjustment factors. *Journal of Research in International Education*, 5(2), 131–154.

Annan, K. (1998). *The causes of conflict and the promotion of durable peace and sustainable development in Africa.* Report of the UN Secretary General. New York: United Nations.

Annan, K. (2015, 20 March). Higher education and Africa's social and political progress. *University World News*, 359. Retrieved 24 March 2015 from www.universityworldnews.com/article.php?story=2015032110423540.

Apusiga, A. A. (2011). Indigenous knowledge, cultural values and sustainable development in Africa. Paper presented at 2nd Annual Ibadan Sustainable Development Summit, Nigeria.

Arephiev, A. (2014). O pokazatelyakh meropriyatiy 'dorozhnykh kart' vuzov proyekta 5–100 i metodike ikh podscheta: sravnitel'nyy analiz [On the performance of 'road maps' of the university under the Project 5–100 and their counting methodology: A comparative analysis]. In F. Sheregi & A. Arephiev (eds), *Metodicheskiye voprosy otsenki realizatsii proyekta 5–100 po reytingam universitetov [Methodological issues for evaluating Project 5–100 on the ratings of universities]* (pp. 90–126). Moscow: Ministry of Education and Science, Center for Sociological Research.

Asante, E. A. (2012). The case of Ghana's President's Special Initiative on oil palm (PSI-oil palm) (DISS Working Paper). Retrieved 5 August 2013 from http://subweb.diis.dk/graphics/Publications/WP2012/WP2012-11-Asante-Ghanas-presidents-special-initiative_web.pdf.

Ashby, E. (1967). *Universities: British, Indian, African.* London: Weidenfeld & Nicolson.

Asociación de Universidades Grupo Montevideo. (2016). *Asociación de Universidades Grupo Montevideo.* Retrieved from http://grupomontevideo.org/sitio.

Ayoubi, R. & Massoud, H. (2007). The strategy of internationalization in universities. *International Journal of Educational Management*, 21, 339–349.

Aziz, M. I. A. & Abdullah, D. (2014). Malaysia: Becoming an education hub to serve national development. In J. Knight (ed.), *International education hubs: Student, talent, knowledge-innovation models* (pp. 101–120). Dordrecht: Springer.

Baba, A. (2004). Future directions of the Ministry of Higher Education. *Bulletin of Higher Education Research*, 4, 1–3.

Baidenko, V. (2002). *Bolonskiy protsess: Strukturnaya reforma vysshego obrazovaniya Evropy [Bologna Process: The structural reform of higher education in Europe]*. Moscow: Issledovatel'skiy tsentr problem kachestva podgotovki spetsialistov, Rossiyskiy Novyy Universitet.

Baidenko, V. (2009). *The Bologna Process: European and national qualifications frameworks (Annex 2). [Bolonsky Protses: yevropeyskiye i natsional'nyye struktury kvalifikatsiy]*. Moscow: Research Center of Problems of Quality of Training, p. 220.

Barakat, S. & Milton, S. (2015a). Houses of wisdom matter: The responsibility to protect and rebuild higher education in the Arab world. Policy Briefing, Foreign Policy at Brookings. Washington, DC: Brookings Institution. Retrieved April 2016 from www.brookings.edu/~/media/Research/Files/Papers/2015/07/08-higher-education-barakat-milton/En-Higher-Ed-Web.pdf?la=en.

Barakat, S. & Milton, S. (2015b, 10 July). Higher education vital to post-conflict rebuilding. *University World News*, 375. Retrieved 11 July 2015 from www.universityworldnews.com/article.php?story=20150710072233289.

Barakat, S. & Zyck, S. (2009). The evolution of post-conflict recovery. *Third World Quarterly*, 30(6), 1069–1086.

Barker, M. C., Hibbins, R. T. & Farrelly, F. (2011). Walking the talk: Fostering a sense of global citizenry amongst staff in higher education. In V. Clifford & C. Montgomery (eds), *Moving towards internationalisation of the curriculum for global citizenship in higher education* (pp. 47–68). Oxford: Oxford Brookes Press.

Bayona, C. & González, R. (2010). *La transferencia de conocimiento en la Universidad Pública de Navarra: Una visión desde la empresa y desde el ámbito universitario*. Pamplona: Universidad Pública de Navarra.

Beanland, D. (2011). *The Birth of RMIT International University Vietnam*. Paper presented at RMIT Vietnam's 10th Anniversary Celebration, Ho Chi Minh City.

Beelen, J. (2014). The other side of mobility: The impact of incoming students on home students. In B. Streitwieser (ed.), *Internationalization of higher education and global mobility* (pp. 287–299). Oxford: Symposium Books.

Beelen, J. & Jones, E. (2015a). Redefining internationalization at home. In A. Curaj, L. Matei, R. Pricopie, J. Salmi & P. Scott (eds), *The European Higher Education Area: Between critical reflections and future policies* (pp. 59–72). Heidelberg: Springer International Publishing.

Beelen, J. & Jones, E. (2015b). Europe calling: A new definition for internationalization at home. *International Higher Education*, 83 (Special Issue), 12–13. Retrieved from http://ejournals.bc.edu/ojs/index.php/ihe/article/view/9080.

Bennett, R. & Kane, S. (2011). Internationalization of U.K. university business schools: A survey. *Journal of Studies in International Education*, 15(4), 351–373.

Bhandari, R. & Blumenthal, P. (2011). Global student mobility and the twenty-first century Silk Road: National trends and new directions. In R. Bhandari & P. Blumenthal (eds), *International students and global mobility in higher education: National trends and new directions* (pp. 1–23). New York: Palgrave Macmillan.

Bhandari, R. & El-Amine, A. (2012). *Classifying higher education institutions in the Middle East and North Africa: A pilot study.* New York: Institute of International Education and Lebanese Association for Educational Studies.

Binns, T., Dixon, A. & Nel, E. (2012). *Africa: Diversity and development.* London: Routledge.

Bologna Process. (2009, 28–29 April). *The Bologna Process 2020: The European Higher Education Area in the new decade.* Communiqué of the Conference of European Ministers Responsible for Higher Education, Leuven and Louvain-la-Neuve. Retrieved from www.ond.vlaanderen.be/hogeronderwijs/bologna/conference/documents/Leuven_Louvain-la-Neuve_Communiqu%C3%A9_April_2009.pdf.

Botha, M. (2010). Compatibility between internationalising and Africanising higher education in South Africa. *Journal of Studies in International Education,* 14, 200–213.

Bourdieu, P. (1979). *Distinction.* London: Routledge.

Bremer, L. & van der Wende, M. C. (1995). *Internationalising the curriculum in higher education: Experiences in the Netherlands.* Amsterdam: Nuffic.

British Council. (2015). *Managing large systems: A comparative analysis – Challenges and opportunities for large higher education systems.* New Delhi: British Council.

Brunner, J. J. & Ferrada, R. (2011). *Educación Superior en Iberoamérica–Informe 2011: Centro Interuniversitario de Desarrollo (CINDA).* Santiago de Chile: CINDA.

Buckland, P. (2006). Post-conflict education: Time for a reality check? In M. Couldrey & T. Morris (eds), *Education and conflict: Research, policy and practice* (pp. 7–8). Oxford: University of Oxford, Refugee Studies Centre, Forced Migration Review.

Buncker, E. (2011). The role of higher education in the Arab state and society: Historical legacies and recent reform patterns. *Comparative & International Higher Education,* 3, 21–26.

CAAM-HP. (n.d.). Retrieved August 2015 from http://caam-hp.org/assessedprogrammes.html.

Callan, H. (1998). Internationalization in Europe. In P. Scott (ed.), *The globalization of higher education* (pp. 44–57). Buckingham: Open University Press/SRHE.

Campbell, J. & Li, M. (2008). Asian students' voices: An empirical study of Asian students' learning experiences at a New Zealand university. *Journal of Studies in International Education,* 12(4), 375–396.

Cannon, H. & Djajanegara, O. (1997). Internationalization of higher education in Indonesia. In J. Knight & H. de Wit (eds), *Internationalization of higher education in Asia Pacific countries* (pp. 65–81). Amsterdam: The EAIE.

CAPES. (2016, 3 January). Retrieved from www.capes.gov.br.

CARPIMS (Caribbean–Pacific Island Mobility Scheme). (n.d.). Retrieved August 2015 from www2.sta.uwi.edu/carpims.

Castells, M. (1999). Information technology, globalization and social development. UNRISD Discussion Paper No. 114, Geneva.

Castro, P. J., Krause, M. & Frisancho, S. (2015). Teoría del Cambio Subjetivo: Aportes desde un Estudio Cualitativo con Profesores. *Revista Colombiana de Psicología,* 24(2), 362–379.

Catalán, J. (2010). Un estudio de TS demostrativo del papel protagónico de los participantes. In J. Catalán (ed.), *Teorías subjetivas: Aspectos teóricos y prácticos.* La Serena: Editorial Universidad de La Serena.

Center for China & Globalization. (2015). *Annual report on the development of Chinese students studying abroad.* Beijing: Social Sciences Academic Press [in Chinese].

Central European University (CEU). (2015, 28 October). *European universities commit to help refugees.* Retrieved April 2016 from www.ceu.edu/article/2015-10-28/european-universities-commit-help-refugees.

Chang, J. (2006). Globalization and English in Chinese higher education. *World Englishes*, 25(3/4), 513–525.

China Education Association for International Exchange (CEAIE). (2015, 13 October). *Report release: Internationalization of higher education in China.* Beijing: China Education Association for International Exchange.

Cleverley, J. & Jones, P. (1976). *Australia and international education: Some critical issues.* Hawthorn: Australian Council for Educational Research.

Clifford, V. (2009). Engaging the disciplines in internationalising the curriculum. *International Journal for Academic Development*, 14(2), 133–143.

Clifford, V. & Montgomery, C. (2011). *Moving towards internationalisation of the curriculum for global citizenship in higher education.* Oxford: Oxford Centre for Staff and Learning Development.

CNPq. (2016, 16 January). *Painel de Investimentos.* Retrieved from http://cnpq.br/painel-de-investimentos.

COLCIENCIAS. (2016, 16 January). Retrieved from www.colciencias.gov.co/ckfinder/userfiles/files/Informe_de_gesti%C3%B3n_Jaime_restrepo_cuartas.pdf.

Collier, P., Hoeffler, A. & Söderbom, M. (2008). Post-conflict risks. *Journal of Peace Research*, 45(4), 461–478.

CONACYT. (2016, 16 January). *Sistema Integrado de Información sobre Investigación Científica, Desarrollo Tecnológico e Innovación (SIICYT).* Retrieved from www.conacyt.mx/siicyt/index.php/estadisticas/publicaciones/informe-de-autoevaluacion.

Concept. (2002). *Kontseptsiya gosudarstvennoy politiki Rossiyskoy Federatsii v oblasti podgotovki natsional'nykh kadrov dlya zarubezhnykh stran v rossiyskikh obrazovatel'nykh uchrezhdeniyakh* [The concept of government policy of the Russian Federation on developing national human resources for foreign countries at Russian higher educational institutions]. Moscow: Russian Federation.

Concept. (2010). *Kontseptsiya eksporta obrazovatel'nykh uslug Rossiyskoy Federatsii na period 2011–2020* [The concept of export of Russian educational services for the period 2011–2020]. Moscow: Russian Federation.

CONICYT. (2016, 16 January). Retrieved from www.conicyt.cl/becas-conicyt/estadisticas/informacion-general.

Cooke, P. (2001). Regional innovation systems, clusters and the knowledge economy. *Industrial and Corporate Change*, 20(4), 945–974.

Crossman, P. (2004). Perceptions of Africanisation and endogenization of African universities: Issues and recommendations. In P. T. Zeleza & A. Olukoshi (eds), *African universities in the twentieth century* (pp. 319–340). Dakar: Codesria.

Crystal, D. (1997). *English as a global language.* Cambridge: Cambridge University Press.

Curry, M. J. & Lillis, T. (2015). The dominance of English in global scholarly publishing. *International Higher Education*, 46, 6–7.

Dang, Q. A. (2011). *Internationalisation of higher education: China and Vietnam – From importers of education to partners in cooperation*. MSc thesis, Copenhagen Business School, Copenhagen. Retrieved 14 May 2016 from http://studenttheses. cbs.dk/bitstream/handle/10417/2017/que_anh_dang.pdf?sequence=1.

Dash, T. R. (2016, 15 January). Internationalisation linked to drive for quality. *University World News*, 396.

Davidson, C. (2015). *After the Sheikhs: The coming collapse of the Gulf monarchies*. London: C. Hurst & Co. Publishers Ltd.

De Hoyos, R., Rogers, H. & Székely, M. (2015). *Out of school and out of work: Risk and opportunities for Latin America's Ninis*. Washington, DC: World Bank.

De Wit, H. (2002). *Internationalization of higher education in the United States of America and Europe: A historical, comparative, and conceptual analysis*. Westport, CT: Greenwood Press.

De Wit, H. (2004). Academic alliances and networks: A new internationalisation strategy in response to the globalisation of our societies. In D. Theather (ed.), *Consortia, international networking, alliances of universities*. Melbourne: University of Melbourne Press.

De Wit, H. (2008). Changing dynamics in international student circulation: Meanings, push and pull factors, trends and data. In P. Agarwal, M. E. Said, M. Sehoole, M. Sirozi & H. de Wit (eds), *The dynamics of international student circulation in a global context* (pp. 15–48). Rotterdam: SensePublishers.

De Wit, H. (2011). Internationalization misconceptions. In *International Higher Education* (No. 64, pp. 6–7). Boston: Boston College Center for International Higher Education.

De Wit, H. (2012, 14 March). Rethinking the concept of internationalization. Paper presented at Going Global, British Council, London.

De Wit, H. (2013a). Rethinking the concept of internationalisation. In *Going global: Identifying trends and drivers of international education* (pp. 213–218). London: Emerald Group Publishing.

De Wit, H. (2013b). Internationalisation of higher education, an introduction on the why, how and what. In H. de Wit (ed.), *An introduction to higher education internationalisation* (pp. 13–46). Milan: Vita e Pensiero.

De Wit, H. (2015a, 14 August). School internationalisation: Whose opportunity? *University World News*, 377.

De Wit, H. (2015b, 13 November). The massive refugee crisis demands a proper response. *University World News*. Retrieved 7 December 2015 from www.univer-sityworldnews.com/article.php?story=20151110181505538&query=dewit.

De Wit, H. (2015c, 20 March). What is an international university? *University World News*, 359. Retrieved 24 March 2015 from www.universityworldnews.com/article. php?story=2015031910180116.

De Wit, H. (2015d). Partnerships for the future: Trends, challenges and oppor-tunities. In N. Jooste, H. de Wit & S. Heleta (eds), *Higher education, partner-ships for the future* (pp. 95–101). Port Elizabeth: Nelson Mandela Metropolitan University.

De Wit, H. (2015e). Internationalisation of the curriculum and learning out-comes: Challenges and opportunities in the European context. Working Paper for Nazarbayev University Graduate School of Education Research Project.

De Wit, H. & Altbach, P. (2015, 15 September). The Syrian refugee crisis: What can universities do? *University World News*. Retrieved April 2016 from www.university-worldnews.com/article.php?story=20150918113842639.

De Wit, H. & Callan, H. (1995). Internationalization of higher education in Europe. In H. de Wit (ed.), *Strategies for internationalization of higher education: A comparative study of Australia, Canada, Europe and the United States of America* (pp. 67–98). Amsterdam: The EAIE.

De Wit, H., Gacel-Ávila, J., Jaramillo, I. & Knight, J. (2005). *Higher education in Latin America*. Washington, DC: The World Bank.

De Wit, H. & Hunter, F. (2015). Understanding internationalisation of higher education in the European context. In H. de Wit, F. Hunter, L. Howard & E. Egron-Polak (eds), *Internationalization of higher education* (pp. 41–58). Brussels: European Parliament, Committee on Culture and Education.

De Wit, H., Hunter, F., Howard, L. & Egron-Polak, E. (2015). *Internationalization of higher education*. Brussels: European Parliament, Committee on Culture and Education. Retrieved May 2016 from www.europarl.europa.eu/RegData/etudes/STUD/2015/540370/IPOL_STU(2015)540370_EN.pdf.

De Wit, H., Hunter, F., Johnson, L. & van Liempd, H.-G. (eds). (2013). *Possible futures: The next 25 years of the internationalization of higher education*. Amsterdam: European Association for International Education.

De Wit, H. & Ripmeester, N. (2013, 16 February). Increasing the stay rate of international students. *University World News*. Retrieved April 2016 from www.universityworldnews.com/article.php?story=20130213165216138&query.

Deardorff, D., de Wit, H., Heyl, J. D. & Adams, T. (eds). (2012). *The Sage handbook of international higher education*. Thousand Oaks, CA: Sage.

Declaración de los Cancilleres Iberoamericanos. (2015, 12 December). Cartagena de Indias. Retrieved December 2015 from www.cancilleria.gov.co/newsroom/news/declaracion-cancilleres-iberoamericanos.

Decree No. 367. (2013). *Ob utverzhdenii Pravil polucheniya mezhdunarodnymi organizatsiyami prava na predostavleniye grantov na territorii Rossiyskoy Federatsii na osushchestvleniye konkretnykh nauchnykh, nauchno-tekhnicheskikh programm i proyektov, provedeniye konkretnykh nauchnykh issledovaniy na usloviyakh, predusmotrennykh grantodatelyami* [On approval of the rules for international organizations to receive grants on the territory of the Russian Federation for specific scientific, technical programmes and projects, and research works under the conditions, which are stipulated by the funders]. Government Decree of 23 April. Moscow: Russian Federation.

Decree No. 803. (2005). *O Federal'noy tselevoy programme razvitiya obrazovaniya na 2006–2010 gody* [On the federal target programme for the development of education in the years 2006–2010]. Government Decree of 23 December. Moscow: Russian Federation.

Decree No. 2293. (2009). *Poryadok predostavleniya informatsii o khode realizatsii program razvitiya natsional'nykh issledovatel'skikh universitetov.* Prilozheniye 1 k prikazu Rosobrazovaniya ot 16 dekabrya 2009 g. N 2293 [The procedure for providing information on the implementation of the programme of the development of national research universities]. Appendix 1 to Government Decree of 16 December. Moscow: Russian Federation.

Deem, R. & Brehony, K. (2005). Management as ideology: The case of new managerialism in higher education. *Oxford Review of Education*, 31(2), 213–231.

Dei, G. J. S. (2002). Rethinking the role of indigenous knowledges in the academy. NALL Working Paper, 58. Retrieved 27 November 2010 from www.nall.oise. utoronto.ca/res/58GeorgeDei.pdf.

Deng, Z. L. (1995). A summary of the symposium on the normalization of indigenization of social studies. *Chinese Social Sciences Quarterly*, 10(Spring), 164–165.

Desjardins, R. (2013). Considerations of the impact of neoliberalism and alternative regimes on learning and its outcome: An empirical example based on the level and distribution of adult learning. *International Studies in Sociology of Education*, 23, 102–203.

DHET (Department of Higher Education and Training, South Africa). (2013). *White Paper for post-school education and training.* Retrieved 5 March 2016 from www.dhet.gov.za/SiteAssets/Latest%20News/White%20paper%20for%20post-school%20education%20and%20training.pdf.

DHET (Department of Higher Education and Training, South Africa). (2015). *Durban statement on transformation in higher education.* Retrieved 3 March 2016 from www.dhet.gov.za/summit/Docs/2015Docs/2015%20Durban%20HE%20 Transformation%20Summit%20Statement.pdf.

Devi, B. & Nair, V. (2008). First year experience of international students in Malaysia: A private higher education viewpoint. In S. Kaur, M. Sirat & N. Azman (eds), *Globalisation and internationalisation of higher education in Malaysia* (pp. 178–209). Penang, Malaysia: Penerbit Universiti Sains Malaysia.

Dirlik, A. (2012). *Zhongguohua*: Worlding China – The case of sociology and anthropology in 20th-century China. In A. Dirlik, G. N. Li & H. P. Yen (eds), *Sociology and anthropology in twentieth-century China* (pp. 1–40). Hong Kong: The Chinese University Press.

Dobbs, R., Madgavkar, A., Barton, D., Labaye, E., Manyika, J., Roxburgh, C., et al. (2012). *The world at work: Jobs, pay, and skills for 3.5 billion people.* McKinsey & Company. Retrieved April 2016 from www.mckinsey.com/global-themes/ employment-and-growth/the-world-at-work.

Douglass, J. A. (ed.). (2016). *A new flagship university: Changing the paradigm from global rankings to national relevancy.* Basingstoke: Palgrave Macmillan.

DREAM Project. (n.d.). Dynamizing research and education for all through mobility in ACP. Retrieved 19 August 2015 from http://dream.up.pt.

Dutch Foundation for Refugee Students (UAF). (n.d.). Resettlement of refugee students. Retrieved April 2016 from www.uaf.nl/wat_doet_het_uaf/projecten/ hervestiging_van_vluchtelingen/resettlement_of_refugee_students.

Economic Commission for Latin America and the Caribbean. (2015). *Inclusive social development.* Santiago: ECLAC.

Education in Russian Federation. (2012). *Obrazovaniye v Rossiyskoy Federatsii: Statistics collection.* Moscow: National Research University, Higher School of Economics, p. 444.

Education in Russian Federation. (2014). *Obrazovaniye v Rossiyskoy Federatsii: Statistics collection.* Moscow: National Research University, Higher School of Economics, p. 464.

Egron-Polak, E. (2012). Internationalization of higher education: An introduction. In *Focus, Re-thinking Internationalization IAU Horizons*, 17.3–18.1, 15.

Egron-Polak, E. & Hudson, R. (2010). *3rd IAU global survey on internationalization of higher education.* Paris: International Association of Universities.

Egron-Polak, E. & Hudson, R. (2014a). *4th IAU global survey on internationalization of higher education.* Paris: International Association of Universities.

Egron-Polak, E. & Hudson, R. (2014b). Internationalization of higher education: Growing expectations, fundamental values. Executive Summary in *4th IAU global survey on internationalization of higher education.* Paris: International Association of Universities.

El-Bushra, J. (2006). Power, agency and identity: Turning vicious circles into virtuous ones. In H. Yanacopulos & J. Hanlon (eds), *Civil war, civil peace* (pp. 206–232). Athens, OH: James Currey.

Elkin, G., Farnsworth, J. & Templer, A. (2008). Strategy and the internationalization of universities. *International Journal of Educational Management*, 22, 239–250.

EUCARINET. Report on science and technology research in the Caribbean: Analysis, monitoring and review. Retrieved 20 August 2015 from www.eucarinet.eu/eudocs/documents/9846c54b3feea46c117659035dfe6bb2.pdf.

European Commission. (2014a, January). *Syrian crisis: EU pledges additional funding for humanitarian aid as needs continue to rise.* Press release. Retrieved April 2016 from http://europa.eu/rapid/press-release_IP-14-17_en.htm.

European Commission. (2014b). *The Erasmus Impact Study: Effects of mobility on the skills and employability of students and the internationalisation of higher education institutions.* Luxembourg: European Commission.

European Commission. (2015). *Higher education co-operation between the European Union, Latin America and the Caribbean: Academic co-operation and mobility – Bringing the two regions together.* European Commission, Education, Audio-Visual and Culture Executive Agency, pp. 28–33. Retrieved August 2015 from https://ec.europa.eu/europeaid/sites/devco/files/higher-education-cooperation_en.pdf.

European University Association (EUA). (2015, 23 October). *European universities' response to the refugee crisis.* Retrieved April 2016 from www.eua.be//Libraries/press/european-universities-response-to-the-refugee-crisis.pdf?sfvrsn=8.

European University Association (EUA). (2016, 3 March). *EUA launches Refugees Welcome Map.* Retrieved April 2016 from www.eua.be/activities-services/news/newsitem/2016/03/03/eua-launches-refugees-welcome-map.

Eurydice. (2007). *Focus on the structure of higher education in Europe 2006/07: National trends in the Bologna Process.* Brussels: Eurydice.

Ezzy, D. (2002). *Qualitative analysis: Practice and innovation.* Crows Nest, NSW: Allen & Unwin.

Fan, B. S. (2000). *An analysis of the contemporary Chinese social sciences newspaper and journal literature.* Shanghai: East China Normal University [in Chinese].

Fanon, F. (2004). *The wretched of the earth.* New York: Grove Press.

Farquhar, R. H. (1999). Integration or isolation: Internationalism and the Internet in Canadian higher education. *Journal of Higher Education Policy and Management*, 21(2), 5–15.

Federal Law No. 83-FZ. (2010). *O vnesenii izmeneniy v otdel'nyye zakonodatel'nyye akty Rossiyskoy Federatsii v svyazi s sovershenstvovaniyem pravovogo polozheniya gosudarstvennykh (munitsipal'nykh) uchrezhdeniy* [On amendments to certain legislative acts of the Russian Federation in connection with the improvement of the legal status of state (municipal) institutions]. Adopted on 8 May. Moscow: Russian Federation.

Federal Law No. 129-FZ. (2015). *O vnesenii izmeneniy v otdel'nyye zakonodatel'nyye akty Rossiyskoy Federatsii* [On amendments to certain legislative acts of the Russian Federation]. Adopted on 23 May. Moscow: Russian Federation.

Federal Statistics Service. (2015). *Demograficheskaya baza dannykh: Obrazovanie* [Demographic database: Education]. Retrieved 26 June 2015 from www.gks.ru/scripts/db_inet/dbinet.cgi.

Feuer, H., Hornidge, A. & Schetter, C. (2013). *Rebuilding knowledge: Opportunities and risks for higher education in post-conflict regions.* ZEF Working Paper Series, No. 121. Bonn: Zentrum für Entwicklungsforschung/Center for Development Research (ZEF), University of Bonn.

Flamboltz, E. & Randle, Y. (2011). *Corporate culture: The ultimate strategic asset.* Stanford, CA: Stanford University Press.

Forrat, N. (2015). The political economy of Russian higher education: Why does Putin support research universities? *Post-Soviet Affairs.* DOI: 10.1080/1060586X.2015.1051749.

Fumasoli, T. & Huisman, J. (2013). Strategic agency and system diversity: Conceptualizing institutional positioning in higher education. *Minerva*, 51, 155–169.

Fundación Bancomer. (2010, November). *BBVA research.* Retrieved from www.bbvaresearch.com/KETD/fbin/mult/1011_SitMigracionMexico_04_tcm346-234630.pdf?ts=12112010.

Gacel-Ávila, J. (2012). Comprehensive internationalisation in Latin America. *Higher Education Policy*, 25(4), 493–510.

Gao, Y., Baik, C. & Arkoudis, S. (2015). Internationalisation of higher education. In J. Huisman, H. de Boer, D. D. Dill & M. Souto-Ottero (eds), *The Palgrave international handbook of higher education policy and governance* (pp. 300–320). London: Palgrave Macmillan.

Government of Canada. (n.d.). International scholarships. Retrieved August 2015 from www.scholarships-bourses.gc.ca/scholarships-bourses/can/institutions/elap-pfla.aspx?lang=eng.

Grayson, J. P. (2005). The application of American models to domestic and international students studying in Canada. *Frontiers: The Interdisciplinary Journal of Study Abroad*, 11(Fall), 71–97.

Gribble, C. (2008). Policy options for managing international student migration: The sending country's perspective. *Journal of Higher Education Policy and Management*, 30(1), 25–39.

Grove, J. (2015, 15 October). How Europe's academy is addressing the refugee crisis. *Times Higher Education.* Retrieved April 2016 from www.timeshighereducation.com/features/how-europes-academy-is-addressing-the-refugee-crisis.

Gu, J. M. (2010). Disparities in the development of higher education internationalization in China: An analysis. *Journal of Zhejiang Education Institute*, 6, 1–6 [in Chinese].

Gyamera, G. O. (2015). The internationalisation agenda: A critical examination of internationalisation strategies in public universities in Ghana. *International Studies in Sociology of Education*, 25(2), 112–131.

Hagenmeier, C. (2013). The future of internationalisation: Perspectives for South African rural-based universities. *Journal of Educational Studies*, 12(2), 56–74. Online: http://reference.sabinet.co.za/document/EJC170587.

Hagenmeier, C. (2015). Ensuring equality in higher education partnerships involving unequal universities in divergent contexts. In N. Jooste, H. de Wit & S. Heleta (eds), *Higher education partnerships for the future*. Port Elizabeth: NMMU.

Haigh, M. (2008). Internationalisation, planetary citizenship and Higher Education Inc. *Compare: A Journal of Comparative and International Education*, 38(4), 427–440.

Haigh, M. J. (2009). Fostering cross-cultural empathy with non-Western curricular structure. *Journal of International Education*, 13(2), 271–284.

Hall, P. A. & Lamont, M. (2009). *Successful societies: How institutions and culture affect health*. Cambridge: Cambridge University Press.

Hardt, M. & Negri, A. (2000). *Empire*. London: Harvard University Press.

Harman, G., Hayden, M. & Nghi, P.T. (2010). Higher education in Vietnam: reform, challenges and priorities. In G. Harman, M. Hayden & T.N. Pham (eds), *Reforming higher education in Vietnam: Challenges and priorities*. Dordrecht: Springer.

Harris, S. (2007). *The governance of education: How neo-liberalism is transforming policy and practice*. London: Continuum Press.

Harris, S. (2008). Internationalising the university. *Educational Philosophy and Theory*, 40, 346–357.

Harris, S. (2011). *University in translation: Internationalising higher education*. London: Continuum International Publishing Group.

Hawthorne, E. (2012). Designer immigrants? International students and two-step migration. In D. Deardorff, H. deWit, J. D. Heyl & T. Adams (eds), *The Sage handbook of international higher education* (pp. 417–435). Thousand Oaks, CA: Sage.

Heleta, S. (2015). Higher education in post-conflict societies: Settings, challenges and opportunities. In S. Heleta (ed.), *Internationalisation of higher education: An EAIE handbook* (Vol. 1). Stuttgart: Raabe Verlag.

Hénard, F., Diamond, L. & Roseveare, D. (2012). Approaches to internationalisation and their implications for strategic management and institutional practice. Retrieved April 2016 from www.oecd.org/edu/imhe/Approaches%20to%20internationalisation%20-%20final%20-%20web.pdf.

Hoa Sen University. (2015). *Core values*. Retrieved 14 May 2016 from www.hoasen.edu.vn/en/569/about-us/core-values.

Hoosen, S., Butcher, N. & Njenga, B. (2009). Harmonization of higher education programmes: A strategy for the African Union. *African Integration Review*, 3(1), 1–36.

Horn, H. (2015). Saving Syria's 'lost generation'. *The Atlantic*. Retrieved April 2016 from www.theatlantic.com/international/archive/2015/10/syria-university-students-education/412174.

Horsthemke, K. (2004). Indigenous knowledge: Conceptions and misconceptions. *Journal of Education*, 32, 31–38.

Horta, H. (2009). Global and national prominent universities: Internationalization, competitiveness and the role of the state. *Higher Education*, 58, 387–405.

Hosein, R., Chen, T. & Singh, R. (2004). *The international supply of tertiary education and services trade negotiations: Implications for CARICOM*. Report prepared for the Caribbean Regional Negotiating Machinery (CRNM).

HSE. (2005). *Byudzhetnoye finansirovaniye obrazovaniya* [Public funding of education]. *Information Bulletin*. Moscow: Higher School of Economics.

Hsu, C. (2001). Chinese encounters with other civilizations. *International Sociology*, 16(3), 438–454.

Hu, G. (2005). English language education in China: Policies, progress and problems. *Language Policy*, 4(1), 5–24.

Huang, F. (2003). Policy and practice of the internationalization of higher education in China. *Journal of Studies in International Education*, 7(3), 225–240.

Hudzik, J. (2011). Comprehensive internationalisation: From concept to action. Washington, DC: NAFSA, Association of International Educators. Retrieved 19 August 2012 from www.nafsa.org/uploadedFiles/NAFSA_Home/Resource_Library_Assets/Publications_Library/2011_Comprehen_Internationalization.pdf.

Hudzik, J. (2015). *Comprehensive internationalization: Institutional pathways for success*. New York: Routledge.

Hudzik, J. & McCarthy, J. (2012). *Leading comprehensive internationalization: Strategy and tactics for action*. Washington, DC: NAFSA, Association of International Educators.

ICEF Monitor. (2015a, 2 September). Four trends that are shaping the future of global student mobility. Retrieved April 2016 from http://monitor.icef.com/2015/09/four-trends-that-are-shaping-the-future-of-global-student-mobility.

ICEF Monitor. (2015b, 15 September). Brazil's Science without Borders programme facing cuts in 2016. Retrieved December 2015 from http://monitor.icef.com/2015/09/brazils-science-without-borders-programme-facing-cuts-in-2016.

IEASA (International Education Association of South Africa). (2014, 17 January). Nelson Mandela Bay global dialogue declaration on the future of internationalisation of higher education. Port Elizabeth, South Africa. Retrieved from www.nafsa.org/_/file/_/ieasa_2014.pdf.

Ilieva, J. & Peak, M. (2016). *The shape of global higher education: National policies framework for international engagement*. British Council. Retrieved from www.britishcouncil.org/education/ihe.

Institute of International Education (IIE). (2014). We will stop here and go no further: Syrian university students and scholars in Lebanon. Retrieved April 2016 from www.iie.org/Research-and-Publications/Publications-and-Reports/IIE-Bookstore/The-War-Follows-Them-Syrian-University-Students-And-Scholars-In-Lebanon.

Institute of International Education (IIE). (2015). *Project Atlas*. Retrieved from www.iie.org/Services/Project-Atlas/Chile/Chiles-Students-Overseas.

International Association of Universities (IAU). (2012). *IAU speaks out*. Paris: International Association of Universities. Retrieved from www.iau-aiu.net.

Jegede, O. (2012, 3 January). African leader wants end to 'slave trade' in education. *Times Higher Education*.

Jones, E. (2013a). Internationalization and student learning outcomes. In H. de Wit (ed.), *An introduction to higher education internationalization* (pp. 107–116). Milan: Vita e Pensiero.

Jones, E. (2013b). The global reach of universities: Leading and engaging academic and support staff in the internationalisation of higher education. In R. Sugden, M. Valania & J. R. Wilson (eds), *Leadership and cooperation in academia: Reflecting on the roles and responsibilities of university faculty and management* (pp. 161–183). Cheltenham: Edward Elgar.

Jones, E. (2013c). Internationalization and employability: The role of intercultural experiences in the development of transferable skills. *Public Money and Management*, 33(2), 95–104.

Jones, E. (2013d, 28 September). Internationalising the curriculum: Future challenges. *University World News*, 289.

Jones, E. & de Wit, H. (2012). Globalization of internationalization: Thematic and regional reflections on a traditional concept. *AUDEM: The International Journal of Higher Education and Democracy*, 3, 35–54.

Jones, E. & de Wit, H. (2014). Globalized internationalization: Implications for policy and practice. *IIEnetworker*, Spring, 28–29 [Chinese translation: *Journal of World Education*, 27 (17)].

Jones, E. & Killick, D. (2007). Internationalisation of the curriculum. In E. Jones & S. Brown (eds), *Internationalising higher education* (pp. 109–119). London: Routledge.

Jooste, N. (2006). *Characteristics of an internationalised university in South Africa: Nelson Mandela Metropolitan University colloquium series* (Vol. 2). Port Elizabeth: NMMU.

Karasapan, O. (2015). Who will help Syria's displaced university students? The World Bank, Voices and Views: Middle East and North Africa. Retrieved April 2016 from http://blogs.worldbank.org/arabvoices/who-will-help-syria-s-displaced-university-students.

Karbo, T. (2008). Peace-building in Africa. In D. Francis (ed.), *Peace and conflict in Africa* (pp. 113–130). London: Zed Books.

Karim, F. & Maarof, N. (2012). Towards understanding the internationalization of higher education and its challenges. In S. Y. Tham (ed.), *Internationalizing higher education in Malaysia: Understanding, practices and challenges* (pp. 18–40). Singapore: Institute of Southeast Asian Studies.

Kaur, S. & Sidhu, G. K. (2009). A qualitative study of postgraduate students' learning experiences in Malaysia. *International Education Studies*, 2(3), 47–56.

Kehm, B. & Teichler, U. (2007). Research on internationalization in higher education. *Journal of Studies in International Education*, 11, 260–273.

Kelly, K. (2000). The higher education system in Vietnam. *World Education News & Reviews*, 13(3). Retrieved 14 May 2016 from http://wenr.wes.org/2000/05/ewenr-mayjune-2000-the-higher-education-system-in-vietnam.

Kenson School of Production Technology. (n.d.). Retrieved August 2015 from http://kspt.edu.tt/index.html.

Kenway, J., Fahey, J., Epstein, D., Koh, A., McCarthy, C. & Rizvi, F. (2016). *Class choreographies: Elite schools in globalizing circumstances*, London: Palgrave.

Khan, S. (2012). *Privilege: The making of an adolescent elite at St. Paul's School*, Princeton, NJ: Princeton University Press.

Killick, D. (2015). *Developing the global student: Higher education in an era of globalization*. New York, NY: Routledge.

Kingston, E. & Forland, H. (2008). Bridging the gap in expectations between international students and academic staff. *Journal of Studies in International Education*, 12(2), 204–221.

Kirby, W. C. (2014). The world of universities in modern China. In L. E. Rumbley, R. M. Helms, P. M. Peterson & P. G. Altbach (eds), *Global opportunities and challenges for higher education leaders* (pp. 73–76). Boston: Sense Publishers.

Klemenčič, M. (2015). Internationalisation of higher education in the peripheries: The 'gear effect' of integrated international engagements. In E. Beerkens, M. Magnan, M. Söderqvist & H.-G. van Liempd (eds), *Handbook of internationalisation* of higher education (A 2.1–11), 22nd supplement (pp. 1–22). Berlin: European Association of International Education and Raabe Verlag.

Klemenčič, M. & Flander, A. (2014). Evaluation of the impact of the ERASMUS Programme on higher education in Slovenia. Ljubljana: Centre of the Republic of Slovenia for Mobility and European Educational and Training Programmes (CMEPIUS). Retrieved from www.cmepius.si/en/files/cmepius/userfiles/publikacije/2014/Eval_en_Erasmus.pdf.

Klemenčič, M. & Zgaga, P. (2013). Internationalisation at the European periphery and academics' geographic preferences for partnership: Focus on the Western Balkans. In A. Labi (ed.), Weaving the future of global partnerships: A conversation starter for the EAIE 2013 Annual Conference (pp. 41–46). Amsterdam: European Association for International Education.

Knight, J. (1994). Internationalization: Elements and checkpoints. Research Monograph, No. 7. Ottawa, Canada: Canadian Bureau for International Education.

Knight, J. (1997). Internationalisation of higher education: A conceptual framework. In J. Knight & H. de Wit (eds), Internationalisation of higher education in Asia Pacific countries (pp. 5–19). Amsterdam: European Association for International Education.

Knight, J. (2003). Updating the definition of internationalization. International Higher Education, 33, 2–3.

Knight, J. (2004). Internationalisation: Meaning and models. Adapted from Internationalisation remodelled: Definition, approaches and rationales. Journal of Studies in International Education, 8(1), 5–31.

Knight, J. (2008a). Higher education in turmoil: The changing world of internationalization. Rotterdam: Sense.

Knight, J. (2008b). Internationalisation: Key concepts and elements. In E. Beerkens, M. Magnan, M. Söderqvist & H.-G. van Liempd (eds), Handbook of internationalisation of higher education (A 1.1). Berlin: European Association of International Education and Raabe Verlag.

Knight, J. (2011a). Regional education hubs: Mobility for the knowledge economy. In R. Bhandari & P. Blumenthal (eds), International students and global mobility in higher education: National trends and new directions (pp. 211–230). New York: Palgrave Macmillan.

Knight, J. (2011b). Internationalisation: Key concepts and elements. In M. Gaebel, L. Purser, B. Waechter & L. Wilson (eds), Internationalisation of European higher education: An EUA/ACA handbook. Berlin: Raabe Academic Publishers.

Knight, J. (2014). Introduction. In J. Knight (ed.), International education hubs: Student, talent, knowledge-innovation models (pp. 1–12). Dordrecht: Springer.

Knight, J. & de Wit, H. (1997). Internationalization of higher education in Asia Pacific countries. Amsterdam: European Association for International Education.

Knight, J. & Lee, J. (2014). An analytical framework for education hubs. In J. Knight (ed.), International education hubs: Student, talent, knowledge-innovation models (pp. 29–42). Dordrecht: Springer.

Kolster, R. (2014). Academic attractiveness of countries: A possible benchmark strategy applied to the Netherlands. European Journal of Higher Education 4(2), 118–134.

Kupriyanova-Ashina, V. & Chang Zhu. (2013). Internatsionalizatsiya vysshego obrazovaniya: rossiyskiye podkhody [The internationalization of higher education: The

Russian approach]. *International Trends Journal of International Relations Theory and World Politics*, 11(2), 33.

Kuraev, A. (2014). *Internationalization of higher education in Russia: Collapse or perpetuation of the Soviet system? A historical and conceptual study.* Unpublished PhD thesis, Boston College Lynch School of Education. Retrieved from http://hdl.handle.net/2345/3799.

Kurlantzick, J. (2006). China's charm: Implications of Chinese soft power. *Policy Brief*, 47, 1–8.

Lambrechts, A. (2015, 16 October). Higher education, global wellbeing and the refugee crisis. University of York, Department of Education. Retrieved April 2016 from https://ergyork.wordpress.com/2015/10/16/higher-education-global-wellbeing-and-the-refugee-crisis.

Lansink, A. (2004). The African university: Contestations in the production of knowledge and identity. In S. Seepe (ed.), *Towards an African identity in higher education*. Pretoria: Vista University and Scottaville Media.

Laredo, P. (2007, 5–6 March). Toward a third mission for universities: Main transformations, challenges and emerging patterns in higher education systems. UNESCO Research Seminar for the Regional Scientific Committee for Europe and North America, Paris. Retrieved May 2016 from http://portal.unesco.org/education/en/files/53913/11858787305Towards_a_third_Mission_universities.pdf/Towards_a_third_Mission_universities.pdf.

Larionova, M. et al. (eds). (2010). *Internatsionalizatsiya vysshego obrazovaniya: tendentsii,strategii, stsenarii budushchego [Internationalization of higher education: Trends, strategies and future scenarios]*. Moscow: Logos, p. 280.

Law, J. (2015, 30 September). Food, shelter or higher education: What's most needed? British Council. Retrieved 15 October 2015 from www.britishcouncil.org/voices-magazine/food-shelter-higher-education-most-needed.

Lawton, W. & Katsomitros, A. (2011). *International branch campuses: Data and developments*. London: Observatory on Borderless Higher Education.

Le Grange, L. (2008). Challenges for enacting an indigenised science curriculum: A reply to Ogunniyi and Ogawa. *South African Journal of Higher Education*, 22, 817–826.

Leask, B. (2005). Internationalisation of the curriculum and intercultural engagement: A variety of perspectives and possibilities. Paper presented at the Australian International Education Conference, Gold Coast, Queensland.

Leask, B. (2009). Using formal and informal curricula to improve interactions between home and international students. *Journal of Studies in International Education*, 13(2), 205–221.

Leask, B. (2012). Internationalisation of the Curriculum (IoC) in action: A guide. Retrieved from http://ioc.global/index.html.

Leask, B. (2015a). *Internationalizing the curriculum*. London: Routledge.

Leask, B. (2015b). Designing an internationalised curriculum. Working Paper for Nazarbayev University Graduate School of Education Research Project.

Leask, B. & Bridge, C. (2013). Comparing internationalisation of the curriculum in action across disciplines: Theoretical and practical perspectives. *Compare: A Journal of Comparative and International Education*, 43(1), 79–101.

Lee, M. N. N. (2004a). *Restructuring higher education in Malaysia*. Penang: Universiti Sains Malaysia, School of Educational Studies.

Lee, M. N. N. (2004b). Global trends, national policies and institutional responses: Restructuring higher education in Malaysia. *Educational Research for Policy and Practice*, 3(1), 31–46.

Lee, M. N. N. (2015). Educational reforms in Malaysia: Towards equity, quality and efficiency. In M. L. Weiss (ed.), *Routledge handbook of contemporary Malaysia*. Abingdon: Taylor & Francis.

Li, G., Chen, W. & Duanmu, J.-L. (2009). Determinants of international students' academic performance: A comparison between Chinese and other international students. *Journal of Studies in International Education OnlineFirst*, 1–17.

Liang, J. (2016). *The lobbying of Chinese elite universities*. PhD thesis, Australian National University.

London, J. D. (2010). Globalization and the governance of education in Viet Nam. *Asia Pacific Journal of Education*, 30(4), 361–379.

London, J. D. (2011). Education in Vietnam: Historical roots, recent trends. In J. D. London (ed.), *Education in Vietnam*. Singapore: Institute of Southeast Asian Studies.

Louw, W. (2009). Africanisation: The dilemma to Africanise or to globalise a curriculum. *Conference of the International Journal of Arts and Sciences*, 1, 62–70. Retrieved 25 September 2013 from http://openaccesslibrary.org/images/MAL150_Willa_Louw.pdf.

Lu, X. (2016, 26 March). Nearly eighty percent Chinese students return, more female than male. BBC. Retrieved 27 March 2016 from www.bbc.com/zhongwen/simp/world/2016/03/160326_china_students_return.

Maathai, W. (2010). *The challenge for Africa*. London: Arrow Books.

MacGregor, K. (2012). Bring internationalization back into academia – Hans De Wit. *University World News*, 306. Retrieved 29 September 2013 from www.universityworldnews.com/article.

Magaziner, J. (2015, 7 December). The importance of higher education for Syrian refugees. *World Education News and Reviews*. Retrieved April 2016 from http://wenr.wes.org/2015/12/the-importance-of-higher-education-for-syrian-refugees/#.VmdQ49fa1A0.email.

Mahmud, Z., Amat, S., Rahman, S. & Ishak, N. M. (2010). Challenges for international students in Malaysia: Culture, climate and care. *Procedia Social and Behavioral Sciences*, 7(C), 289–293.

Makgopa, M. & Seepe, S. (2004). Knowledge and identity: An African vision of higher education transformation. In S. Seepe (ed.), *Towards an African identity of higher education* (pp. 13–57). Pretoria: Vista University.

Maldonado Maldonado, A. (2013, 8 April). Caci la tercera parte de los doctores mexicanos está en EU. Retrieved from www.cronica.com.mx/notas/2013/743250.html.

Marcos, A. (2015, 12 December). Iberoamérica pacta la movilidad regional de sus estudiantes. *El País*. Retrieved December 2015 from http://internacional.elpais.com/internacional/2015/12/12/colombia/1449947767_688348.html.

Marginson, S. (2006). Dynamics of national and global competition in higher education. *Higher Education*, 52(1), 1–39.

Marginson, S. (2011). Strategizing and ordering the global. In R. King, S. Marginson & R. Naidoo (eds), *Handbook on globalization and higher education* (pp. 394–414). Cheltenham: Edward Elgar Publishing.

Marginson, S. (2013). We are becoming more global. In H. de Wit, F. Hunter, L. Johnson & H.-G. van Liempd (eds), *Possible futures: The next 25 years of the internationalization of higher education* (pp. 48–51). Amsterdam: European Association for International Education.

Marginson, S. & van der Wende, M. (2009). The new global landscape of nations and institutions. In OECD (ed.), *Higher education to 2030*, Vol. 2: *Globalisation*. Paris: OECD.

Marimuthu, T. (2008). The role of the private sector in higher education in Malaysia. In D. Johnson & R. Maclean (eds), *Teaching: Professionalization, development and leadership*. Dordrecht: Springer.

Maringe, F. & Carter, S. (2007). International students' motivations for studying in UKHE: Insights into the choice and decision-making of African students. *International Journal of Educational Management*, 21(6), 459–475.

Marmolejo, F., Manley-Casimir, S. & Vincent-Lancrin, S. (2008). Immigration and access to tertiary education: Integration or marginalisation? In OECD (ed.), *Higher Education to 2030*, Vol. 1: *Demography*. Paris: OECD.

Matthews, Z. K. (1957). *The University College of Fort Hare* [Originally published in 1957 *South African Outlook*]. Retrieved 5 March 2016 from http://uir.unisa.ac.za/bitstream/handle/10500/5795/ZKM_C4_13.pdf?sequence=1.

Mazzarol, T. & Soutar, G. N. (2002). Push–pull factors influencing student destination choice. *International Journal of Education Management*, 16(2), 82–90.

McCormick, A. C., Pike, G. R., Kuh, G. D. & Chen, P.-S. (2008). Comparing the utility of the 2000 and 2005 Carnegie classification system in research on students' college experiences and outcomes. *Research Higher Education*, 50, 144–167.

McNamara, J. (2013). *The shape of things to come: The evolution of transnational education – Data, definitions, opportunities and impacts analysis*. London: British Council.

Melikhov, V. (2009). Avtonomnost' vysshey shkoly: mif ili real'nost [Autonomy of higher school: Myth or reality]. *Journal of Socioeconomic Phenomena and Processes*, 3, 60–66.

Metz, T. (2007). Ubuntu as a moral theory: Reply to four critics. *South African Journal of Philosophy*, 26, 369–387.

Middlehurst, R. (2009). Developing institutional internationalisation policies and strategies: An overview of key issues. In E. Beerkens, M. Magnan, M. Söderqvist & H.-G. van Liempd (eds), *Handbook of internationalisation of higher education* (B1.1–1). Berlin: European Association of International Education and Raabe Verlag.

Ministry of Education Malaysia. (2004). *Establishment of research universities in Malaysia: A concept paper*. Ministry of Education, Kuala Lumpur, Malaysia.

Ministry of Education Malaysia. (2014). *National education statistic: Higher education sector 2013*. Kuala Lumpur: Ministry of Education.

Ministry of Education Malaysia. (n.d.). *Malaysian higher education indicators 2011–2012*. Kuala Lumpur: Ministry of Education.

Ministry of Education and Science of the Republic of Kazakhstan. (2010). *State Program of Education Development in the Republic of Kazakhstan for 2011–2020*.

Ministry of Higher Education. (2012). *Malaysia higher education statistics 2011*. Kuala Lumpur: Ministry of Higher Education.

Mitchell, D. E. & Yildiz Nielsen, S. (2012). Internationalization and globalization in higher education. In H. Cuadra-Montiel (ed.), *Globalization: Education*

and management agendas. Rijeka: Intech. Retrieved from http://idl.isead.edu.
es:8080/jspui/bitstream/10954/1776/1/9789535107026.pdf.

MOET. (2013). *Approved foreign programs*. Hanoi: Ministry of Education and Training.

MOHE Malaysia. (2007). *The national higher education strategic plan: Laying the foundation beyond 2020*. Kuala Lumpur: Ministry of Higher Education.

MOHE Malaysia. (2010). *Malaysia higher education statistics 2009*. Kuala Lumpur: Ministry of Higher Education.

MOHE Malaysia. (2011a). *Internationalisation policy for higher education Malaysia 2011*. Kuala Lumpur: Ministry of Higher Education.

MOHE Malaysia. (2011b). *National higher education strategic plan 2: Malaysia's global reach – A new dimension*. Kuala Lumpur: Ministry of Higher Education.

Molesworth, M., Scullion, R. & Nixon, E. (2011). *The marketisation of higher education and the student as consumer*. London: Routledge.

Montgomery, C. & McDowell, L. (2009). Social networks and the international student experience: An international community of practice? *Journal of Studies in International Education*, 13(4), 455–466.

Moosavi, L. (2016). Internationalised higher education as a conflict zone. *EAIE Forum*, Spring, 35–37.

Muda, W. A. M. W. (2008). *The Malaysian national higher education action plan: Redefining autonomy and academic freedom under the APEX experiment*. Paper presented at the Association of South East Asian Institutions of Higher Learning Conference, Penang, Malaysia.

Naidoo, R. & Jamieson, I. (2005). Knowledge in the marketplace: The global commodification of teaching and learning in higher education. In P. Ninnes & M. Hellsten (eds), *Internationalizing higher education* (pp. 37–51). Dordrecht: Springer.

Najafi, T. & Lea-Baranovich, D. (2013). The need for Iranian counsellors for Iranian undergraduate students in Malaysia: A qualitative study. *International Journal of Advanced Research*, 1(9), 875–881.

Netshandama, V., Hagenmeier, C., Dillingham, R., Smith, J. & Louis, G. (2011). The impact of internationalisation on the quality of higher education: A case of selected programmes at the University of Venda. Paper presented at the 2011 Annual IEASA Conference in Durban, South Africa.

Nguyen, D. P., Vickers, M., Ly, T. M. C. & Tran, M. D. (2016). Internationalizing higher education in Vietnam. *Education + Training*, 58(2), 193–208.

Nguyen, T. A. (2009). *The internationalization of higher education in Vietnam: National policies and institutional implementation at Vietnam National University, Hanoi*. Tokyo: Waseda University Global Institute for Asian Regional Integration.

Nikolaev, D. & Suslova, D. (2010). Russia in the Bologna Process. *Issues of Education*, 1, 6–25.

Nkomo, M. & Sehoole, N. (2007). *Rural-based universities: Albatrosses or potential nodes for sustainable development*? Pretoria, South Africa: openUP. Retrieved 10 August 2012 from http://repository.up.ac.za/handle/2263/2544.

Observatory on Borderless Higher Education (OBHE). (2011). *Perspectives on the future*. Retrieved 3 January 2016 from www.obhe.org.

OECD. (2009). *Higher education to 2030*, Vol. 2: *Globalisation*. Paris: OECD.

OECD. (2013). *Education at a glance 2013: OECD indicators*. Paris: OECD.

OECD & World Bank. (2007). *Review of national policies for education: Higher education in Kazakhstan*. Paris: OECD & World Bank. Retrieved April 2016 from www.usp.ac.fj/worldbank2009/frame/Documents/Publications_regional/Kazakhstan%20Higher%20Education.pdf.

Olsen, C., Green, M. & Hill, B. (2005). *Building a strategic framework for comprehensive internationalisation*. Washington, DC: American Council on Education.

Olutokunbo, A. S., Ismail, I. A. & Suandi, T. (2013). Academic experience of international students on scholarships in Malaysian universities: The case of a private university college. *International Journal of Learning and Development*, 3(6), 7–18.

Open University. (n.d.). Open University to deliver academic programmes for Syrian refugees in Jordan and Lebanon. Retrieved April 2016 from www3.open.ac.uk/media/fullstory.aspx?id=29403.

Oregioni, M.-S. (2013). La universidad como actor de cooperación Sur-Sur. *Integración y Conocimiento*, 2, 52–67.

Ortiz, A., Li Chang & Yuanyuan Fang (2015). International student mobility trends 2015: An economic perspective. *World Education News and Reviews*. New York: World Educational Services.

Oxford Martin School. (2013). *Now for the long term: The report of the Oxford Martin Commission for Future Generations*. Oxford: University of Oxford.

The Pacific Alliance. (2015, 14 December). Home page. Retrieved from https://alianzapacifico.net/en/#home.

Pan, L. (2011). English language ideologies in the Chinese foreign language education policies: A world-system perspective. *Language Policy*, 10, 245–263.

Pandian, A. (2008). Multiculturalism in higher education: A case study of Middle Eastern students' perceptions and experiences in a Malaysian university. *International Journal of Asia-Pacific Studies*, 4(1), 33–59.

Parmenter, L. (2013). Power and place in the discourse of global citizenship education. In V. Andreotti (ed.), *The political economy of global citizenship education*. London: Routledge.

Perez, R. H. (2005). Internationalization of higher education in Cuba. in H. de Wit, I. C. Jaramillo, J. Gacel-Ávila & J. Knight (eds), *Higher education in Latin America: The international dimension*. Washington, DC: World Bank.

Perkins, D. (2014). *Future wise: Educating our children for a changing world*. San Francisco, CA: Jossey-Bass.

Perna, L., Orosz, K., Jumakulov, Z., Kishkentayeva, M. & Ashirbekov, A. (2015). Understanding the programmatic and contextual forces that influence participation in a government-sponsored international student mobility program. *Higher Education*, 69(2), 173–188.

Ping, J. (2016). On ne peut plus ignorer l'Afrique. *Géopolitique Africaine*, 57.

Pinheiro, R., Langa, P. V. & Pausits, A. (2015). One and two equals three? The third mission of universities. *European Journal of Higher Education*, 5(3), 233–249.

Popova, E. (2015). Rossiyskiye universitety: mezhdu internatsionalizatsiyey i etnonatsionalizmom [Russian Universities between Internationalization and Technonationalism]. *Sociologia Vlasti*, 27(3), 174–196.

Postiglione, G. A. & Altbach, P. G. (2013). Professors: The key to internationalization. *International Higher Education*, 73, 11–12.

Program 5–100. (2012). *Povysheniye konkurentosposobnosti vedushchikh universitetov Rossiyskoy Federatsii sredi vedushchikh mirovykh nauchno-obrazovatel'nykh tsentrov*

(5–100) [Enhancing the competitiveness of the leading universities of the Russian Federation among the world's leading research and education centers (5–100)]. Adopted on 29 October. Retrieved June 2015 from http://минобрнауки.рф/проекты/5–100.

Pusser, B. & Marginson, S. (2013). University rankings in critical perspective. *The Journal of Higher Education*, 84(4), 544–568.

Ralyk, N. (2008). *Integrating internationalization into higher education: Reconceptualizing the 'why', 'what', and 'how'*. Educational Leadership and Policy Integrative Paper. Salt Lake City, UT: University of Utah.

Red Macro. (2015, 25 November). *Informe Ejecutivo 2002–2015*. Retrieved from www.redmacro.unam.mx/VIAsamblea2015/1%20INFORME%20GRAL%20VI%20Asamblea%20RED%20MACRO%20VF.pdf.

Redden, E. (2015, 25 September). The refugee crisis and higher education. *Inside Higher Ed*. Retrieved April 2016 from www.insidehighered.com/news/2015/09/25/syrian-refugee-crisis-and-higher-education.

Riggs, F. W. (2001). *Social science in a global context*. Retrieved 27 July 2013 from www2.hawaii.edu/~fredr/glosci.htm.

Rizvi, F. (2009). Towards cosmopolitan learning. *Discourse: Studies in the Cultural Politics of Education*, 30(3), 253–268.

Rizvi, F. & Lingard, R. (2010). *Globalizing education policy*. London: Routledge.

Rizvi, F., Lingard, B. & Lavia, J. (2006). Postcolonialism and education: Negotiating a contested terrain. *Pedagogy, Culture & Society*, 14, 249–262.

RMIT. (2015). Program enrolments by campus (2014 headcounts and load). Retrieved 14 May 2016 from www1.rmit.edu.au/sr/http:/www.rmit.edu.au/sr/studentstats2014.

Rochester-King, N. (2015, April). Internationalisation of the higher education services and institutional partnerships. Background brief for the 3rd CARIFORUM–EU Business Forum.

Romani, V. (2009). The politics of higher education in the Middle East: Problems and prospects. Brandeis University: Crown Center for Middle East Studies. Retrieved 28 December 2015 from www.brandeis.edu/crown/publications/meb/MEB36.pdf.

Rumbley, L. & Altbach, P. G. (2015). The local and the global in higher education internationalization. In E. Jones, R. Coelen, J. Beelen & H. de Wit (eds), *Global and local internationalization* (pp. 7–13). Rotterdam: Sense Publishers.

Rumbley, L., Altbach, P. & Reisberg, L. (2012). Internationalisation within the higher education context. In D. Deardorff, H. de Wit, J. Heyl & T. Adams (eds), *The Sage handbook of international higher education* (pp. 3–26). Thousand Oaks, CA: Sage Publications.

Russian Federation. (2002). On Education Law. Adopted 10 July 1992, No. 3266-1. Retrieved 25 May 2015 from www.rg.ru/oficial/doc/federal_zak/71-fz.shtm.

Salmi, J. (2009). *The challenge of establishing world-class universities*. Washington, DC: World Bank.

Sandel, M. (2012). *What money can't buy: The moral limits of markets*. New York, NY: Penguin Group.

Sato, M. (2005). Education, ethnicity and economics: Higher education reforms in Malaysia 1957–2003. *NUCB Journal of Language, Culture and Communication*, 7(1), 73–88.

Saw, S.-H. (2006). Population trends and patterns in multicultural Malaysia. In S.-H. Saw & K. Kesavapany (eds), *Malaysia: Recent trends and challenges*. Singapore: Institute of Southeast Asian Studies.

Sawyerr, A. (2004). African universities and the challenge of research capacity development. *JHEA/RESA*, 2, 211–240.

Schütz, A. (1999). *Estudios sobre teoría social*. Buenos Aires: Amorrortu Editores. Retrieved May 2016 from http://html.rincondelvago.com/estudios-sobre-teoria-social_alfred-schutz_1.html.

SCIMAGO. (2015, 1 December). *SCImago journal & country rank*. Retrieved from www.scimagojr.com.

Scott, P. (1998). Massification, internationalization and globalization. In P. Scott (ed.), *The globalization of higher education* (pp. 108–129). Buckingham: The Society for Research into Higher Education/Open University Press.

Scott, P. (2011). The internationalisation of higher education and research: Purposes and drivers. In M. Gaebel, L. Purser, B. Waechter & L. Wilson (eds), *Internationalisation of European higher education: An EUA/ACA handbook*. Berlin: Raabe Academic Publishers.

Scott, P. (2013). Future trends in international education. In H. de Wit, F. Hunter, L. Johnson & H.-G. van Liempd (eds), *Possible futures: The next 25 years of the internationalization of higher education* (pp. 52–56). Amsterdam: European Association for International Education.

Seepe, S. (2004). Editorial notes. *South African Journal of Higher Education*, 18, 9–16.

Selvaratnam, V. (1988). Ethnicity, inequality and higher education in Malaysia. *Comparitive Education Review*, 32(2), 173–196.

SENESCYT. (2016, 21 January). *Programa de Becas SENESCYT*. Retrieved from http://programasbecas.educacionsuperior.gob.ec/ensena-ingles.

Shambaugh, D. (2005). Return to the Middle Kingdom: China and Asia in the early twenty-first century. In D. Shambaugh (ed.), *Power shift: China and Asia's new dynamics* (pp. 23–47). Berkeley, CA: University of California Press.

Sheregi, F., Konstantinovsky, D. & Arephiev, A. (2006). *Vzaimodeystviye rossiyskikh vuzov s mezhdunarodnymi fondami i organizatsiyami [Interplay of Russian HEIs with international foundations and universities: Monitoring and performance evaluation]*. Moscow: Center of Social Forecasting.

Singh, J. K. N. (2009). *A case-study of the impact of the research university policy on research universities in Malaysia*. Unpublished masters dissertation, Monash University, Melbourne, Victoria, Australia.

Singh, J. K. N., Jack, G. & Schapper, J. (2012). Factors that contribute to academic success of international students: A literature review. *Bulletin of Higher Education Research*, 19(June), 4–6.

Singh, J. K. N., Schapper, J. & Jack, G. (2014). The importance of place for international students' choice of university: A case study at a Malaysian university. *Journal of Studies in International Education*, 18(5), 463–474.

Sirat, M. (2008a). Strategic planning directions of Malaysia's higher education: University autonomy in a politcally turbulent time. Paper presented at the Research Institute for Higher Education Seminar, Hiroshima University, Japan.

Sirat, M. (2008b). The impact of September 11 on international student flow into Malaysia: Lessons learned. *International Journal of Asia-Pacific Studies*, 4(1), 79–95.

Sirat, M. (2009). *Trends in international higher education and regionalism: Issues and challenges for Malaysia.* Retrieved 24 October 2009 from www.waseda-giari.jp/sysimg/imgs/wp2008-E-17.pdf.

Siufi, G. (2009). Cooperación internacional e internacionalización de la educación superior. *Educación Superior y Sociedad,* 14(1), 119–146.

Skribic, Z. & Woodward, I. (2013). *Cosmopolitanism: Uses of the idea.* London: Sage.

Smith, L. (2005). On tricky ground: Researching the native in the age of uncertainty. In N. Denzin & Y. Lincoln (eds), *The Sage handbook of qualitative research* (3rd ed., pp. 113–144). Thousand Oaks, CA: Sage.

Socialist Republic of Vietnam. (2012). *Decision approving the 2011–2020 education development strategy 711/QD-TTg.* Hanoi: Socialist Republic of Vietnam.

Sorokova, L. (2012). Perekhod obrazovatel'nykh uchrezhdeniy v status avtonom-nykh: potentsial vzaimodeystviya vuzov i shkol dlya povysheniya kachestva obrazovatel'nykh uslug [Transition of educational institutions in the status of autonomous: The potential interaction between universities and schools to improve the quality of educational services]. *Herald of Tomsk State University,* 358, 198–205.

Soutar, G. & Turner, J. (2002). Students' preferences for university: A conjoint analysis. *International Journal of Educational Management,* 16(1), 40–45.

Southern African Development Community (SADC). (1997). Protocol on education and training. Retrieved from www.sadc.int/files/3813/5292/8362/Protocol_on_Education__Training1997.pdf.

Sparks, J., Ashirbekov, A., Parmenter, L., Jumakulov, Z. & Sagintayeva, A. (2015). Becoming Bologna capable: Strategic cooperation and capacity building in international offices in Kazakhstani HEIs. In A. Curaj, L. Matei, R. Pricopie & J. Salmi (eds), *The European higher education area: Between critical reflections and future policies* (pp. 121–138). New York: Springer.

SST (School of Science and Technology, Singapore). (n.d.). Global citizenship program (GCP). Retrieved from www.sst.edu.sg/student-life/student-development/global-citizenship-program-gcp.

St. Augustine Education City. (n.d.). Retrieved 29 December 2015 from http://stte.gov.tt/EduCity.

St George, E. (2010). Higher education in Vietnam 1986–1998: education in transition to a new era?. In G. Harman, M. Hayden & T.N. Pham (eds), *Reforming higher education in Vietnam: Challenges and priorities.* Dordrecht: Springer.

Stake, R. E. (1995). *The art of case study research.* Thousand Oaks, CA: Sage.

Statistical Collection. (2015a). *Obucheniye inostrannykh grazhdan v vysshikh ucheb-nykh zavedeniyakh Rossiyskoy Federatsii: Statisticheskiy sbornik.* [Education of foreign citizens in the higher educational institutions of the Russian Federation: Statistical collection]. Issue 12. Moscow: Center for Sociological Research, Ministry of Education and Science, p. 196.

Statistical Collection. (2015b). *Eksport rossiyskikh obrazovatel'nykh uslug: Statisticheskiy sbornik* [Russian export of educational services: Statistical collection]. Issue 5. Moscow: Center for Sociological Research, Ministry of Education and Science, p. 416.

Stevenson, J. & Willott, J. (2015). Refugees: Home students with international needs. In E. Jones (ed.), *Internationalisation and the student voice: Higher education perspectives* (pp. 193–202). London: Routledge.

Streitwieser, B. (ed.). (2014). *Internationalisation of higher education and global mobility*. Oxford: Symposium Books.

Su, Y. (2009). *Numbers of students going abroad to study* [in Chinese]. Retrieved 19 December 2011 from http://learning.sohu.com/20090326/n263029186.shtml.

Sunders, S. (2013). Defining internationalization vs. globalisation within higher education. *University Outlook*, 203. Retrieved from http://universityoutlook.com/topics/international/defining-internationalization-vs-globalization-within-higher-education.

Sutton, S. B., Eggington, E. & Favela, R. (2012). Collaborating on the future: Strategic partnerships and linkages. In D. K. Deardorff, H. de Wit, J. D. Heyl & T. Adams (eds), *The SAGE handbook of international higher education*. Thousand Oaks, CA: SAGE Publishers.

Tadaki, M. & Christopher, T. (2013). Reimagining internationalization in higher education: International consortia as transformative space? *Studies in Higher Education*, 38(3), 367–387.

Taylor, J. (2010). The management of internationalisation in higher education. In F. Maringe & K. Foskett (eds), *Globalisation in higher education: Theoretical, strategic and management perspectives* (pp. 97–108). London: Continuum.

Tibbetts, P. K. (2007). *Resistance and change: A century of education reform in Vietnam*. Doctor of Education thesis, George Washington University, Washington, DC.

Tố, T. T. (2012). Việt Nam 'xuất siêu' du học [Vietnam 'surplus' study]. Retrieved 14 May 2016 from http://dantri.com.vn/giao-duc-khuyen-hoc/viet-nam-xuat-sieu-du-hoc-556901.htm.

Tobenkin, D. (2014). Revitalizing education in Afghanistan: Overcoming decades of devastation. *International Educator*, 23(4).

Torres, C. A. (2011). Public universities and the neoliberal common sense: Seven iconoclastic theses. *International Studies in Sociology of Education*, 21, 177–197.

Torres, C. A. & Jones, G. (2013). Neoliberal common sense in education, part two. *International Studies in Sociology of Education*, 23, 179–181.

Trading Economics. (n.d.). School enrollment: Tertiary (% gross) in Middle East and North Africa. Retrieved April 2016 from www.tradingeconomics.com/middle-east-and-north-africa/school-enrollment-tertiary-percent-gross-wb-data.html.

Trahar, S. (2014). 'This is Malaysia. You have to follow the custom here': Narratives of the student and academic experience in international higher education in Malaysia. *Journal of Education for Teaching: International Research and Pedagogy*, 40(3), 217–231.

Tran, H. P. (1998). *Vietnamese higher education at the intersection of French and Soviet influences*. Buffalo, NY: State University of New York at Buffalo.

Tran, Q. T. & Swierczek, F. W. (2009). Skills development in higher education in Vietnam. *Asia Pacific Business Review*, 15(4), 565–586.

Tran, T. T. (2015). Is graduate employability the 'whole-of-higher-education-issue'?. *Journal of Education and Work*, 28(3), 207–227.

Trostyanskaya, I. & Tolstikov, D. (2014). O finansirovanii proyekta 5–100 v 2013 godu [On the financing of Project 5–100 in 2013]. In F. Sheregi & A. Arephiev (eds), *Metodicheskiye voprosy otsenki realizatsii proyekta 5–100 po reytingam universitetov [Methodological issues for evaluating Project 5–100 on the ratings of universities]* (pp. 139–157). Moscow: Center for Sociological Research, Ministry of Education and Science.

Tuyết, T. N. T. (2014). Internationalization of higher education in Vietnam: Opportunities and challenges. *VNU Journal of Science: Foreign Studies*, 30(3), 61–69.

UDUAL. (2014). Plan de desarrollo estratégico de ENLACES. Retrieved December 2015 from www.udual.org/pdf/Plan%20de%20Desarrollo%20Estrategico%20 de%20ENLACES.pdf.

ULB. (2014). A bit of history. Solvay Business School, Université Libre de Bruxelles. Retrieved 9 September 2016 from http://solvay-mba.edu.vn/about/page/11.

UNESCO. (2008). Declaration of the Regional Conference of Higher Education in Latin America. Retrieved December 2015 from www.unesco.de/fileadmin/ medien/Dokumente/Bildung/WCHE_Vorkonferenz_Lateinamerika_Karibik_ Abschlussdokument_ENG_fuer_Web.pdf.

UNESCO. (2009, July). A decade of higher education in the Arab states: Achievements & challenges. Regional report, Arab Regional Conference on Higher Education, Cairo, 31 May, 1–2 June. Retrieved from www.unesco.org/new/fileadmin/ MULTIMEDIA/FIELD/Beirut/pdf/Regional_Report_on_Higher_Education_ in_the_Arab_States.pdf.

UNESCO. (2011). *The hidden crisis: Armed conflict and education*. EFA Global Monitoring Report. Paris: UNESCO.

UNESCO. (2014–2017). Culture: Extracts from approved programme and budget 2014–2017 37 C/5 major programme IV. Retrieved from www.unesco.org/ new/ en/culture/about-us/how-we-work/strategy.

UNESCO. (2015). A growing number of children and adolescents are out of school as aid fails to meet the mark (Policy paper 22, Factsheet 31). UNESCO Institute for Statistics and EFA Global Monitoring Report. Paris: UNESCO.

UNESCO-UIS. (2012). *Global education digest 2012*. Montreal: UNESCO.

UNESCO-UIS. (2015, 22 November). *UIS UNESCO*. Retrieved from www.uis. unesco.org/Education/Pages/tertiary-education.aspx.

United Nations. (2015). Transforming our world: The 2030 Agenda for Sustainable Development. Retrieved from https://sustainabledevelopment.un.org/post2015/ transformingourworld.

United Nations. (n.d.). Sustainable development knowledge platform: Sustainable development goal 4. Retrieved from https://sustainabledevelopment.un.org/sdg4.

United Nations & OECD. (2013). *World migration in figures*. UN-DESA & OECD. Retrieved from www.oecd.org/els/mig/World-Migration-in-Figures.pdf.

University of Venda. (2009). *2009–2013 strategic plan*. Thohoyandou, South Africa: University of Venda.

University of Venda. (2013). Internationalisation policy. Policy approved by the University of Venda Council on 19 April 2013. University of Venda, Thohoyandou, South Africa.

University of Venda. (2014). Buddy programme to link students: 'We seek to create a spirit of Ubuntu'. *Nendila Newsletter*. Retrieved 11 August 2014 from www. univen.ac.za/docs/Nendila%20May%202014%20lowres-final.pdf.

University of Venda. (2015a). Annual report. Retrieved 11 September 2016 from www.univen.ac.za/docs/UnivenAnnRep2014lowres.pdf.

University of Venda. (2015b). Univen celebrates cultural diversity and internationalisation. *Nendila Newsletter*. Retrieved 5 March 2016 from www.univen.ac.za/ docs/nendila/NendilaNovDec2015_lowres.pdf.

University of Venda. (2015c). *Univen transformation charter.* Thohoyandou, South Africa: University of Venda.

University of Venda. (2016). *2016–2020 strategic plan.* Thohoyandou, South Africa: University of Venda.

US Department of State. (2015, 6 June). *Joint U.S.–Mexico statement on the U.S.– Mexico Bilateral Forum on Higher Education, Innovation, and Research: Connecting Tomorrow's Leaders Today.* Retrieved from www.state.gov/r/pa/prs/ps/2015/ 01/235641.htm.

UWI. (2012). *Strategic plan 2012–2017.* Retrieved July 2015 from www.uwi.edu/ sf-docs/default-source/planningdocs/UWI_Strategic_Plan_2012-2017_Final. pdf?sfvrsn=0.

UWI. (n.d.a). Arthur Lok Jack Graduate School of Business. Retrieved 24 August 2015 from http://lokjackgsb.edu.tt/international-relations.html.

UWI. (n.d.b). Open campus. Retrieved 26 July 2015 from www.open.uwi.edu/ about/welcome-uwi-open-campus.

UWI. (n.d.c). Programmes in engineering. Retrieved from http://sta.uwi.edu/eng/ Accreditation.asp.

Van der Wende, M. (1996). Internationalizing the curriculum in higher education: Report on a OECD/CERI study. *Tertiary Education and Management,* 2(2), 186–195.

Van der Wende, M. C. (2001). Internationalisation policies: About new trends and contrasting paradigms. *Higher Education Policy,* 14(3), 249–259.

Van Winden, W. (2014). EUniverCities: City & university – Co-creating a more attractive city. URBACT II Programme. Retrieved from www.urbact.eu.

Veevers, N. & Pete, A. (2011). *Kurt Hahn: Inspirational, visionary, outdoor and experiential educator.* Rotterdam: Sense Publishers.

Vigil Taquechel, C. A. (2015, 24 March). *Innovación e internacionalización universitaria.* Retrieved December 2015 from http://cavtaquechel.blogspot.com/2015/ 03/innovacion-e-internacionalizacion.html.

Wagner, A.-C. (2007). *Les classes sociales dans la mondialisation.* Paris: La découverte.

Wagner, P. (1999). The twentieth century: The century of the social sciences? In A. Kazancigil & D. Makinson (eds), *World social sciences report 1999* (pp. 16–31). Paris: UNESCO Publishing/Elsevier.

Wang, J. B. & Xue, R. L. (2004). Some reflections on educational sovereignty in Chinese–foreign joint programs. *Journal of Shandong Normal University (Humanities and Social Sciences),* 49(5), 119–122 [in Chinese].

Watenpaugh, K. D., Fricke, A. L. & King, J. R. (2014). *The war follows them: Syrian university students and scholars in Lebanon.* Institute of International education and UC Davis. Retrieved from www.iie.org/Research-and-Publications/Publications-and-Reports/IIE-Bookstore/The-War-Follows-Them-Syrian-University-Students-And-Scholars-In-Lebanon#.V-Rn0ZMrKCQ.

Watermeyer, R. (2015). Lost in the 'third space': The impact of public engagement in higher education on academic identity, research practice and career progression. *European Journal of Higher Education,* 5(3), 331–347.

Welch, A. R. (2010). Internationalisation of Vietnamese higher education: Retrospect and prospect. In G. Harman, M. Hayden & T.N. Pham (eds), *Reforming higher education in Vietnam: Challenges and priorities.* Dordrecht: Springer.

Welch, A., Yang, R. & Wolhouter, C. (2004). Internationalising a rural, historically disadvantaged black South African university. *Journal of Studies in International Education*, 8(3), 317–331.

Williams, T. R. (2005). Exploring the impact of study abroad on students' intercultural communication skills: Adaptability and sensitivity. *Journal of Studies in International Education*, 9(4), 356–371.

Wilmoth, D. (2004). RMIT Vietnam and Vietnam's development: Risk and responsibility. *Journal of Studies in International Education*, 8(2), 186–206.

Woodward, S. (2011). State-building for peace-building: What theory and whose role? In R. Kozul-Wright & P. Fortunato (eds), *Securing peace: State-building and economic development in post-conflict countries* (pp. 87–111). London: Bloomsbury Academic.

World Bank. (2000). *Higher education in developing countries: Peril and promise*. Washington, DC: World Bank.

World Bank. (2008). *Vietnam higher education and skills for growth*. Washington, DC: World Bank.

World Bank. (2012). *Putting higher education to work: Skills and research for growth in East Asia*. Washington, DC: World Bank.

World Bank. (2013). *Skilling up Vietnam: Preparing the workforce for a modern market economy – Vietnam development report 2014*. Washington, DC: World Bank.

World Bank. (2015). *What matters in tertiary education: Conceptual framework and policy data collection rubric*. Washington, DC: World Bank.

World Bank Data. (n.d.). Retrieved 8 December 2015 from http://data.worldbank.org/indicator/SE.TER.ENRR.

Yamane, T. (1967). *Statistics: An introductory analysis* (2nd edn). New York: Harper & Row.

Yang, R. (2001). An obstacle or a useful tool? The role of the English language in internationalizing Chinese universities. *Journal of Studies in International Education*, 5(3), 339–356.

Yang, R. (2002). *Third delight: Internationalization of higher education in China*. New York: Routledge.

Yang, R. (2003). Globalisation and higher education development: A critical analysis. *International Review of Education*, 49(3–4), 269–291.

Yang, R. (2009). Enter the dragon? China's higher education returns to the world community: The case of the Peking University personnel reforms. In J. Smart & W. Tierney (eds), *Higher education: Handbook of theory and practice* (pp. 427–461). Dordrecht: Springer.

Yang, R. (2011). Self and the other in the Confucian cultural context: Implications of China's higher education development for comparative studies. *International Review of Education*, 57(3–4), 337–355.

Yang, R. (2012a). Scholarly publishing, knowledge mobility and internationalization of Chinese universities. In T. Fenwick & L. Farrell (eds), *Knowledge mobilization and educational research: Politics, languages and responsibilities* (pp. 185–167). New York: Routledge.

Yang, R. (2012b). Internationalization, regionalization and soft power: China's relations with ASEAN member countries in higher education. *Frontiers of Education in China*, 7(4), 486–507.

Yang, R. (2012c). Soft power and higher education: An examination of China's Confucius Institutes. In E. Hartmann (ed.), *The internationalization of higher education: Towards a new research agenda in critical higher education studies* (pp. 65–76). New York: Routledge.

Yonezawa, A. (2003). The impact of globalisation on higher education governance in Japan. *Higher Education Research & Development*, 22(2), 145–154.

York Accord. (2015). *The responsibility to protect and rebuild higher education during and after conflict*. Doha: Brookings Doha Center.

Yu, J. H. (2016). *Student mobility in internationalization: Recent developments, new viewpoints and latest changes* [in Chinese]. Retrieved 4 February 2016 from www.th-chinaembassyedu.org/publish/portal125/tab5220/info119220.htm.

Yusoff, Y. M. (2012). Self-efficacy, perceived social support and psychological adjustment in international undergraduate students in a public higher education institution in Malaysia. *Journal of Studies in International Education*, 16(4), 353–371.

Yusoff, Y. M. & Chelliah, S. (2010). Adjustment in international students in Malaysian public university. *International Journal of Innovation, Management and Technology*, 1(3), 275–278.

Zhang, X. Q. (2013, 26 November). Global student mobility and characteristics of international students in China. China Education Daily. Retrieved 7 February 2016 from http://edu.sina.com.cn/a/2013-11-26/1054236574.shtml.

Zhang, L. & Yuan, Y. (2011, 4 December). China's scientific publications: Happy and sorrow news. Guangming Daily [in Chinese]. Retrieved 17 August 2012 from www.stdaily.com/stdaily/content/2011-12/04/content_393697.htm.

Ziguras, C. & Law, S. F. (2006). Recruiting international students as skilled migrants: The global 'skills race' as viewed from Australia and Malaysia. *Globalisation, Societies and Education*, 4(1), 59–76.

Ziguras, C. & McBurnie, G. (2015). *Governing cross-border higher education*. London: Routledge.

Ziguras, C. & Pham, A. (2014). Assessing participation in cross-border higher education in cities: Foreign education provision in Ho Chi Minh City. *Asia Pacific Viewpoint*, 55(2), 169–181.

Index